SCEPTICISM AND ANIMAL FAITH

SCEPTICISM
AND
ANIMAL FAITH

*Introduction to a System
of Philosophy*

RXTSA

GEORGE SANTAYANA

DOVER PUBLICATIONS, INC.
NEW YORK

This Dover edition, first published in 1955, is an unabridged and unaltered republication of the work first published in 1923.

Standard Book Number: 486-20236-4

Library of Congress Catalog Card Number: 55-14672

Manufactured in the United States of America

Dover Publications, Inc.
180 Varick Street
New York, N. Y. 10014

PREFACE

HERE is one more system of philosophy. If the reader
is tempted to smile, I can assure him that I smile with
him, and that my system—to which this volume is
a critical introduction—differs widely in spirit and
pretensions from what usually goes by that name.
In the first place, *my system is not mine, nor new.* I
am merely attempting to express for the reader the
principles to which he appeals when he smiles. There
are convictions in the depths of his soul, beneath all
his overt parrot beliefs, on which I would build our
friendship. I have a great respect for orthodoxy ;
not for those orthodoxies which prevail in particular
schools or nations, and which vary from age to age,
but for a certain shrewd orthodoxy which the sentiment and practice of laymen maintain everywhere. I
think that common sense, in a rough dogged way, is
technically sounder than the special schools of philosophy, each of which squints and overlooks half the
facts and half the difficulties in its eagerness to find
in some detail the key to the whole. I am animated
by distrust of all high guesses, and by sympathy with
the old prejudices and workaday opinions of mankind : they are ill expressed, but they are well grounded.
What novelty my version of things may possess is
meant simply to obviate occasions for sophistry by
giving to everyday beliefs a more accurate and circum-
spect form. I do not pretend to place myself at the

heart of the universe nor at its origin, nor to draw its
periphery. I would lay siege to the truth only as
animal exploration and fancy may do so, first from
one quarter and then from another, expecting the
reality to be not simpler than my experience of it,
but far more extensive and complex. I stand in
philosophy exactly where I stand in daily life ; I
should not be honest otherwise. I accept the same
miscellaneous witnesses, bow to the same obvious
facts, make conjectures no less instinctively, and admit
the same encircling ignorance.

My system, accordingly, is *no system of the universe*.
The Realms of Being of which I speak are not parts
of a cosmos, nor one great cosmos together : they are
only kinds or categories of things which I find con-
spicuously different and worth distinguishing, at least
in my own thoughts. I do not know how many
things in the universe at large may fall under each of
these classes, nor what other Realms of Being may
not exist, to which I have no approach or which I
have not happened to distinguish in my personal
observation of the world. Logic, like language, is
partly a free construction and partly a means of
symbolising and harnessing in expression the existing
diversities of things ; and whilst some languages,
given a man's constitution and habits, may seem more
beautiful and convenient to him than others, it is a
foolish heat in a patriot to insist that only his native
language is intelligible or right. No language or logic
is right in the sense of being identical with the facts
it is used to express, but each may be right by being
faithful to these facts, as a translation may be faithful.
My endeavour is to think straight in such terms as
are offered to me, to clear my mind of cant and free
it from the cramp of artificial traditions ; but I do
not ask any one to think in my terms if he prefers
others. Let him clean better, if he can, the windows

of his soul, that the variety and beauty of the prospect may spread more brightly before him.

Moreover, my system, save in the mocking literary sense of the word, is *not metaphysical*. It contains much criticism of metaphysics, and some refinements in speculation, like the doctrine of essence, which are not familiar to the public ; and I do not disclaim being metaphysical because I at all dislike dialectic or disdain immaterial things : indeed, it is of immaterial things, essence, truth, and spirit that I speak chiefly. But logic and mathematics and literary psychology (when frankly literary) are not metaphysical, although their subject-matter is immaterial, and their application to existing things is often questionable. Metaphysics, in the proper sense of the word, is dialectical physics, or an attempt to determine matters of fact by means of logical or moral or rhetorical constructions. It arises by a confusion of those Realms of Being which it is my special care to distinguish. It is neither physical speculation nor pure logic nor honest literature, but (as in the treatise of Aristotle first called by that name) a hybrid of the three, materialising ideal entities, turning harmonies into forces, and dissolving natural things into terms of discourse. Speculations about the natural world, such as those of the Ionian philosophers, are not metaphysics, but simply cosmology or natural philosophy. Now in natural philosophy I am a decided materialist—apparently the only one living ; and I am well aware that idealists are fond of calling materialism, too, metaphysics, in rather an angry tone, so as to cast discredit upon it by assimilating it to their own systems. But my materialism, for all that, is not metaphysical. I do not profess to know what matter is in itself, and feel no confidence in the divination of those *esprits forts* who, leading a life of vice, thought the universe must be composed of nothing but dice and billiard-balls. I wait for the men of science to tell me what matter is, in so far as they can discover it, and am not at all surprised or troubled at the abstractness and vagueness of their ultimate conceptions : how should our notions of things so remote from the scale and scope of our senses be anything but schematic ? But whatever matter may be, I call it matter boldly, as I call my acquaintances Smith and Jones without knowing their secrets : whatever it may be, it must present the aspects and undergo the motions of the gross objects that fill the world : and if belief in the existence of hidden parts and movements in nature be metaphysics, then the kitchen-maid is a metaphysician whenever she peels a potato.

My system, finally, though, of course, formed under the fire of contemporary discussions, is *no phase of any current movement*. I cannot take at all seriously the present flutter of the image-lovers against intelligence. I love images as much as they do, but images must be discounted in our waking life, when we come to business. I also appreciate the other reforms and rebellions that have made up the history of philosophy. I prize their sharp criticism of one another and their several discoveries ; the trouble is that each in turn has denied or forgotten a much more important truth than it has asserted. The first philosophers, the original observers of life and nature, were the best ; and I think only the Indians and the Greek naturalists, together with Spinoza, have been right on the chief issue, the relation of man and of his spirit to the universe. It is not unwillingness to be a disciple that prompts me to look beyond the modern scramble of philosophies : I should gladly learn of them all, if they had learned more of one another. Even as it is, I endeavour to retain the positive insight of each, reducing it to the scale of nature and keeping it in its place ; thus I am a Platonist in logic and morals, and a transcendentalist in romantic soliloquy, when I choose to indulge in it. Nor is it necessary, in being teachable by any master, to become eclectic. All these vistas give glimpses of the same wood, and a fair and true map of it must be drawn to a single scale, by one method of projection, and in one style of calligraphy. All known truth can be rendered in any language, although the accent and poetry of each may be incommunicable ; and as I am content to write in English, although it was not my mother-tongue, and although in speculative matters I have not much sympathy with the English mind, so I am content to follow the European tradition in philosophy, little as I respect its rhetorical metaphysics, its human-ism, and its worldliness.

There is one point, indeed, in which I am truly sorry not to be able to profit by the guidance of my contemporaries. There is now a great ferment in natural and mathematical philosophy and the times seem ripe for a new system of nature, at once ingenuous and comprehensive, such as has not appeared since the earlier days of Greece. We may soon be all believing in an honest cosmology, comparable with that of Heraclitus, Pythagoras, or Democritus. I wish such scientific systems joy, and if I were com-petent to follow or to forecast their procedure, I should gladly avail myself of their results, which are bound to be no less picturesque than instructive. But what exists to-day is so tentative, obscure, and confused by bad philosophy, that there is no knowing what parts may be sound and what parts merely personal and scatter-brained. If I were a mathe-matician I should no doubt regale myself, if not the reader, with an electric or logistic system of the universe expressed in algebraic symbols. For good or ill, I am an ignorant man, almost a poet, and I can only spread a feast of what everybody knows.

Fortunately exact science and the books of the learned are not necessary to establish my essential doctrine, nor can any of them claim a higher warrant than it has in itself : for it rests on public experience. It needs, to prove it, only the stars, the seasons, the swarm of animals, the spectacle of birth and death, of cities and wars. My philosophy is justified, and has been justified in all ages and countries, by the facts before every man's eyes ; and no great wit is requisite to discover it, only (what is rarer than wit) candour and courage. Learning does not liberate men from superstition when their souls are cowed or perplexed ; and, without learning, clear eyes and honest reflection can discern the hang of the world, and distinguish the edge of truth from the might of imagination. In the past or in the future, my language and my borrowed knowledge would have been different, but under whatever sky I had been born, since it is the same sky, I should have had the same philosophy.

CONTENTS

xi

SCEPTICISM AND ANIMAL FAITH

CHAPTER I

A PHILOSOPHER is compelled to follow the maxim of epic poets and to plunge *in medias res*. The origin of things, if things have an origin, cannot be revealed to me, if revealed at all, until I have travelled very far from it, and many revolutions of the sun must precede my first dawn. The light as it appears hides the candle. Perhaps there is no source of things at all, no simpler form from which they are evolved, but only an endless succession of different complexities. In that case nothing would be lost by joining the procession wherever one happens to come upon it, and following it as long as one's legs hold out. Every one might still observe a typical bit of it ; he would not have understood anything better if he had seen more things ; he would only have had more to explain. The very notion of understanding or explaining any-thing would then be absurd ; yet this notion is drawn from a current presumption or experience to the effect that in some directions at least things do grow out of simpler things : bread can be baked, and dough and fire and an oven are conjoined in baking it. Such an episode is enough to establish the notion of origins and explanations, without at all implying that the dough and the hot oven are themselves primary facts. A philosopher may accordingly perfectly well undertake to find *episodes of evolution* in the world : parents

with children, storms with shipwrecks, passions with
tragedies. If he begins in the middle he will still begin
at the beginning of something, and perhaps as much
at the beginning of things as he could possibly begin.

On the other hand, this whole supposition may be
wrong. Things may have had some simpler origin,
or may contain simpler elements. In that case it will
be incumbent on the philosopher to prove this fact ;
that is, to find in the complex present objects
evidence of their composition out of simples. But
in this proof also he would be beginning in the middle ;
and he would reach origins or elements only at the
end of his analysis.

The case is similar with respect to first principles
of discourse. They can never be discovered, if
discovered at all, until they have been long taken for
granted, and employed in the very investigation which
reveals them. The more cogent a logic is, the fewer
and simpler its first principles will turn out to have
been ; but in discovering them, and deducing the rest
from them, they must first be employed unawares, if
they are the principles lending cogency to actual discourse ; so that the mind must trust current presumptions no less in discovering that they are logical
—that is, justified by more general unquestioned presumptions—than in discovering that they are arbitrary
and merely instinctive.

It is true that, quite apart from living discourse, a
set of axioms and postulates, as simple as we like, may
be posited in the air, and deductions drawn from them
ad libitum ; but such pure logic is otiose, unless we
find or assume that discourse or nature actually follows
it ; and it is not by deduction from first principles,
arbitrarily chosen, that human reasoning actually
proceeds, but by loose habits of mental evocation
which such principles at best may exhibit afterwards
in an idealised form. Moreover, if we could strip our

thought for the arena of a perfect logic, we should be performing, perhaps, a remarkable dialectical feat ; but this feat would be a mere addition to the complexities of nature, and no simplification. This motley world, besides its other antics, would then contain logicians and their sports. If by chance, on turning to the flowing facts, we found by analysis that they obeyed that ideal logic, we should again be beginning with things as we find them in the gross, and not with first principles.

It may be observed in passing that no logic to which empire over nature or over human discourse has ever been ascribed has been a cogent logic ; it has been, in proportion to its exemplification in existence, a mere description, psychological or historical, of an actual procedure ; whereas pure logic, when at last, quite recently, it was clearly conceived, turned out instantly to have no necessary application to anything, and to be merely a parabolic excursion into the realm of essence.

In the tangle of human beliefs, as conventionally expressed in talk and in literature, it is easy to distinguish a compulsory factor called facts or things from a more optional and argumentative factor called suggestion or interpretation ; not that what we call facts are at all indubitable, or composed of immediate data, but that in the direction of fact we come much sooner to a stand, and feel that we are safe from criticism. To reduce conventional beliefs to the facts they rest on — however questionable those facts themselves may be in other ways—is to clear our intellectual conscience of voluntary or avoidable delusion. If what we call a fact still deceives us, we feel we are not to blame ; we should not call it a fact, did we see any way of eluding the recognition of it. To reduce conventional belief to the recognition of matters of fact is empirical criticism of knowledge.

The more drastic this criticism is, and the more revolutionary the view to which it reduces me, the clearer will be the contrast between what I find I know and what I thought I knew. But if these plain facts were all I had to go on, how did I reach those strange conclusions ? What principles of interpretation, what tendencies to feign, what habits of inference were at work in me ? For if nothing in the facts justified my beliefs, something in me must have suggested them. To disentangle and formulate these subjective principles of interpretation is transcendental criticism of knowledge.

Transcendental criticism in the hands of Kant and his followers was a sceptical instrument used by persons who were not sceptics. They accordingly imported into their argument many uncritical assumptions, such as that these tendencies to feign must be the same in everybody, that the notions of nature, history, or mind which they led people to adopt were the right or standard notions on these subjects, and that it was glorious, rather than ignominious or sophistical, to build on these principles an encyclopædia of false sciences and to call it knowledge. A true sceptic will begin by throwing over all those academic conventions as so much confessed fiction ; and he will ask rather if, when all that these arbitrary tendencies to feign import into experience has been removed, any factual element remains at all. The only critical function of transcendentalism is to drive empiricism home, and challenge it to produce any knowledge of fact whatsoever. And empirical criticism will not be able to do so. Just as inattention leads ordinary people to assume as part of the given facts all that their unconscious transcendental logic has added to them, so inattention, at a deeper level, leads the empiricist to assume an existence in his radical facts which does not belong to them. In standing helpless and resigned before them he is, for all his assurance, obeying his illusion rather than their evidence. Thus transcendental criticism, used by a thorough sceptic, may compel empirical criticism to show its hand. It had mistaken its cards, and was bluffing without knowing it.

CHAPTER II

DOGMA AND DOUBT

CUSTOM does not breed understanding, but takes its place, teaching people to make their way contentedly through the world without knowing what the world is, nor what they think of it, nor what they are. When their attention is attracted to some remarkable thing, say to the rainbow, this thing is not analysed nor examined from various points of view, but all the casual resources of the fancy are called forth in conceiving it, and this total reaction of the mind precipitates a dogma ; the rainbow is taken for an omen of fair weather, or for a trace left in the sky by the passage of some beautiful and elusive goddess. Such a dogma, far from being an interpenetration or identification of thought with the truth of the object, is a fresh and additional object in itself. The original passive perception remains unchanged ; the thing remains unfathomed ; and as its diffuse influence has by chance bred one dogma to-day, it may breed a different dogma to-morrow. We have therefore, as we progress in our acquaintance with the world, an always greater confusion. Besides the original fantastic inadequacy of our perceptions, we have now rival clarifications of them, and a new uncertainty as to whether these dogmas are relevant to the original object, or are themselves really clear, or if so, which of them is true.

6

A prosperous dogmatism is indeed not impossible. We may have such determinate minds that the suggestions of experience always issue there in the same dogmas ; and these orthodox dogmas, perpetually revived by the stimulus of things, may become our dominant or even our sole apprehension of them. We shall really have moved to another level of mental discourse ; we shall be living on ideas. In the gardens of Seville I once heard, coming through the tangle of palms and orange trees, the treble voice of a pupil in the theological seminary, crying to his playmate : " You booby ! of course angels have a more perfect nature than men." With his black and red cassock that child had put on dialectic ; he was playing the game of dogma and dreaming in words, and was insensible to the scent of violets that filled the air. How long would that last ? Hardly, I suspect, until the next spring ; and the troubled awakening which puberty would presently bring to that little dogmatist, sooner or later overtakes all elder dogmatists in the press of the world. The more perfect the dogmatism, the more insecure. A great high topsail that can never be reefed nor furled is the first carried away by the gale.

To me the opinions of mankind, taken without any contrary prejudice (since I have no rival opinions to propose) but simply contrasted with the course of nature, seem surprising fictions ; and the marvel is how they can be maintained. What strange religions, what ferocious moralities, what slavish fashions, what sham interests ! I can explain it all only by saying to myself that intelligence is naturally forthright ; it forges ahead ; it piles fiction on fiction ; and the fact that the dogmatic structure, for the time being, stands and grows, passes for a proof of its rightness. Right indeed it is in one sense, as vegetation is right ; it is vital ; it has plasticity and warmth, and a certain indirect correspondence with its soil and climate. Many obviously fabulous dogmas, like those of religion, might for ever dominate the most active minds, except for one circumstance. In the jungle one tree strangles another, and luxuriance itself is murderous. So is luxuriance in the human mind. What kills spontaneous fictions, what recalls the impassioned fancy from its improvisation, is the angry voice of some contrary fancy. Nature, silently making fools of us all our lives, never would bring us to our senses ; but the maddest assertions of the mind may do so, when they challenge one another. Criticism arises out of the conflict of dogmas.

May I escape this predicament and criticise without a dogmatic criterion ? Hardly ; for though the criticism may be expressed hypothetically, as for instance in saying that if any child knew his own father he would be a wise child, yet the point on which doubt is thrown is a point of fact, and that there are fathers and children is assumed dogmatically. If not, however obscure the essential relation between fathers and children might be ideally, no one could be wise or foolish in assigning it in any particular instance, since no such terms would exist in nature at all. Scepticism is a suspicion of error about facts, and to suspect error about facts is to share the enterprise of knowledge, in which facts are presupposed and error is possible. The sceptic thinks himself shrewd, and often is so ; his intellect, like the intellect he criticises, may have some inkling of the true hang and connection of things ; he may have pierced to a truth of nature behind current illusions. Since his criticism may thus be true and his doubt well grounded, they are certainly assertions ; and if he is sincerely a sceptic, they are assertions which he is ready to maintain stoutly. Scepticism is accordingly a form of belief. Dogma cannot be abandoned ; it can only be revised in view of some more elementary dogma which it has not yet occurred to the sceptic to doubt ; and he may be right in every point of his criticism, except in fancying that his criticism is radical and that he is altogether a sceptic.

This vital compulsion to posit and to believe something, even in the act of doubting, would nevertheless be ignominious, if the beliefs which life and intelligence forced upon me were always false. I should then be obliged to honour the sceptic for his heroic though hopeless effort to eschew belief, and I should despise the dogmatist for his willing subservience to illusion. The sequel will show, I trust, that this is not the case ; that intelligence is by nature veridical, and that its ambition to reach the truth is sane and capable of satisfaction, even if each of its efforts actually fails. To convince me of this fact, however, I must first justify my faith in many subsidiary beliefs concerning animal economy and the human mind and the world they flourish in.

That scepticism should intervene in philosophy at all is an accident of human history, due to much unhappy experience of perplexity and error. If all had gone well, assertions would be made spontaneously in dogmatic innocence, and the very notion of a *right* to make them would seem as gratuitous as in fact it is ; because all the realms of being lie open to a spirit plastic enough to conceive them, and those that have ears to hear, may hear. Nevertheless, in the confused state of human speculation this embarrassment obtrudes itself automatically, and a philosopher to-day would be ridiculous and negligible who had not strained his dogmas through the utmost rigours of scepticism, and who did not approach every opinion, whatever his own ultimate faith, with the courtesy and smile of the sceptic.

The brute necessity of believing something so long

as life lasts does not justify any belief in particular ; nor does it assure me that not to live would not, for this very reason, be far safer and saner. To be dead and have no opinions would certainly not be to discover the truth ; but if all opinions are necessarily false, it would at least be not to sin against intellectual honour. Let me then push scepticism as far as I logically can, and endeavour to clear my mind of illusion, even at the price of intellectual suicide.

CHAPTER III

WAYWARD SCEPTICISM

CRITICISM surprises the soul in the arms of convention. Children insensibly accept all the suggestions of sense and language, the only initiative they show being a certain wilfulness in the extension of these notions, a certain impulse towards private superstition. This is soon corrected by education or broken off rudely, like the nails of a tender hand, by hard contact with custom, fact, or derision. Belief then settles down in sullenness and apathy to a narrow circle of vague assumptions, to none of which the mind need have any deep affinity, none of which it need really understand, but which nevertheless it clings to for lack of other footing. The philosophy of the common man is an old wife that gives him no pleasure, yet he cannot live without her, and resents any aspersions that strangers may cast on her character.

Of this homely philosophy the tender cuticle is religious belief; really the least vital and most arbitrary part of human opinion, the outer ring, as it were, of the fortifications of prejudice, but for that very reason the most jealously defended; since it is on being attacked there, at the least defensible point, that rage and alarm at being attacked at all are first aroused in the citadel. People are not naturally sceptics, wondering if a single one of their intellectual habits can be reasonably preserved; they are dogmatists angrily confident of maintaining them all. Integral minds, pupils of a single coherent tradition, regard their religion, whatever it may be, as certain, as sublime, and as the only rational basis of morality and policy. Yet in fact religious belief is terribly precarious, partly because it is arbitrary, so that in the next tribe or in the next century it will wear quite a different form ; and partly because, when genuine, it is spontaneous and continually remodelled, like poetry, in the heart that gives it birth. A man of the world soon learns to discredit established religions on account of their variety and absurdity, although he may good-naturedly continue to conform to his own ; and a mystic before long begins fervently to condemn current dogmas, on account of his own different inspiration. Without philosophical criticism, therefore, mere experience and good sense suggest that all positive religions are false, or at least (which is enough for my present purpose) that they are all fantastic and insecure.

Closely allied with religious beliefs there are usually legends and histories, dramatic if not miraculous ; and a man who knows anything of literature and has observed how histories are written, even in the most enlightened times, needs no satirist to remind him that all histories, in so far as they contain a system, a drama, or a moral, are so much literary fiction, and probably disingenuous. Common sense, however, will still admit that there are recorded facts not to be doubted, as it will admit that there are obvious physical facts ; and it is here, when popular philosophy has been reduced to a kind of positivism, that the speculative critic may well step upon the scene.

Criticism, I have said, has no first principle, and its desultory character may be clearly exhibited at this point by asking whether the evidence of science or that of history should be questioned first. I might impugn the belief in physical facts reported by the senses and by natural science, such as the existence of a ring of Saturn, reducing them to appearances, which are facts reported by personal remembrance ; and this is actually the choice made by British and German critics of knowledge, who, relying on memory and history, have denied the existence of anything but experience. Yet the opposite procedure would seem more judicious ; knowledge of the facts reported by history is mediated by documents which are physical facts ; and these documents must first be discovered and believed to have subsisted unknown and to have had a more or less remote origin in time and place, before they can be taken as evidence for any mental events ; for if I did not believe that there had been any men in Athens I should not imagine they had had any thoughts. Even personal memory, when it professes to record any distant experience, can recognise and place this experience only by first reconstructing the material scene in which it occurred. Memory records moral events in terms of their physical occasions ; and if the latter are merely imaginary, the former must be doubly so, like the thoughts of a personage in a novel. My remembrance of the past is a novel I am constantly recomposing ; and it would not be a historical novel, but sheer fiction, if the material events which mark and ballast my career had not their public dates and characters scientifically discoverable.

Romantic solipsism, in which the self making up the universe is a moral person endowed with memory and vanity, is accordingly untenable. Not that it is unthinkable or self - contradictory ; because all the complementary objects which might be requisite to give point and body to the idea of oneself might be only ideas and not facts ; and a solitary deity imagining a world or remembering his own past constitutes a perfectly conceivable universe. But this imagination

would have no truth and this remembrance no control ;
so that the fond belief of such a deity that he knew
his own past would be the most groundless of dogmas ;
and while by chance the dogma might be true, that
deity would have no reason to think it so. At the
first touch of criticism he would be obliged to confess
that his alleged past was merely a picture now before
him, and that he had no reason to suppose that this
picture had had any constancy in successive moments,
or that he had lived through previous moments at all ;
nor could any new experience ever lend any colour or
corroboration to such a pathological conviction. This is
obvious ; so that romantic solipsism, although perhaps
an interesting state of mind, is not a position capable of
defence ; and any solipsism which is not a solipsism
of the present moment is logically contemptible.

The postulates on which empirical knowledge and
inductive science are based—namely, that there has
been a past, that it was such as it is now thought
to be, that there will be a future and that it must,
for some inconceivable reason, resemble the past and
obey the same laws—these are all gratuitous dogmas.
The sceptic in his honest retreat knows nothing of
a future, and has no need of such an unwarrantable
idea. He may perhaps have images before him of
scenes somehow not in the foreground, with a sense
of before and after running through the texture of
them ; and he may call this background of his sentiency
the past ; but the relative obscurity and evanescence
of these phantoms will not prompt him to suppose
that they have retreated to obscurity from the light
of day. They will be to him simply what he experiences them as being, denizens of the twilight. It
would be a vain fancy to imagine that these ghosts
had once been men ; they are simply nether gods,
native to the Erebus they inhabit. The world present
to the sceptic may continue to fade into these opposite

abysses, the past and the future ; but having renounced all prejudice and checked all customary faith, he will regard both as painted abysses only, like the opposite exits to the country and to the city on the ancient stage. He will see the masked actors (and he will invent a reason) rushing frantically out on one side and in at the other ; but he knows that the moment they are out of sight the play is over for them ; those outlying regions and those reported events which the messengers narrate so impressively are pure fancy ; and there is nothing for him but to sit in his seat and lend his mind to the tragic illusion.

The solipsist thus becomes an incredulous spectator of his own romance, thinks his own adventures fictions, and accepts a solipsism of the present moment. This is an honest position, and certain attempts to refute it as self-contradictory are based on a misunderstanding. For example, it is irrelevant to urge that the present moment cannot comprise the whole of existence because the phrase " a present moment " implies a chain of moments ; or that the mind that calls any moment the present moment virtually transcends it and posits a past and a future beyond it. These arguments confuse the convictions of the solipsist with those of a spectator describing him from outside. The sceptic is not committed to the implications of other men's language ; nor can he be convicted out of his own mouth by the names he is obliged to bestow on the details of his momentary vision. There may be long vistas in it ; there may be many figures of men and beasts, many legends and apocalypses depicted on his canvas ; there may even be a shadowy frame about it, or the suggestion of a gigantic ghostly some-thing on the hither side of it which he may call him-self. All this wealth of objects is not inconsistent with solipsism, although the implication of the conventional terms in which those objects are described may render it difficult for the solipsist always to remember his solitude. Yet when he reflects, he perceives it ; and all his heroic efforts are concentrated on *not* asserting and *not* implying anything, but simply noticing what he finds. Scepticism is not concerned to abolish ideas ; it can relish the variety and order of a pictured world, or of any number of them in succession, without any of the qualms and exclusions proper to dogmatism. Its case is simply not to credit these ideas, not to posit any of these fancied worlds, nor this ghostly mind imagined as viewing them. The attitude of the sceptic is not inconsistent ; it is merely difficult, because it is hard for the greedy intellect to keep its cake without eating it. Very voracious dogmatists like Spinoza even assert that it is impossible, but the impossibility is only psychological, and due to their voracity ; they no doubt speak truly for themselves when they say that the idea of a horse, if not contradicted by some other idea, *is* a belief that the horse exists ; but this would not be the case if they felt no impulse to ride that imagined horse, or to get out of its way. Ideas become beliefs only when by precipitating tendencies to action they persuade me that they are signs of things ; and these things are not those ideas simply hypostatised, but are believed to be compacted of many parts, and full of ambushed powers, entirely absent from the ideas. The belief is imposed on me surreptitiously by a latent mechanical reaction of my body on the object producing the idea ; it is by no means implied in any qualities obvious in that idea. Such a latent reaction, being mechanical, can hardly be avoided, but it may be discounted in reflection, if a man has experience and the poise of a philosopher ; and scepticism is not the less honourable for being difficult, when it is inspired by a firm determination to probe this confused and terrible apparition of life to the bottom.

So far is solipsism of the present moment from being self-contradictory that it might, under other circumstances, be the normal and invincible attitude of the spirit ; and I suspect it may be that of many animals. The difficulties I find in maintaining it consistently come from the social and laborious character of human life. A creature whose whole existence was passed under a hard shell, or was spent in a free flight, might find nothing paradoxical or acrobatic in solipsism ; nor would he feel the anguish which men feel in doubt, because doubt leaves them defenceless and undecided in the presence of on-coming events. A creature whose actions were pre-determined might have a clearer mind. He might keenly enjoy the momentary scene, never conceiving himself as a separate body or as anything but the unity of that scene, nor his enjoyment as anything but its beauty : nor would he harbour the least suspicion that it would change or perish, nor any objection to its doing so if it chose. Solipsism would then be selflessness and scepticism simplicity. They would not be open to disruption from within. The ephemeral insect would accept the evidence of his ephemeral object, whatever quality this might chance to have ; he would not suppose, as Descartes did, that in think-ing anything his own existence was involved. Being new-born himself, with only this one innate (and also experimental) idea, he would bring to his single experience no extraneous habits of interpretation or inference ; and he would not be troubled by doubts, because he would believe nothing.

For men, however, who are long-lived and teachable animals, solipsism of the present moment is a violent pose, permitted only to the young philosopher, in his first intellectual despair ; and even he often cheats himself when he thinks he assumes it, and professing to stand on his head really, like a clumsy acrobat, rests on his hands also. The very terms " solipsism " and " present moment " betray this impurity. An actual intuition, which by hypothesis is fresh, absolute, and not to be repeated, is called and is perhaps conceived as an *ipse*, a self-same man. But identity (as I shall have occasion to observe in discussing identity in essences) implies two moments, two instances, or two intuitions, between which it obtains. Similarly, a " present moment " suggests other moments, and an adventitious limitation either in duration or in scope ; but the solipsist and his wòrld (which are not distinguishable) have by hypothesis no environment whatsoever, and nothing limits them save the fact that there is nothing more. These irrelevances and side glances are imported into the mind of the sceptic because in fact he is retreating into solipsism from a far more ambitious philosophy. A thought naturally momentary would be immune from them.

A perfect solipsist, therefore, hardly is found amongst men ; but some men are zealous in bringing their criticism down to solipsism of the present moment just because this attitude enables them to cast away everything that is not present in their prevalent mood, or in their deepest thought, and to set up this chosen object as the absolute. Such a compensatory dogma is itself not critical ; but criticism may help to raise it to a specious eminence by lopping off everything else. What remains will be different in different persons : some say it is Brahma, some that it is Pure Being, some that it is the Idea or Law of the moral world. Each of these absolutes is the sacred residuum which the temperament of different philosophers or of different nations clings to, and will not criticise, and in each case it is contrasted with the world in which the vulgar believe, as something deeper, simpler, and more real. Perhaps when solipsism of the present moment is reached by a philosopher trained in abstraction and inclined to ecstasy, his experience, at this depth of concentration, will be that of an extreme tension which is also liberty, an emptiness which is intensest light; and his denial of all natural facts and events, which he will call illusions, will culminate in the fervent assertion that all is One, and that One is Brahma, or the breath of life. On the other hand, a scientific observer and reasoner, who has pried into substance, and has learned that all the aspects of nature are relative and variable, may still not deny the existence of matter in every object; and this element of mere intensity, drawn from the sense of mere actuality in himself, may lead him to assert that pure Being is, and everything else is not. Finally, a second-ary mind fed on books may drop the natural emphasis which objects of sense have for the living animal, and may retain, as the sole filling of its present moment, nothing but the sciences. The philosopher will then balance his denial of material facts by asserting the absolute reality of his knowledge of them. This reality, however, will extend no farther than his information, as some intensest moment of recollection may gather it together; and his personal idea of the world, so composed and so limited, will seem to him the sole existence. His universe will be the after-image of his learning.

We may notice that in these three instances scepti-cism has not suspended affirmation but has rather intensified it, pouring it all on the devoted head of one chosen object. There is a tireless and deafening vehemence about these sceptical prophets; it betrays the poor old human Psyche labouring desperately within them in the shipwreck of her native hopes, and refusing to die. Her sacrifice, she believes, will be her salvation, and she passionately identifies what remains to her with all she has lost and by an audacious falsehood persuades herself she has lost nothing.

Thus the temper of these sceptics is not at all sceptical. They take their revenge on the world, which eluded them when they tried to prove its existence, by asserting the existence of the remnant which they have still by them, insisting that this, and this only, is the true and perfect world, and a much better one than that false world in which the heathen trust. Such infatuation in the solipsist, however, is not inevitable ; no such exorbitant credit need be given to the object, perhaps a miserable one, which still fills the sceptical mind, and a more dispassionate scepticism, while contemplating that object, may disallow it.

CHAPTER IV

DOUBTS ABOUT SELF-CONSCIOUSNESS

Do I know, can I know, anything ? Would not knowledge be an impossible inclusion of what lies outside ? May I not rather renounce all beliefs ? If only I could, what peace would descend into my perturbed conscience ! The spectacle of other men's folly continually reawakens in me the suspicion that I too am surely fooled ; and the character of the beliefs which force themselves upon me — the fantasticality of space and time, the grotesque medley of nature, the cruel mockery called religion, the sorry history and absurd passions of mankind—all invite me to disown them and to say to what I call the world, " Come now ; how do you expect me to believe in *you* ? " At the same time this very incredulity and wonder in me are baseless and without credentials. What right have I to any presumptions as to what would be natural and proper ? Is not the most extravagant fact as plausible as any other ? Is not the most obvious axiom a wanton dogma ? Yet turn whichever way I will, and refine as I may, the pressure of existence, of tyrannical absolute present being, seems to confront me. Something is evidently going on, at least in myself. I feel an instant complex strain of existence, forcing me to say that I think and that I am. Certainly the words I use in such reflection bring many images with them which may possess no truth.

Thus when I say " I," the term suggests a man, one of many living in a world contrasted with his thinking, yet partly surveyed by it. These suggestions of the word " I " might well be false. This thinking might not belong to a member of the human family, and no such race as this mankind that I am thinking of might ever have existed. The natural world in which I fancy that race living, among other races of animals, might also be imaginary. Yet, in that case, what is imagination ? Banish myself and my world as much as I will, the present act of banishing them subsists and is manifest ; and it was this act, now unrolling itself consciously through various phases, not any particular person in any environment, that I meant when I said, " I find that I think and am."

In like manner the terms thinking and finding, which I use for want of anything better, imply contrasts and antecedents which I may disregard. It is not a particular process called thinking, nor a particular conjunction called finding, that I need assert to exist, but merely this passing unrest, whatever you choose to call it : these pulsations and phantoms which to deny is to produce and to strive to banish is to redouble.

It might seem for a moment as if this pressing actuality of experience implied a relation between subject and object, so that an indescribable being called the ego or self was given with and involved in any actual fact. This analysis, however, is merely grammatical, and if pressed issues in mythical notions. Analysis can never find in the object what, by hypothesis, is not there ; and the object, by definition, is all that is found. But there is a biological truth, discovered much later, under this alleged analytic necessity : the truth that animal experience is a product of two factors, antecedent to the experience and not parts of it, namely, organ and stimulus, body and environment, person and situation. These two natural conditions must normally come together, like flint and steel, before the spark of experience will fly. But scepticism requires me to take the spark itself as my point of departure, since it alone lives morally and lights up with its vital flame the scene I seem to discover. This spark is single, though changeful. Experience has no conditions for a critic of knowledge who proceeds transcendentally, that is, from the vantage-ground of experience itself. To urge, therefore, that a self or ego is presupposed in experience, or even must have created experience by its absolute fiat, is curiously to fail in critical thinking, and to renounce the transcendental method. All transcendental system - makers are in fact false to the very principle by which they criticise dogmatism ; a principle which admits of no system, tolerates no belief, but recalls the universe at every moment into the absolute experience which posits it here and now.

This backsliding of transcendentalism, when it forgets itself so far as to assign conditions to experience, might have no serious consequences, if transcendentalism were clearly recognised to be simply a romantic episode in reflection, a sort of poetic madness, and no necessary step in the life of reason. That its professed scepticism should so soon turn into mythology would then seem appropriate in such a disease of genius. But the delusion becomes troublesome to the serious critic of knowledge when it perhaps inclines him to imagine that, in asserting that experience is a product, and has two terms, he is describing the inner nature of experience, and not merely its external conditions, as natural history reports them. He may then be tempted to assign a metaphysical status and logical necessity to a merely material fact. Instead of the body, which is the true " subject " in experience, he may think he finds an absolute ego, and instead of the natural environment of the body, which is the true "object," he may think he finds an illimitable reality; and, to make things simpler, he may proceed to declare that these two are one; but all this is myth.

The fact of experience, then, is single and, from its own point of view, absolutely unconditioned and groundless, impossible to explain and impossible to exorcise. Yet just as it comes unbidden, so it may fade and lapse of its own accord. It constantly seems to do so; and my hold on existence is not so firm that non-existence does not seem always at hand and, as it were, always something deeper, vaster, and more natural than existence. Yet this apprehension of an imminent non-existence — an apprehension which is itself an existing fact—cannot be trusted to penetrate to a real nothingness yawning about me unless I assert something not at all involved in the present being, and something most remarkable, namely, that I know and can survey the *movement* of my existence, and that it can actually have lapsed from one state into another, as I conceive it to have lapsed.

Thus the sense of a complex strain of existence, the conviction that I am and that I am thinking, involve a sense of at least possible change. I should not speak of complexity nor of strain, if various opposed developments into the not-given were not, to my feeling, striving to take place. Doors are about to open, cords to snap, blows to fall, pulsations to repeat themselves. The flux and perspectives of being seem to be open within me to my own intuition.

Caution is requisite here. All this may be simply a present obsession, destitute of all prophetic or retrospective truth, and carrying me no further, if I wish to be honest, than a bare confession of how I feel. Anything given in intuition is, by definition, an appearance and nothing but an appearance. Of course, if I am a thorough sceptic, I may discredit the existence of anything else, so that this appearance will stand in my philosophy as the only reality. But, then, I must not enlarge nor interpret nor hypostatise it : I must keep it as the mere picture it is, and revert to solipsism of the present moment. One thing is the *feeling* that something is happening, an intuition which finds what it finds and cannot be made to find anything else. Another thing is the *belief* that what is found is a report or description of events that have happened already, in such a manner that the earlier phases of the flux I am aware of existed first, before the later phases and without them ; whereas in my intuition now the earlier phases are merely the first part of the given whole, exist only together with the later phases, and are earlier only in a perspective, not in a flux of successive events. If anything had an actual beginning, that first phase must have occurred out of relation to the subsequent phases which had not yet arisen, and only became manifest in the sequel : as the Old Testament, if really earlier than the New Testament, must have existed alone first, when it could not be called old. If it had existed only in the Christian Bible, under that perspective which renders and calls it old, it would be old only speciously and for Christian intuition, and all revelation would have been really simultaneous. In a word, specious change is not actual change. The unity of apperception which yields the sense of change renders change specious, by relating the terms and directions of change together in a single perspective, as respectively receding, passing, or arriving. In so uniting and viewing these terms, intuition of change excludes actual change in the given object. If change has been actual, it must have been prior to, and independent of, the intuition of that change.

Doubtless, as a matter of fact, this intuition of change is itself lapsing, and yielding its place in

physical time to vacancy or to the intuition of changelessness ; and this lapse of the intuition in physical
time is an actual change. Evidently, however, it is
not a given change, since neither vacancy nor the
intuition of changelessness can reveal it. It is revealed,
if revealed at all, by a further intuition of specious
change *taken as a report*. Actual change, if it is to
be known at all, must be known by belief and not
by intuition. Doubt is accordingly always possible
regarding the existence of actual change. Having
renounced my faith in nature, I must not weakly
retain faith in experience. This intuition of change
might be false ; it might be the only fact in the universe, and perfectly changeless. I should then be that
intuition, but it would not bring me any true knowledge
of anything actual. On the contrary, it would be an
illusion, presenting a false object, since it would
present nothing but change, when the only actual
reality, namely its own, was unchanging. On the
other hand, if this intuition of change was no illusion,
but a change was actually occurring and the universe
had passed into its present state out of a previous
state which was different (if, for instance, this very
intuition of change had grown more articulate or more
complex), I should then be right in hazarding a very
bold assertion, namely, that it is known to me that
what now is was not always, that there are things not
given, that there is genesis in nature, and that time
is real.

CHAPTER V

DOUBTS ABOUT CHANGE

As I watch a sensible object the evidence of variation is often irresistible. This flag is flapping. This flame is dancing. How shall I deny that almost everything, in nature and in fancy, like the Ghost in *Hamlet*, is here, is there, is gone ? Of course I witness these appearances and disappearances. The intuition of change is more direct and more imperious than any other. But *belief* in change, as I found just now, asserts that before this intuition of change arose the first term of that change had occurred separately. This no intuition of change can prove. The belief is irresistible in animal perception, for reasons which biology can plausibly assign ; and it cannot be long suspended in actual thinking ; but it may be suspended for a moment theoretically, in the interests of a thorough criticism. The criticism too may prove persuasive. Many solemn if not serious philosophers have actually maintained that this irresistible assertion is false, and that all diversity and change are illusion. In denying time, multiplicity, and motion, their theory has harked back—and it is no mean feat of concentration—almost to the infancy of thought, and reversed the whole life of reason. This mystical retraction of all the beliefs necessary to life, and suspension, almost, of life itself, have been sometimes defended by dialectical arguments, to the effect that change is impossible, because the idea of it is incoherent or self-contradictory. Such arguments, however, are worthless for a critic of knowledge, because they involve an assumption much grosser than that which they discard. They assume that if a thing is dialectically unintelligible, as change is, or inexpressible in terms other than its own, it cannot be true ; whereas, on the contrary, *only* when dialectic passes its own frontiers and, fortified by a passport countersigned by experience, enters the realm of brute fact, has dialectic itself any claim to truth or any relevance to the facts. Dialectical difficulties, therefore, are irrelevant to valid knowledge, the terms of which are irrational, no less than is their juxtaposition in existence.

The denial of change may rest on more sceptical grounds, and may have a deeper and more tragic character. It may come from insight into the temerity of asserting change. Why, indeed, do men believe in it ? Because they see and feel it : but this fact is not denied. They may see and feel all the changes they like : what reason is that for believing that over and above this actual intuition, with the specious change it regards, one state of the universe has given place to another, or different intuitions have existed ? You feel you have changed ; you feel things changing ? Granted. Does this fact help you to feel an earlier state which you do not feel, which is not an integral part of what is now before you, but a state from which you are supposed to have passed into the state in which you now are ? If you feel that earlier state now, there is no change involved. That datum, which you now designate as the past, and which exists only in this perspective, is merely a term in your present feeling. It was never anything else. It was never given otherwise than as it is given now, when it is given as past. Therefore, if things are such only as intuition makes them, every suggestion of a past is false. For if the event now called past was ever actual and in its day a present event, then it is not merely a term in the specious change now given in intuition. Thus the feeling of movement, on which you so trustfully rely, cannot vouch for the reality of movement, I mean, for the existence of an actual past, once present, and not identical with the specious past now falling within the compass of intuition. By a curious fatality, the more you insist on the sense of change the more you hedge yourself in in the changeless and the immediate. There is no avenue to the past or future, there is no room or breath for progressive life, except through faith in the intellect and in the reality of things not seen.

I think that if the sense of change, primordial and continual as it is, were ever pure, this fact that in itself it is changeless would not seem strange or confusing : for evidently the idea of *pure* change would be always the same, and changeless ; it could change only by yielding to the idea of rest or of identity. But in animals of a human complexity the sense of change is never pure ; larger terms are recognised and felt to be permanent, and the change is seen to proceed within one of these or the other, without being pervasive, or changing everything in the picture. These are matters of animal sensibility, to be decided empirically—that is, never to be decided at all. Every new animal is free to feel in a new way. The gnat may begin with a sense of flux, like Heraclitus, and only diffidently and sceptically ask himself *what* it is that is rushing by ; and the barnacle may begin, like Parmenides, with a sense of the unshakable foundations of being, and never quite reconcile himself to the thought that reality could ever move from its solid bottom, or exchange one adhesion for another. But, after all, the mind of Heraclitus, seeing nothing but flux, would be as constant a mind as that of

Parmenides, seeing nothing but rest ; and if the philosophy of Heraclitus were the only one in the world, there would be no change in the world of philosophy.

Accordingly, when I have removed the instinctive belief in an environment beyond the given scene, and in a past and future beyond the specious present, the lapse in this specious present itself and the sensible events within it lose all the urgency of actual motions. They become pictures of motions and ideas of events : I no longer seem to live in a changing world, but an illusion of change seems to play idly before me, and to be contained in my changelessness. This pictured change is a particular quality of being, as is pain or a sustained note, not a passage from one quality of being to another, since the part called earlier never disappears and the part called later is given from the first. Events, and the reality of change they involve, may therefore be always illusions. The sceptic can ultimately penetrate to the vision of a reality from which they should be excluded. All he need do, in order to attain to this immunity from illusion, is to extirpate from his own nature every vestige of anxiety, not to regret nor to fear nor to attempt anything. If he can accomplish this he has exorcised belief in change.

Moreover, the animal compulsion to believe in change may not only be erroneous, but it may not operate at all times. I may remain alive, and be actually changing, and yet this change in me, remaining unabated, may be undiscerned. Very quick complete changes, cutting up existence into discrete instants, the inner order of which would not be transmitted from one to the other, would presumably exclude memory. There would be no intuition of change, and therefore not even a possible belief in it. A certain actual persistence is requisite to perceive a flux, and an absolute flux, in which nothing was carried over from moment to moment, would yield, in each of these moments, nothing but an intuition of permanence. So far is the actual instability of things, even if I admit it, from involving a sense of it, or excluding a sense of its opposite. I may, therefore, occasionally deny it; and nothing can persuade me, during those moments, that my insight then is not truer than at other times, when I perceive and believe in change. The mystic must confess that he spends most of his life in the teeming valleys of illusion : but he may still maintain that truth and reality are disclosed to him only on those almost inaccessible mountain tops, where only the One and Changeless is visible. That the believer in nature perceives that this mystical conviction is itself a natural event, and a very ticklish and unstable illusion, does not alter that conviction while it lasts, nor enter into its deliverance : so that under its sway the mystic may disallow all change and multiplicity, either virtually by forgetting it, or actually by demonstrating it to be false and impossible. Being without irrational expectation (and all expectation is irrational) and without belief in memory (which is a sort of expectation reversed), he will lack altogether that sagacity which makes the animal believe in latent events and latent substances, on which his eventual action might operate ; and his dialectic not being rebuked by any contrary buffets of experience, he will prove to his heart's content that change is unthinkable. For if discrete altogether, without a continuous substance or medium, events will not follow one another, but each will simply exist absolutely ; and if a substance or medium be posited, no relation can be conceived to obtain between it and the events said to diversify it : for in so far as the substance or medium permeates the events nothing will happen or change ; and in so far as the events really occur and are not merely specious changes given in one intuition, they will be discrete altogether, without foothold in that medium or substance postulated in vain to sustain them.   Thus the mystic, on the wings of a free dialectic, will be wafted home to his ancient and comforting assurance that all is One, that Being is, and that Non-Being is not.

CHAPTER VI

WHY should the mystic, in proportion as he dismisses the miscellany of experience as so much illusion, feel that he becomes one with reality and attains to absolute existence ? I think that the same survival of vulgar presumptions which leads the romantic solipsist to retain his belief in his personal history and destiny, leads the mystic to retain, and fondly to embrace, the feeling of existence. His speculation is indeed inspired by the love of security : his grand objection to the natural world, and to mortal life, is that they are deceptive, that they cheat the soul that loves them, and prove to be illusions : the assumption apparently being that reality must be permanent, and that he who has hold on reality is safe for ever. In this the mystic, who so hates illusions, is the victim of an illusion himself : for the reality he has hold of is but the burden of a single moment, which in its solipsism thinks itself absolute. What is reality ? As I should like to use the term, reality is being of any sort. If it means character or essence, illusions have it as much as substance, and more richly. If it means substance, then sceptical concentration upon inner experience, or ecstatic abstraction, seems to me the last place in which we should look for it. The immediate and the visionary are at the opposite pole from substance ; they are on the surface or, if you like, at the top ;

whereas substance if it is anywhere is at the bottom. The realm of immediate illusion is as real as any other, and very attractive ; many would wish it to be the only reality, and hate substance ; but if substance exists (which I am not yet ready to assert) they have no reason to hate it, since it is the basis of those immediate feelings which fill them with satisfaction. Finally, if reality means existence, certainly the mystic and his meditation may exist, but not more truly than any other natural fact ; and what would exist in them would be a pulse of animal being, kindling that momentary ecstasy, as animal life at certain intensities is wont to do.   The theme of that meditation, its visionary object, need not exist at all ; it may be incapable of existing if it is essentially timeless and dialectical.   The animal mind treats its data as facts, or as signs of facts, but the animal mind is full of the rashest presumptions, positing time, change, a particular station in the midst of events yielding a particular perspective of those events, and the flux of all nature precipitating that experience at that place.   None of these posited objects is a datum in which a sceptic could rest.   Indeed, existence or fact, in the sense which I give to these words, cannot be a datum at all, because existence involves external relations and actual (not merely specious) flux : whereas, however complex a datum may be, with no matter what perspectives opening within it, it must be embraced in a single stroke of apperception, and nothing outside it can belong to it at all.   The datum is a pure image ; it is essentially illusory and unsubstantial, however thunderous its sound or keen its edge, or however normal and significant its presence may be.   When the mystic asserts enthusiastically the existence of his immediate, ideal, unutterable object, Absolute Being, he is peculiarly unfortunate in his faith : it would be impossible to choose an image less relevant to the agencies that actually bring that image before him. The burden and glow of existence which he is conscious of come entirely from himself ; his object is eminently empty, impotent, non-existent ; but the heat and labour of his own soul suffuse that emptiness with light, and the very hum of change within him, accelerated almost beyond endurance and quite beyond discrimination, sounds that piercing note.

The last step in scepticism is now before me. It will lead me to deny existence to any datum, whatever it may be ; and as the datum, by hypothesis, is the whole of what solicits my attention at any moment, I shall deny the existence of everything, and abolish that category of thought altogether. If I could not do this, I should be a tyro in scepticism. Belief in the existence of anything, including myself, is something radically incapable of proof, and resting, like all belief, on some irrational persuasion or prompting of life. Certainly, as a matter of fact, when I deny existence I exist ; but doubtless many of the other facts I have been denying, because I found no evidence for them, were true also. To bring me evidence of their existence is no duty imposed on facts, nor a habit of theirs : I must employ private detectives The point is, in this task of criticism, to discard every belief that is a belief merely ; and the belief in existence, in the nature of the case, can be a belief only. The datum is an idea, a description ; I may contemplate it without belief ; but when I assert that such a thing exists I am hypostatising this datum, placing it in presumptive relations which are not internal to it, and worshipping it as an idol or thing. Neither its existence nor mine nor that of my belief can be given in any datum. These things are incidents involved in that order of nature which I have thrown over ; they are no part of what remains before me.

Assurance of existence expresses animal watchfulness : it posits, within me and round me, hidden and imminent events. The sceptic can easily cast a doubt on the remoter objects of this belief ; and nothing but a certain obduracy and want of agility prevents him from doubting present existence itself. For what could present existence mean, if the imminent events for which animal sense is watching failed altogether, failed at the very roots, so to speak, of the tree of intuition, and left nothing but its branches flowering *in vacuo* ? Expectation is admittedly the most hazardous of beliefs : yet what is watchfulness but expectation ? Memory is notoriously full of illusion ; yet what would experience of the present be if the veracity of primary memory were denied, and if I no longer believed that anything had just happened, or that I had ever been in the state from which I suppose myself to have passed into this my present condition ?

It will not do for the sceptic to take refuge in the confused notion that expectation *possesses* the future, or memory the past. As a matter of fact, expectation is like hunger ; it opens its mouth, and something probably drops into it, more or less, very often, the sort of thing it expected ; but sometimes a surprise comes, and sometimes nothing. Life involves expectation, but does not prevent death : and expectation is never so thoroughly stultified as when it is not undeceived, but cancelled. The open mouth does not then so much as close upon nothing. It is buried open. Nor is memory in a better case. As the whole world might collapse and cease at any moment, nullifying all expectation, so it might at any moment have sprung out of nothing : for it is thoroughly contingent, and might have begun to-day, with this degree of complexity and illusive memory, as well as long ago, with whatever energy or momentum it was first endowed with. The backward perspective of time is perhaps really an inverted expectation ; but for the momentum of life forward, we might not be able to space the elements active in the present so as to assign to them a longer or a shorter history ; for we should not attempt to discriminate amongst these elements such as we could still count on in the immediate future, and such as we might safely ignore : so that our conception of the past implies, perhaps, a distinction between the living and the dead. This distinction is itself practical, and looks to the future. In the absolute present all is specious ; and to pure intuition the living are as ghostly as the dead, and the dead as present as the living.

In the sense of existence there is accordingly something more than the obvious character of that which is alleged to exist. What is this complement ? It cannot be a feature in the datum, since the datum by definition is the whole of what is found. Nor can it be, in my sense at least of the word existence, the intrinsic constitution or specific being of this object, since existence comports external relations, variable, contingent, and not discoverable in a given being when taken alone : for there is nothing that may not lose its existence, or the existence of which might not be conceivably denied. The complement added to the datum when it is alleged to exist seems, then, to be added by *me* ; it is the finding, the occurrence, the assault, the impact of that being here and now ; it is the experience of it. But what can experience be, if I take away from it the whole of what is experienced ? And what meaning can I give to such words as impact, assault, occurrence, or finding, when I have banished and denied my body, my past, my residual present being, and everything except the datum which I find ? The sense of existence evidently belongs to the intoxication, to the *Rausch*, of existence itself ; it is the strain of life within me, prior to all intuition, that in its precipitation and terror, passing as it continually must from one untenable condition to another, stretches my attention absurdly over what is not given, over the lost and the unattained, the before and after which are wrapped in darkness, and confuses my breathless apprehension of the clear presence of all I can ever truly behold.

Indeed, so much am I a creature of movement, and of the ceaseless metabolism of matter, that I should never catch even these glimpses of the light, if there were not rhythms, pauses, repetitions, and nodes in my physical progress, to absorb and reflect it here and there : as the traveller, hurried in a cloud of smoke and dust through tunnel after tunnel in the Italian Riviera, catches and loses momentary visions of blue sea and sky, which he would like to arrest, but cannot ; yet if he had not been rushed and whistled along these particular tunnels, even those snatches, in the form in which they come to him, would have been denied him. So it is the rush of life that, at its open moments, floods me with intuitions, partial and confused, but still revelations ; the landscape is wrapped in the smoke of my little engine, and turned into a tantalising incident of my hot journey. What appears (which is an ideal object and not an event) is thus confused with the event of its appearance ; the picture is identified with the kindling or distraction of my attention falling by chance upon it ; and the strain of my material existence, battling with material accidents, turns the ideal object too into a temporal fact, and makes it seem substantial. But this fugitive existence which I egotistically attach to it, as if its fate was that of my glimpses of it, is no part of its true being, as even my intuition discerns it ; it is a practical dignity or potency attributed to it by the irrelevant momentum of my animal life. Animals, being by nature hounded and hungry creatures, spy out and take alarm at any datum of sense or fancy, supposing that there is something substantial there, something that will count and work in the world. The notion of a moving world is brought implicitly with them ; they fetch it out of the depths of their vegetating psyche, which is a small dark cosmos, silently revolving within. By being noticed, and treated as a signal for I know not what material opportunity or danger, the given image is taken up into the business world, and puts on the garment of existence. Remove this frame, strip off all suggestion of a time when this image was not yet present, or a time when it shall be past, and the very notion of existence is removed. The datum ceases to be an appearance, in the proper and pregnant sense of this word, since it ceases to imply any substance that appears or any mind to which it appears. It is an appearance only in the sense that its nature is wholly manifest, that it is a specific being, which may be mentioned, thought of, seen, or defined, if any one has the wit to do so. But its own nature says nothing of any hidden circumstances that shall bring it to light, or any adventitious mind that shall discover it. It lies simply in its own category. If a colour, it is just this colour ; if a pain, just this pain. Its appearance is not an event : its presence is not an experience ; for there is no surrounding world in which it can arise, and no watchful spirit to appropriate it. The sceptic has here withdrawn into the intuition of a surface form, without roots, without origin or environment, without a seat or a locus ; a little universe, an immaterial absolute theme, rejoicing merely in its own quality. This theme, being out of all adventitious relations and not in the least threatened with not being the theme it is, has not the contingency nor the fortunes proper to an existence ; it is simply that which it inherently, logically, and unchangeably is.

Existence, then, not being included in any

immediate datum, is a fact always open to doubt. I call it a fact notwithstanding, because in talking about the sceptic I am positing his existence. If he has any intuition, however little the theme of that intuition may have to do with any actual world, certainly I who think of his intuition, or he himself thinking of it afterwards, see that this intuition of his must have been an event, and his existence at that time a fact ; but like all facts and events, this one can be known only by an affirmation which posits it, which may be suspended or reversed, and which is subject to error. Hence all this business of intuition may perfectly well be doubted by the sceptic : the existence of his own doubt (however confidently I may assert it for him) is not given to him then : all that is given is some ambiguity or contradiction in images ; and if afterwards he is sure that he has doubted, the sole cogent evidence which that fact can claim lies in the psychological impossibility that, so long as he believes he has doubted, he should not believe it. But he may be wrong in harbouring this belief, and he may rescind it. For all an ultimate scepticism can see, therefore, there may be no facts at all, and perhaps nothing has ever existed.

Scepticism may thus be carried to the point of denying change and memory, and the reality of all facts. Such a sceptical dogma would certainly be false, because this dogma itself would have to be entertained, and that event would be a fact and an existence : and the sceptic in framing that dogma discourses, vacillates, and lives in the act of contrasting one assertion with another—all of which is to exist with a vengeance. Yet this false dogma that nothing exists is tenable intuitively and, while it prevails, is irrefutable. There are certain motives (to be discussed later) which render ultimate scepticism precious to a spiritual mind, as a sanctuary from grosser illusions.

For the wayward sceptic, who regards it as no truer than any other view, it also has some utility : it accustoms him to discard the dogma which an introspective critic might be tempted to think self-evident, namely, that he himself lives and thinks. That he does so is true ; but to establish that truth he must appeal to animal faith. If he is too proud for that, and simply stares at the datum, the last thing he will see is himself.

CHAPTER VII

NOTHING GIVEN EXISTS

SCEPTICISM is not sleep, and in casting a doubt on any belief, or proving the absurdity of any idea, the sceptic is by no means losing his sense of what is proposed. He is merely doubting or denying the *existence* of any such object. In scepticism, therefore, everything turns on the meaning of the word existence, and it will be worth while to stop a moment here to consider it further.

I have already indicated roughly how I am using the word existence, namely, to designate such being as is in flux, determined by external relations, and jostled by irrelevant events. Of course this is no definition. The term existence is only a name. In using it I am merely pointing out to the reader, as if by a gesture, what this word designates in my habits of speech, as if in saying Cæsar I pointed to my dog, lest some one should suppose I meant the Roman emperor. The Roman emperor, the dog, and the sound Cæsar are all indefinable ; but they might be described more particularly, by using other indicative and indefinable names, to mark their characteristics or the events in which they figured. So the whole realm of being which I point to when I say existence might be described more fully ; the description of it would be physics or perhaps psychology ; but the exploration of that realm, which is open only to animal faith, would not concern the sceptic.

The sceptic turns from such indefinite confusing objects to the immediate, to the datum ; and perhaps for a moment he may fancy he has found true existence there ; but if he is a good sceptic he will soon be undeceived. Certainly in the immediate he will find freedom from the struggle of assertion and counter-assertion : no report there, no hypothesis, no ghostly reduplication of the obvious, no ghostly imminence of the not-given. Is not the obvious, he might ask, the truly existent ? Yet the obvious is only the apparent ; and this in both senses of this ambiguous word. The datum is apparent in the sense of being self-evident and luminous ; and it is apparent also in the sense of merely appearing and being unsubstantial. In this latter sense, the apparent threatens to become the non-existent. Does not the existent profess to be more than apparent : to be not so much the self-evident as that which I am seeking evidence for, in the sense of testimony ? Is not the existent, then (which from its own point of view, or physically, is more than the apparent), cognitively and from my point of view less than the apparent ? Does it not need witnesses to bear testimony to its being ? And what can recommend those witnesses to me except their intrinsic eloquence ? I shall prove no sceptic if I do not immediately transfer all my trust from the existence reported to the appearance reporting it, and substitute the evidence of my senses for all lawyer's evidence. I shall forget the murders and embroglios talked about in the court, and gaze at the judge in his scarlet and ermine, with the pale features of an old fox under his grey wig ; at the jury in their stolidity ; at the witness stammering ; at the counsel, officially insolent, not thinking of what he is saying mechanic-ally, but whispering something that really interests him in an aside, almost yawning, and looking at the clock to see if it is time for luncheon ; and at the flood of hazy light falling aslant on the whole scene from the high windows. Is not the floating picture, in my waking trance, the actual reality, and the whole world of existence and business but a perpetual fable, which this trance sustains ?

The theory that the universe is nothing but a flux of appearances is plausible to the sceptic ; he thinks he is not believing much in believing it. Yet the residuum of dogma is very remarkable in this view ; and the question at once will assail him how many appearances he shall assert to exist, of what sort, and in what order, if in any, he shall assert them to arise ; and the various hypotheses that may be suggested concerning the character and distribution of appearances will become fresh data in his thought ; and he will find it impossible to decide whether any such appearances, beyond the one now passing before him, are ever actual, or whether any of the suggested systems of appearances actually exists. Thus existence will loom again before him, as something problematical, at a distance from that immediacy into which he thought he had fled.

Existence thus seems to re-establish itself in the very world of appearances, so soon as these are regarded as facts and events occurring side by side or one after the other. In each datum taken separately there would be no occasion to speak of existence. It would be an obvious appearance ; whatever appeared there would be simply and wholly apparent, and the fact that it appeared (which would be the only fact involved) would not appear in it at all. This fact, the existence of the intuition, would not be asserted until the appearance ceased to be actual, and was viewed from the outside, as something that presumably had occurred, or would occur, or was occurring elsewhere.

In such an external view there might be truth or error ; not so in each appearance taken in itself, because in itself and as a whole each is a pure appearance and bears witness to nothing further. Nevertheless, when some term within this given appearance comes to be regarded as a sign of some other appearance not now given, the question is pertinent whether that other appearance exists or not. Thus existence and non-existence seem to be relevant to appearances in so far as they are problematical and posited from outside, not in so far as they are certain and given.

Hence an important conclusion which at first seems paradoxical but which reflection will support ; namely, that the notion that the datum exists is un-meaning, and if insisted upon is false. That which exists is the fact that the datum is given at that parti-cular moment and crisis in the universe ; the intuition, not the datum, is the fact which occurs ; and this fact, if known at all, must be asserted at some other moment by an adventurous belief which may be true or false. That which is certain and given, on the contrary, is something of which existence cannot be predicated, and which, until it is used as a description of some-thing else, cannot be either false or true.

I see here how halting is the scepticism of those modern philosophers who have supposed that to exist is to be an idea in the mind, or an object of consciousness, or a fact of experience, if by these phrases no more is meant than to be a datum of intuition. If there is any existence at all, presence to consciousness is neither necessary nor sufficient to render it an existence. Imagine a novelist whose entire life was spent in conceiving a novel, or a deity whose only function was to think a world. That world would not exist, any more than the novel would comprise the feelings and actions of existing persons. If that novelist, in the heat of invention, believed his personages real, he would be deceived : and so would that deity if he supposed his world to exist merely because he thought of it. Before the creation could be actual, or the novel historical, it would have to be enacted elsewhere than in the mind of its author. And if it was so enacted, it would evidently not be requisite to its existence that any imaginative person, falsely conceiving himself to be its author, should form an image of it in his mind. If he did so, that remarkable clairvoyance would be a fact requiring explanation ; but it would be an added harmony in the world, not the ground of its existence.

If for the sake of argument I accept the notion that presence to intuition is existence, I may easily disprove it by a *reductio ad absurdum*. If nothing not given in intuition can exist, then all those beliefs in existing facts beyond my intuition, by which thought is diversified when it is intelligent, would be necessarily false, and all intelligence would be illusion. This implication might be welcome to me, if I wished not to entertain any opinions which might conceivably be wrong. But the next implication is more disconcerting, namely, that the intuitions in which such illusion appears can have no existence themselves : for being instances of intuition they could not be data for any intuition. At one moment I may *believe* that there are or have been or will be other moments ; but evidently they would not be *other* moments, if they were data to me now, and nothing more. If presence to intuition were necessary to existence, intuition itself would not exist ; that is, no other intuition would be right in positing it ; and as this absence of transcendence would be mutual, nothing would exist at all. And yet, since presence to intuition would be sufficient for existence, everything mentionable would exist without question, the non-existent could never be thought of, to deny anything (if I knew what I was denying) would be impossible, and there would be no such thing as fancy, hallucination, illusion, or error.

I think it is evidently necessary to revise a vocabulary which lends itself to such equivocation, and if I keep the words existence and intuition at all, to lend them meanings which can apply to something possible and credible. I therefore propose to use the word existence (in a way consonant, on the whole, with ordinary usage) to designate not data of intuition but facts or events believed to occur in nature. These facts or events will include, *first*, intuitions themselves, or instances of consciousness, like pains and pleasures and all remembered experiences and mental discourse ; and *second*, physical things and events, having a transcendent relation to the data of intuition which, in belief, may be used as signs for them ; the same transcendent relation which objects of desire have to desire, or objects of pursuit to pursuit ; for example, such a relation as the fact of my birth (which I cannot even remember) has to my present persuasion that I was once born, or the event of my death (which I conceive only abstractly) to my present expectation of some day dying. If an angel visits me, I may intelligibly debate the question whether he exists or not. On the one hand, I may affirm that he came in through the door, that is, that he existed before I saw him ; and I may continue in perception, memory, theory, and expectation to assert that he was a fact of nature : in that case I believe in his existence. On the other hand, I may suspect that he was only an event in me, called a dream ; an event not at all included in the angel as I saw him, nor at all like an angel in the conditions of its existence ; and in this case I disbelieve in my vision : for visiting angels cannot honestly be said to exist if I entertain them only in idea.

Existences, then, from the point of view of knowledge, are facts or events affirmed, not images seen or topics merely entertained. Existence is accordingly not only doubtful to the sceptic, but odious to the logician. To him it seems a truly monstrous excrescence and superfluity in being, since anything existent is more than the description of it, having suffered an unintelligible emphasis or materialisation to fall upon it, which is logically inane and morally comic. At the same time, existence suffers from defect of being and obscuration ; any ideal nature, such as might be exhaustively given in intuition, when it is materialised loses the intangibility and eternity proper to it in its own sphere ; so that existence doubly injures the forms of being it embodies, by ravishing them first and betraying them afterwards.

Such is existence as approached by belief and affirmed in animal experience ; but I shall find in the sequel that considered physically, as it is unrolled amidst the other realms of being, existence is a conjunction of natures in adventitious and variable relations. According to this definition, it is evident that existence can never be given in intuition ; since no matter how complex a datum may be, and no matter how many specious changes it may picture, its specious order and unity are just what they are : they can neither suffer mutation nor acquire new relations : which is another way of saying that they cannot exist. If this whole evolving world were merely given in idea, and were not an external object posited in belief and in action, it could not exist nor evolve. In order to exist it must enact itself ignorantly and successively, and carry down all ideas of it in its own current.

CHAPTER VIII

SOME AUTHORITIES FOR THIS CONCLUSION

THE ultimate position of the sceptic, that nothing given exists, may be fortified by the authority of many renowned philosophers who are accounted orthodox ; and it will be worth while to stop for a moment to invoke their support, since the scepticism I am defending is not meant to be merely provisional ; its just conclusions will remain fixed, to remind me perpetually that all alleged knowledge of matters of fact is faith only, and that an existing world, whatever form it may choose to wear, is intrinsically a questionable and arbitrary thing. It is true that many who have defended this view, in the form that all appearance is illusion, have done so in order to insist all the more stoutly on the existence of something occult which they call reality ; but as the existence of this reality is far easier to doubt than the existence of the obvious, I may here disregard that compensatory dogma. I shall soon introduce compensatory dogmas of my own, more credible, I think, than theirs ; and I shall attribute existence to a flux of natural events which can never be data of intuition, but only objects of a belief which men and animals, caught in that flux themselves, hazard instinctively. Although a sceptic may doubt all existence, none being involved in any indubitable datum, yet I think good human reasons, apart from irresistible impulse, can be found for positing existing intuitions to which data appear, no less than other existing events and things, which the intuited data report or describe. For the moment, however, I am concerned to justify further the contention of the sceptic that, if we refuse to bow to the yoke of animal faith, we can find in pure intuition no evidence of any existence whatsoever.

There is notably one tenet, namely, that all change is illusion, proper to many deep-voiced philosophers, which of itself suffices to abolish all existence, in the sense which I give to this word. Instead of change they probably posit changeless substance or pure Being; but if substance were not subject to change, at least in its distribution, it would not be the substance of anything found in the world or happening in the mind; it would, therefore, have no more lodgement in existence than has pure Being, which is evidently only a logical term. Pure Being, as far as it goes, is no doubt a true description of everything, whether existent or non-existent; so that if anything exists, pure Being will exist in it; but it will exist merely as pure colour does in all colours, or pure space in all spaces, and not separately nor exclusively. These philosophers, in denying change, accordingly deny all existence. But though many of them have prized this doctrine, few have lived up to it, or rather none have; so that I may pass over the fact that in denying change they have inadvertently denied existence, even to substance and pure Being, because they have inadvertently retained both existence and change. The reality they attributed with so much unction and conviction to the absolute was not that proper to this idea—one of the least impressive which it is possible to contemplate—but was obviously due to the strain of existence and movement within themselves, and to the vast rumble, which hypnotised them, of universal mutation.

It is the Indians who have insisted most sincerely and intrepidly on the non-existence of everything given, even adjusting their moral regimen to this insight. Life is a dream, they say : and all experienced events are illusions. In dreaming of nature and of ourselves we are deceived, even in imagining that we exist and are deceived and dreaming. Some aver, indeed, that there is a universal dreamer, Brahma, slumbering and breathing deeply in all of us, who is the reality of our dreams, and the negation of them. But as Brahma is emphatically not qualified by any of the forms of illusory existence, but annuls them all, there is no need, for my purpose, of distinguishing him from the reported state of redeemed souls (where many souls are admitted) nor from the Nirvana into which lives flow when they happily cease, becoming at last aware, as it were, that neither they nor anything else has ever existed.

It would be rash, across the chasm of language and tradition that separates me from the Indians, to accuse their formidable systems of self-contradiction. Truth and reality are words which, in the mouths of prophets, have often a eulogistic rather than a scientific force ; and if it is *better* to elude the importunities of existence and to find a sanctuary of intense safety and repose in the notion of pure Being, there may be a dramatic propriety in saying that the view of the saved, from which all memory of the path to salvation is excluded, is the true view, and their condition the only reality ; so that they are right in thinking that they have never existed, and we wrong in thinking that we now exist.

Here is an egotism of the redeemed with which, as with other egotisms, I confess I have little sympathy. The blessed, in giving out that I do not exist in my sins, because they cannot distinguish me, appear to me to be deceived. The intrinsic blessedness of their

condition cannot turn into a truth this small oversight
on their part, however excusable. I suspect, or I like
to imagine, that what the Indians mean is rather that
the principle of my existence, and of my persuasion
that I exist, is an *evil* principle. It is sin, guilt,
passion, and mad will, the natural and universal source
of illusion—very much what I am here calling animal
faith ; and since this assertiveness in me (according
to the Indians) is wrong morally, and since its influence
alone leads me to posit existence in myself or in
anything else, if I were healed morally I should cease
to assert existence ; and I should, in fact, have ceased
to exist.

Now in this doctrine, so stated, lies a great confirmation of my thesis that nothing given exists ;
because it is only a dark principle, transcendental in
respect to the datum (that is, on the hither side of the
footlights) that calls up this datum at all, or leads me
to posit its existence. It is this sorry self of mine
sitting here in the dark, one in this serried pack of
open-mouthed fools, hungry for illusion, that is
responsible for the spectacle ; for if a foolish instinct
had not brought me to the playhouse, and if avid eyes
and an idealising understanding had not watched the
performance, no part of it would have abused me :
and if no one came to the theatre, the actors would
soon flit away like ghosts, the poets would starve, the
scenery would topple over and become rubbish, and
the very walls would disappear. Every part of experience, as it comes, is illusion ; and the source of
this illusion is my animal nature, blindly labouring in
a blind world.

Such is the ancient lesson of experience itself,
when we reflect upon experience and turn its illusions
into instruction : a lesson which a bird-witted empiricism can never learn, though it is daily repeated. But
the Indian with a rare sensitiveness joined a rare

recollection. He *lived*: a religious love, a childish absorption in appearances as they come (which busy empiricists do not share), led him to remember them truly, in all their beauty, and therefore to perceive that they were illusions. The poet, the disinterested philosopher, the lover of things distilled into purity, frees himself from belief. This infinite chaos of cruel and lovely forms, he cries, is all deceptive, all unsubstantial, substituted at will for nothing, and soon found to sink into nothing again, and to be nothing in truth.

I will disregard the vehemence with which these saintly scholastics denounce the world and the sinful nature that attaches me to it. I like the theatre, not because I cannot perceive that the play is a fiction, but because I do perceive it ; if I thought the thing a fact, I should detest it : anxiety would rob me of all my imaginative pleasure. Even as it is, I often wish the spectacle were less barbarous ; but I am not angry because each scene does not last for ever, and is likely to be followed by a thousand others which I shall not witness. Such is the nature of endless comedy, and of experience. But I wish to retain the valuable testimony of the Indians to the non-existence of the obvious. This testimony is the more valuable because the spectacle present to their eyes was tropical ; harder, therefore, to master and to smile at than are the political and romantic medleys which fill the mind of Europe. Yet amidst the serpents and hyænas, the monkeys and parrots of their mental jungle, those sages could sit unmoved, too holily incredulous for fear. How infinite, how helpless, how deserving of forgiveness creative error becomes to the eye of understanding, that loves only in pity, and has no concupiscence for what it loves ! How like unhappy animals western philosophers seem in comparison, with their fact-worship, their thrift, their moral

intolerance, their imaginative poverty, their political
zeal, and their subservience to intellectual fashion !

It makes no difference for my purposes if the
cosmology of the Indians was fanciful. It could
hardly be more extraordinary than the constitution
of the material world is in fact, nor more decidedly
out of scale with human data ; truth and fancy in this
matter equally convict the human senses of illusion.
Nor am I out of sympathy with their hope of escaping
from the universal hurly-burly into some haven of
peace. A philosopher has a haven in himself, of
which I suspect the fabled bliss to follow in other
lives, or after total emancipation from living, is only
a poetic symbol : he has pleasure in truth, and an
equal readiness to enjoy the scene or to quit it.   Liberation is never complete while life lasts, and is nothing
afterwards ; but it flows in a measure from this very
conviction that all experience is illusion, when this
conviction is morally effective, as it was with the
Indians. Their belief in transmigration or in Karma
is superfluous in this regard, since a later experience
could only change the illusion without perfecting the
liberation. Yet the mention of some ulterior refuge
or substance is indispensable to the doctrine of illusion,
and though it may be expressed mythically must be
taken to heart too. It points to other realms of being
—such as those which I call the realms of matter,
truth, and spirit—which by nature cannot be data of
intuition but must be posited (if recognised by man
at all) by an instinctive faith expressed in action.
Whether these ulterior realms exist or not is their
own affair : existence may be proper to some, like
matter or spirit, and not to others, like truth.   But as
to the data of intuition, their non-existent and illusory
character is implied in the fact that they are given.
A datum is by definition a theme of attention, a term
in passing thought, a visioned universal.   The realm

in which it lies, and in which flying intuition discloses it for a moment, is the very realm of non-existence, of inert or ideal being. The Indians, in asserting the non-existence of every term in possible experience, not only free the spirit from idolatry, but free the realm of spirit (which is that of intuition) from limitation ; because if nothing that appears exists, anything may appear without the labour and expense of existing ; and fancy is invited to range innocently—fancies not murdering other fancies as an existence must murder other existences. While life lasts, the field is thus cleared for innocent poetry and infinite hypothesis, without suffering the judgement to be deceived nor the heart enslaved.

European philosophers, even when called idealists, have seldom reconciled themselves to regarding experience as a creature of fancy. Instead of looking beneath illusion for some principle that might call it forth or perhaps dispel it, as they would if endeavouring to interpret a dream, they have treated it as dreams are treated by the superstitious ; that is, they have supposed that the images they saw were themselves substances, or powers, or at least imperfect visions of originals resembling them. In other words, they have been empiricists, regarding appearances as constituents of substance. There have been exceptions, but some of them only prove the rule. Parmenides and Democritus certainly did not admit that the data of sense or imagination existed otherwise than as illusions or conventional signs : but their whole interest, for this reason, skipped over them, and settled heavily on " Being," or on the atoms and the void, which they severally supposed underlay appearance. Appearance itself thereby acquired a certain vicarious solidity, since it was thought to be the garment of substance ; somehow within the visionary datum, or beneath it, the most unobjectionable substance was always to be found. Parmenides could not have admitted, and Democritus had not discovered, that the sole basis of appearances was some event in the brain, in no way resembling them ; and that the relation of data to the external events they indicated was that of a spontaneous symbol, like an exclamatory word, and not that of a copy or emanation. The simple ancients supposed (as some of my contemporaries do also) that perception stripped material things of their surface properties, or was actually these surface properties peeled off and lodged in the observer's head. Accordingly the denial of existence to sensibles and to intelligibles was never hearty until substance was denied also, and nothing existent was any longer supposed to lurk within these appearances or behind them.

All modern idealists have perceived that an actual appearance cannot be a part of a substance that does not appear ; the given image has only the given relations ; if I assign other relations to it (which I do if I attribute existence to it) I substitute for the pure datum one of two other things : either a substance possessing the same form as that datum, but created and dissolved in its own medium, at its own periods, apart from all observation ; or else, a perception of my own, a moment in my experience, carrying the vision of such an image. The former choice simply puts me back at the beginning of physics, when a merely pictorial knowledge of the material world existed, and nothing of its true mechanism and history had been discovered. The latter choice posits human discourse, or as these philosophers call it, experience : and it is certain that the status of a datum in discourse or experience is that of a mere appearance, fluctuating, intermittent, never twice the same, and dependent for its specious actuality on the movement of attention and the shuffling of confused images in the fancy. In other words, what exists—that is, what is carried on through the flux and has changing and external relations—is a *life*, discourse itself, the voluminous adventures of the mind in its wholeness. This is also what novelists and literary psychologists endeavour to record or to imagine ; and the particular data, hardly distinguishable by the aid of a word clapped on to them, are only salient sparks or abstract points of reference for an observer intent on ulterior events. It is ulterior events, the whole of human experience and history as conventionally reported, that is the object of belief in this school, and the true existence.

Ostensibly empiricists seek to reduce this unmanageable object to particular data, and to attribute existence to each scintilla taken separately ; but in reality all the relations of these intuitions (which are not relations between the data), their temporal order, subordination to habit and passion, associations, meaning, and embosoming intelligence, are interpolated as if they were matters of course ; and indeed they are, because these are the tides of animal life on which the datum sparkles for a moment. Empiricists are interested in practice, and wish to work with as light an intellectual equipment as possible ; they therefore attribute existence to " ideas "—meaning intuitions but professing to mean data. If they were interested in these data for their own sake, they would perceive that they are only symbols, like words, used to mark or express the crises in their practical career ; and becoming fervid materialists again in their beliefs, as they have always been in their allegiances, they might soon go so far as to deny that there is intuition of data at all : which is a radical way of denying their existence. Discourse and experience would thus drop out of sight altogether, and instead of data of intuition there would be only the pictorial elements of physics—the other possible form in which anything given may be asserted to exist.

If anything, therefore, exists at all when an appearance arises, this existence is not the unit that appears, but either a material fact presenting such an appearance, though constituted by many other relations, or else an actual intuition evoking, creating, or dreaming that non-existent unit.   Idealists, if they are thorough, will deny both ; for neither a material thing nor an actual intuition has its being in being perceived : both, by definition, exist on their own account, by virtue of their internal energy and natural relations.   Therefore either existence apart from givenness is admitted, inconsistently with idealism, or existence is denied altogether.   It is allowed, and in fact urged, by all complete idealists that appearance, far from involving the existence of what appears, positively excludes it.   *Esse est percipi* was a maxim recalled by an intelligible literary impulse, as Faust said, *Gefühl ist Alles !*   Yet that maxim was uttered without reflection, because what those who uttered it really meant was the exact opposite, namely, that only spirits, or perhaps one spirit, existed, which were beings perfectly imperceptible.   It was the beautiful and profound part of such a sentiment that whatever is pictorial is non-existent.   Data could be only forms assumed by animal sensibility, like the camel and the weasel seen by Hamlet in a cloud ; as these curious creatures could have no zoological existence in that nebula, so the units of human apperception have no existence anywhere.

When idealists say, therefore, that ideas are the only objects of human knowledge and that they exist only in the mind, their language is incoherent, because knowledge of ideas is not knowledge, and presence to intuition is not existence.   But this incoherence enables two different philosophies to use the same formula, to the extreme confusion both of doctrine and feeling.   One philosophy under the name idea conceives of a fact or phenomenon, a phase in the flux of fortune or experience, existing at a given moment, and known at other moments to have existed there : in other words, its ideas are recollected events in nature, the subject-matter of psychology and physics. This philosophy, when carried out, becomes materialism ; its psychology turns into a record of behaviour and its phenomenalistic view of nature into a mathematical calculus of invisible processes. The other philosophy (which alone concerns me here) under the name idea understands the terms of sensation and thought, and their pictorial or rhetorical synthesis. Since these themes of intuition are called upon to absorb all reality, and no belief is accepted as more than a fresh datum in thought, this philosophy denies the transcendence of knowledge and the existence of anything.

Although the temper of absolute idealists is often far from sceptical, their method is scepticism itself : as appears not only in their criticism of all dogma, but in the reasons they give for their own views. What are these reasons ? That the criticism of knowledge proves that actual thinking is the only reality ; that the objects of knowledge can live, move, and have their being only within it ; that existence is something merely imputed ; and that truth is coherence among views having themselves no objects. A fact, these critics say, is a concept. This statement might seem absurd, since a concept means at most the idea or supposition of a fact ; but if the statement is taken sympathetically, for what the malicious criticism of knowledge means by it, it amounts to this : that there are no facts, but that what we call facts, and believe to be such, are really only conventional fictions, imaginations of what facts would be if facts were possible at all. That facts are ideals, impossible to realise, is clear on transcendental principles, since a fact would be an event or existence which knowledge would have to approach and lay siege to somehow from the outside, so that for knowledge (the only reality on this system) they would always remain phantoms, creatures of a superstitious instinct, terms for ever posited but never possessed, and therefore perpetually unreal. If fact or truth had any separate being it could not be an integral part of knowledge ; what modicum of reality facts or truths can possess they must borrow from knowledge, in which they perforce remain ideals only ; so that it is only as unreal that they are real at all. Transcendentalists are sure that knowledge is everything, not because they presume that everything is known, but precisely because they see that there is nothing to know. If anything existed actually, or if there was any independent truth, it would be unknowable, as these voracious thinkers conceive knowledge. The glorious thing about knowledge, in their eyes, is that, as there is nothing to know, knowledge is a free and a sure creation, new and self-grounded for ever.

Transcendentalism, when it is thorough, accordingly agrees with the Indian systems in maintaining that the illusion that given objects exist has itself no existence. Any actual sensation, any instance of thinking, would be a self-existing fact ; but facts are only concepts, that is, inert terms in absolute thought : if illusions occurred actually, they would not be concepts but events, and though their visionary objects might be non-existent, the vision of them would exist ; and they would be the sort of independent facts which transcendental logic excludes as impossible. Acts of judging or positing or imagining cannot be admitted on this system until they in their turn have been posited in another judgement ; that is, until they cease to hide their heads in the obscurity of self-existence, and become purely ideal themes of actual

intuition. When they have thus become phenomenal, intent and judgement may posit them and
depute them to exist ; but the belief that they exist
otherwise than as present postulates is always false.
Imputed existence is the only existence possible, but
must always be imputed falsely. For example, the
much-talked-of opinions of ancient philosophers, if
they had existed at all, would have had to exist before
they became objects of intuition to the historian, or
to the reader of history, who judges them to have
existed ; but such self-existence is repugnant to transcendental logic : it is a ghost cut off from knowledge
and from the breath of life in me here and now.
Therefore the opinions of philosophers exist only in
history, history exists only in the historian, and the
historian only in the reader ; and the reader himself
exists only for his self-consciousness, which is not
really his own, but absolute consciousness thinking
about him or about all things from his point of view.
Thus everything exists only ideally, by being falsely
supposed to exist. The only knowable reality is
unreal because specious, and all other reality is unreal because unknowable.

Transcendentalists are thus driven, like Parmenides
and the Vedanta philosophy, to withdraw into a dark
interior yet omnipresent principle, the unfathomable
force that sets all this illusion going, and at the same
time rebukes and annuls the illusion. I am here
concerned, let me repeat, with scepticism, not with
compensatory dogmas ; but for the transcendentalist,
who fundamentally abhors substance, the compensatory dogma itself is one more denial of existence.
For what, in his system, is this transcendental seat of
all illusion, this agent in all judgements and positings ?
Not an existing spirit, if such a phrase could have a
meaning. Absolute thought cannot exist first, before
it imputes existence to other things or to itself. If it

needed to possess existence before imputing it, as the inexpert in logic might suppose, the whole principle of transcendental criticism would be abandoned and disproved, and nothing would any longer prevent the existence of intuitions or of material things before any one posited them. But if non-existent, what can absolute spirit be ? Just a principle, a logic to be embodied, a self-creating programme or duty, asserting itself without any previous instrument, ground, or occasion. Existence is something utterly unworthy of such a transcendental spirit, and repugnant to it. Spirit is here only a name for absolute law, for the fatality or chance that one set of appearances instead of another insists upon arising. No doubt this fatality is welcome to the enthusiast in whom this spirit is awake, and its very groundlessness takes on the form of freedom and creative power to his apprehension : but this sympathy with life, being expressly without any natural basis, is itself a happy accident, and precarious : and sometimes conscience may suddenly turn against it, and call it vain, mad, and criminal. Fichte once said that he who truly wills anything must will that very thing for ever ; and this saying may be interpreted consistently with transcendentalism, if it is understood to mean that, since transcendental will is dateless and creates its own universe wherever it exerts itself, the character of this will is unalterable in that phase of it, producing just that vision and that world, which being out of time cannot be devoured by time. But perhaps even Fichte was not free from human weakness, and he may also have meant, or half-meant, that a thorough education, such as Prussia was called to create, could fix the will of mankind and turn it into an unalterable habit ; and that a philosopher could pledge the absolute always to posit the same set of objects. So understood, the maxim would be contrary to transcendentalism and to the fervent conviction of Fichte himself, which demanded "new worlds for ever." Even if he meant only that the principle of perpetual novelty at least was safe and could never be betrayed by the event, he would have contradicted the absolute freedom of " Life " to be what it willed, and his own occasional fears that, somewhere and some day, Life might grow weary, and might consent to be hypnotised and enslaved by the vision of matter which it had created.

But the frailty even of the greatest idealists is nothing against idealism, and the principle that existence is something always imputed, and never found, is not less cogent if idealists, for the sake of courtesy, sometimes say that when existence is imputed necessarily it is imputed truly ; and it makes no difference for my object whether they call fiction truth because it is legal, or call legality illusion because it is false. In any case, I can invoke the authority of this whole school, in which consciousness has been studied and described with admirable sincerity, for the thesis I have at heart. They deny with one voice that anything given can exist on its own account, or can be anything but a theme chosen by the spirit, a theme which no substantial thing or event existing outside could ever force the spirit to conceive or to copy. Nothing existent can appear, and nothing specious can exist. An apparition is a thought, its whole life is but mine in thinking it ; and whatever monition or significance I may attribute to its presence, it can never be anything but the specious thing it is. In the routine of animal life, an appearance may be normal or abnormal, and animal faith or practical intellect may interpret it in a way practically right or wrong ; but in itself every appearance, just because it is an appearance, is an illusion.

Confirmation of this thesis may also be found in an entirely different quarter, in natural history. The sensibility of animals, as judged by their motions and behaviour, is due to their own structure. The surrounding facts and forces are like the sun shining and the rain falling on the just and the unjust ; they condition the existence of the animal and reward any apt habits which he may acquire ; but he survives mainly by insensibility, and by a sort of pervasive immunity to most of the vibrations that run through him. It is only in very special directions, to very special occasional stimulations, that he develops instinctive responses in special organs : and his intuitions, if he has them, express these reactions. If the stimulus is cut off, the material sources of it may continue to be what they were, but they will not be perceived. If the stimulus, or anything equivalent to it, reaches the brain from any source, as in dreams, the same intuition will appear, in the absence of the material object. The feelings of animals express their bodily habit ; they do not express directly either the existence or the character of any external thing. The intent to react on these external things is independent of any presumptive data of intuition and antecedent to their appearance : it is an animal endeavour in pursuit or avoidance, or an animal expectation ; but the signals by which intuition may mark the crises of this animal watch or animal struggle are the same signals as appear in a dream, when nothing is afoot. The immediate visionary datum is never the intended object, but always a pathological symptom, a term in discourse, a description proffered at that moment by that feeling for that object, different for each channel of sense, translating digestibility into taste, salubrity into freshness, distance into size, refraction into colour, attitude into outline, distribution into perspective, and immersing everything in a moral medium, where it becomes a good or an evil, as it cannot be save to animal sympathy.

All these transcripts, however original in character, remain symbols in function, because they arise in the act of focussing animal sensibility or animal endeavour upon some external influence. In a healthy life they become the familiar and unmistakable masks of nature, lending to everything in the environment its appropriate aspect in human discourse, its nick-name in the human family. For this reason, when imagination works in a void (as it can do in dreams or under the influence of violent passion) it becomes illusion in the bad sense of this word ; that is, it is still taken for a symbol, when it is the symbol of nothing. All these data, if by a suspension of practical reference they came to be regarded in themselves, would cease to be illusions cognitively, since no existence would be suggested by any of them ; but a practical man might still call them illusions for that very reason, because although free from error they would be devoid of truth. In order to reach existences intent must transcend intuition, and take data for what they mean, not for what they are ; it must credit them, as understanding credits words, accepting the passing vision as a warrant for something that once was, or that will be, or that lies in an entirely different medium, that of material being, or of discourse else-where. Intuition cannot reveal or discriminate any fact ; it is pure fancy ; and the more I sink into it, and the more absolute I make it, the more fanciful it becomes. If ever it ceases to mean anything at all, it becomes pure poetry if placid, and mere delirium if intense. So a pain, when it is not sorrow at some event or the sign of some injury or crisis in bodily life, becomes sheer horror, and a sort of wanton little hell, existing absolutely ; because the rending of the organism has raised intuition to an extreme intensity without giving it direction upon anything to be found or done in the world, or contemplated in the fancy ;

and pain, when it reaches distraction, may be said to be that moral monster, intuition devouring itself, or wasted in agony upon nothing.

Thus scientific psychology confirms the criticism of knowledge and the experience of life which proclaim that the immediate objects of intuition are mere appearances and that nothing given exists as it is given.

CHAPTER IX

THE DISCOVERY OF ESSENCE

THE loss of faith, as I have already observed, has no tendency to banish ideas ; on the contrary, since doubt arises on reflection, it tends to keep the imagination on the stretch, and lends to the whole spectacle of things a certain immediacy, suavity, and humour. All that is sordid or tragic falls away, and everything acquires a lyric purity, as if the die had not yet been cast and the ominous choice of creation had not been made. Often the richest philosophies are the most sceptical ; the mind is not then tethered in its home paddock, but ranges at will over the wilderness of being. The Indians, who deny the existence of the world, have a keen sense for its infinity and its variegated colours ; they play with the monstrous and miraculous in the grand manner, as in the *Arabian Nights*. No critic has had a sharper eye for the outlines of ideas than Hume, who found it impossible seriously to believe that they revealed anything. In the critic, as in the painter, suspension of belief and of practical understanding is favourable to vision ; the arrested eye renders every image limpid and unequivocal. And this is not merely an effect of physiological compensation, in that perhaps the nervous energy withdrawn from preparations for action is allowed to intensify the process of mere sensation. There ensues a logical clarification as well ; because so long as belief, interpretation, and significance entered in, the object in hand was ambiguous ; in seeking the fact the mind overlooked or confused the datum. Yet each element in this eager investigation —including its very eagerness—is precisely what it is ; and if I renounce for the moment all transitive intelligence, and give to each of these elements its due definition, I shall have a much richer as well as clearer collection of terms and relations before me, than when I was clumsily attempting to make up my mind. Living beings dwell in their expectations rather than in their senses. If they are ever to *see* what they see, they must first in a manner stop living ; they must suspend the will, as Schopenhauer put it ; they must photograph the idea that is flying past, veiled in its very swiftness. This swiftness is not its own fault, but that of my haste and inattention ; my hold is loose on it, as in a dream ; or else perhaps those veils and that swiftness are the truth of the picture ; and it is they that the true artist should be concerned to catch and to eternalise, restoring to all that the practical intellect calls vague its own specious definition. Nothing is vague in itself, or other than just what it is. Symbols are vague only in respect to their signification, when this remains ambiguous.

It is accordingly an inapt criticism often passed upon Berkeley and Hume that they overlooked vagueness in ideas, although almost every human idea is scandalously vague. No, their intuition of ideas, at least initially, was quite direct and honest. The ambiguity they overlooked lay in the relation of ideas to physical things, which they wished to reduce to groups or series of these pellucid ideas—a chimerical physics. Had they abstained altogether from identifying ideas with objects of natural knowledge (which are events and facts), and from trying to construct material things out of optical and tactile images, they might have much enriched the philosophy of specious reality, and discerned the innocent realm of ideas as directly as Plato did, but more accurately. In this they need not have confused or undermined faith in natural things. Perception *is* faith ; more perception may extend this faith or reform it, but can never recant it except by sophistry. These virgin philosophers were like the cubists or futurists in the painting of to-day. They might have brought to light curious and neglected forms of direct intuition. They could not justly have been charged with absurdity for seeing what they actually saw. But they lapse into absurdity, and that irremediably, if they pretend to be the first and only masters of anatomy and topography.

Far from being vague or abstract the obvious ideas remaining to a complete sceptic may prove too absorbing, too multitudinous, or too sweet. A moral reprobation of them is no less intelligible than is the scientific criticism which rejects them as illusions and as no constituents of the existing world. Conscience no less than business may blame the sceptic for a sort of luxurious idleness ; he may call himself a lotus-eater, may heave a sigh of fatigue at doing nothing, and may even feel a touch of the vertigo and wish to close the eyes on all these images that entertain him to no purpose. But scepticism is an exercise, not a life ; it is a discipline fit to purify the mind of prejudice and render it all the more apt, when the time comes, to believe and to act wisely ; and meantime the pure sceptic need take no offence at the multiplicity of images that crowd upon him, if he is scrupulous not to trust them and to assert nothing at their prompting. Scepticism is the chastity of the intellect, and it is shameful to surrender it too soon or to the first comer : there is nobility in preserving it coolly and proudly through a long youth, until at last, in the ripeness of instinct and discretion, it can be safely exchanged for fidelity and happiness. But the philosopher, when he is speculative only, is a sort of perpetual celibate ; he is bent on not being betrayed, rather than on being annexed or inspired ; and although if he is at all wise he must see that the true marriage of the mind is with nature and science and the practical arts, yet in his special theoretic vocation, it will be a boon to him to view all experience simply, in the precision and distinctness which all its parts acquire when not referred to any substance which they might present confusedly, nor to any hypothesis or action which they might suggest.

The sceptic, then, as a consequence of carrying his scepticism to the greatest lengths, finds himself in the presence of more luminous and less equivocal objects than does the working and believing mind ; only these objects are without meaning, they are only what they are obviously, all surface. They show him everything thinkable with the greatest clearness and force ; but he can no longer imagine that he sees in these objects anything save their instant presence and their face-value. Scepticism therefore suspends all knowledge worthy of the name, all that transitive and presumptive knowledge of facts which is a form of belief ; and instead it bestows intuition of ideas, contemplative, æsthetic, dialectical, arbitrary. But whereas transitive knowledge, though important if true, may always be challenged, intuition, on the contrary, which neither has nor professes to have any ulterior object or truth, runs no risks of error, because it claims no jurisdiction over anything alien or eventual.

In this lucidity and calmness of intuition there is something preternatural. Imagine a child accustomed to see clothes only on living persons and hardly distinguishing them from the magical strong bodies that agitate them, and suddenly carry this child into a costumer's shop, where he will see all sorts of garments hung in rows upon manikins, with hollow breasts all

of visible wire, and little wooden nobs instead of heads :
he might be seriously shocked or even frightened.
How should it be possible for clothes standing up like
this not to be people ?   Such abstractions, he might
say to himself, are metaphysically impossible.   Either
these figures must be secretly alive and ready, when he
least expects it, to begin to dance, or else they are not
real at all, and he can only fancy that he sees them.
Just as the spectacle of all these gaunt clothes without
bodies might make the child cry, so later might the
whole spectacle of nature, if ever he became a sceptic.
The little word *is* has its tragedies ; it marries and
identifies different things with the greatest innocence ;
and yet no two are ever identical, and if therein lies the
charm of wedding them and calling them one, therein
too lies the danger.   Whenever I use the word *is*,
except in sheer tautology, I deeply misuse it ; and
when I discover my error, the world seems to fall
asunder and the members of my family no longer
know one another.   Existence is the strong body and
familiar motion which the young mind expects to find
in every dummy.   The oldest of us are sometimes no
less recalcitrant to the spectacle of the garments of
existence—which is all we ever saw of it—when the
existence is taken away.   Yet it is to these actual and
familiar, but now disembowelled objects, that scepticism introduces us, as if to a strange world ; a vast
costumer's gallery of ideas where all sorts of patterns
and models are on exhibition, without bodies to wear
them, and where no human habits of motion distract
the eye from the curious cut and precise embroideries of
every article.   This display, so complete in its spec-
tacular reality, not a button nor a feather wanting or
unobserved, is not the living crowd that it ought to
be, but a mockery of it, like the palace of the Sleeping
Beauty.   To my conventional mind, clothes without
bodies are no less improper than bodies without

clothes ; yet the conjunction of these things is but human. All nature runs about naked, and quite happy ; and I am not so remote from nature as not to revert on occasion to that nakedness—which is unconsciousness—with profound relief. But ideas without things and apparel without wearers seem to me a stranger condition ; I think the garments were made to fit the limbs, and should collapse without them. Yet, like the fig leaves of Eden, they are not garments essentially. They become such by accident, when one or another of them is appropriated by the providential buyer—not necessarily human—whose instinct may choose it ; or else it is perfectly content to miss its chance, and to lie stacked for ever among its motley neighbours in this great store of neglected finery.

It was the fear of illusion that originally disquieted the honest mind, congenitally dogmatic, and drove it in the direction of scepticism ; and it may find three ways, not equally satisfying to its honesty, in which that fear of illusion may be dispelled. One is death, in which illusion vanishes and is forgotten ; but although anxiety about error, and even positive error, are thus destroyed, no solution is offered to the previous doubt : no explanation of what could have called forth that illusion or what could have dissipated it. Another way out is by correcting the error, and substituting a new belief for it : but while in animal life this is the satisfying solution, and the old habit of dogmatism may be resumed in consequence without practical inconvenience, speculatively the case is not at all advanced ; because no criterion of truth is afforded except custom, comfort, and the accidental absence of doubt ; and what is absent by chance may return at any time unbidden. The third way, at which I have now arrived, is to entertain the illusion without succumbing to it, accepting it openly as an illusion, and forbidding it to claim any sort of being but that which it obviously has ; and then, whether it profits me or not, it will not deceive me. What will remain of this non-deceptive illusion will then be a truth, and a truth the being of which requires no explanation, since it is utterly impossible that it should have been otherwise. Of course I may still ask why the identity of this particular thing with itself should have occurred to *me* ; a question which could only be answered by plunging into a realm of existence and natural history every part and principle of which would be just as contingent, just as uncalled-for, and just as inexplicable as this accident of my being ; but that this particular thing, or any other which might have occurred to me instead, should be constituted as it is raises no problem ; for how could *it* have been constituted otherwise ? Nor is there any moral offence any longer in the contingency of my view of it, since my view of it involves no error. The error came from a wild belief about it ; and the possibility of error came from a wild propensity to belief. Relieve now the pressure of that animal haste and that hungry presumption ; the error is washed out of the illusion ; it is no illusion now, but an idea. Just as food would cease to be food, and poison poison, if you removed the stomach and the blood that they might nourish or infect ; and just as beautiful things would cease to be beautiful if you removed the wonder and the welcome of living souls, so if you eliminate your anxiety, deceit itself becomes entertainment, and every illusion but so much added acquaintance with the realm of form. For the unintelligible accident of existence will cease to appear to lurk in this manifest being, weighting and crowding it, and threatening it with being swallowed up by nondescript neighbours. It will appear dwelling in its own world, and shining by its own light, however brief may be my glimpse of it : for no date will be written on it, no frame of full or of empty time will shut it in ; nothing in it will be addressed to me, nor suggestive of any spectator. It will seem an event in no world, an incident in no experience. The quality of it will have ceased to exist : it will be merely the quality which it inherently, logically, and inalienably is. It will be an ESSENCE.

Retrenchment has its rewards. When by a difficult suspension of judgement I have deprived a given image of all adventitious significance, when it is taken neither for the manifestation of a substance nor for an idea in a mind nor for an event in a world, but simply if a colour for that colour and if music for that music, and if a face for that face, then an immense cognitive certitude comes to compensate me for so much cognitive abstention. My scepticism at last has touched bottom, and my doubt has found honourable rest in the absolutely indubitable. Whatever essence I find and note, that essence and no other is established before me. I cannot be mistaken about it, since I now have no object of intent other than the object of intuition. If for some private reason I am dissatisfied, and wish to change my entertainment, nothing prevents ; but the change leaves the thing I first saw possessed of all its quality, for the sake of which I perhaps disliked or disowned it. That, while one essence is before me, some one else may be talking of another, which he calls by the same name, is nothing to the purpose ; and if I myself change and correct myself, choosing a new essence in place of the old, my life indeed may have shifted its visions and its interests, but the characters they had when I harboured them are theirs without change. Indeed, only because each essence is the essence defined by instant apprehension can I truly be said to have changed my mind ; for I can have discarded any one of them only by substituting something different. This new essence could not be different from the former one, if each was not unchangeably itself.

There is, then, a sort of play with the non-existent, or game of thought, which intervenes in all alleged knowledge of matters of fact, and survives that knowledge, if this is ever questioned or disproved. To this mirage of the non-existent, or intuition of essence, the pure sceptic is confined ; and confined is hardly the word ; because though without faith and risk he can never leave that thin and bodiless plane of being, this plane in its tenuity is infinite ; and there is nothing possible elsewhere that, as a shadow and a pattern, is not prefigured there. To consider an essence is, from a spiritual point of view, to enlarge acquaintance with true being ; but it is not even to broach knowledge of fact ; and the ideal object so defined may have no natural significance, though it has æsthetic immediacy and logical definition. The modest scope of this speculative acquaintance with essence renders it infallible, whilst the logical and æsthetic ideality of its object renders that object eternal. Thus the most radical sceptic may be consoled, without being rebuked nor refuted ; he may leap at one bound over the whole human tangle of beliefs and dogmatic claims, elude human incapacity and bias, and take hold of the quite sufficient assurance that any essence or ideal quality of being which he may be intuiting has just the characters he is finding in it, and has them eternally.

This is no idle assurance. After all, the only thing that can ultimately interest me in other men's experience or, apart from animal egotism, in my own, is just this character of the essences which at any time have swum into our ken ; not at all the length of time through which we may have beheld them, nor the circumstances that produced that vision ; unless these circumstances in turn, when considered, place before the mind the essences which it delights to entertain. Of course, the choice and the interest of essences come entirely from the bent of the animal that elicits the vision of them from his own soul and its adventures ; and nothing but affinity with my animal life lends the essences I am able to discern their moral colour, so that to my mind they are beautiful, horrible, trivial, or vulgar. The good essences are such as accompany and express a good life. In them, whether good or bad, that life has its eternity. Certainly when I cease to exist and to think, I shall lose hold on this assurance ; but the theme in which for a moment I found the fulfilment of my expressive impulses will remain, as it always was, a theme fit for consideration, even if no one else should consider it, and I should never consider it again.

Nor is this all. Not only is the character of each essence inalienable, and, so long as it is open to intuition, indubitable, but the realm of essences is infinite. Since any essence I happen to have hit upon is independent of me and would possess its precise character if I had never been born, or had never been led by the circumstances of my life and temperament to apprehend that particular essence, evidently all other essences, which I have not been led to think of, rejoice in the same sort of impalpable being—impalpable, yet the only sort of being that the most rugged experience can ever actually find. Thus a mind enlightened by scepticism and cured of noisy dogma, a mind discounting all reports, and free from all tormenting anxiety about its own fortunes or existence, finds in the wilderness of essence a very sweet and marvellous solitude. The ultimate reaches of doubt and renunciation open out for it, by an easy transition, into fields of endless variety and peace, as if through the gorges of death it had passed into a paradise where all things are crystallised into the image of themselves, and have lost their urgency and their venom.

CHAPTER X

SOME USES OF THIS DISCOVERY

THERE is some danger in pointing out the obvious. Quick wits, perceiving at once how obvious the obvious is (though they may never have noticed it before), will say it is futile and silly to dwell upon it. Pugnacious people will assume that you mean more than you say, and are attempting to smuggle in some objectionable dogma under your truisms. Finally, docile minds, pleased to think you are delivering an oracle for their edification, will bow before your plain words as before some sacred mystery. The discernment of essence is subject, I know, to all these misunderstandings, and before going further I will endeavour to remove them.

In the first place, a warning to tender idealists. This recognition that the data of experience are essences is Platonic, but it is a corrective to all that is sentimental in Platonism, curing it as it were homœopathically. The realm of essence is not peopled by choice forms or magic powers. It is simply the unwritten catalogue, prosaic and infinite, of all the characters possessed by such things as happen to exist, together with the characters which all different things would possess if they existed. It is the sum of mentionable objects, of terms about which, or in which, something might be said. Thus although essences have the texture and ontological status of Platonic ideas, they can lay claim to none of the cosmological, metaphysical, or moral prerogatives attributed to those ideas. They are infinite in number and neutral in value. Greek minds had rhetorical habits ; what told in debate seemed to them final ; and Socrates thought it important to define in disputation the common natures designated by various words. Plato, who was initially a poet, had a warmer intuition of his ideas ; but it was still grammar and moral prejudice that led him to select and to deify them. The quality or function that makes all shepherds shepherds or all goods good is an essence ; but so are all the remaining qualities which make each shepherd and each good distinguishable from every other. Far from gathering up the fluidity of existence into a few norms for human language and thought to be focussed upon, the realm of essence infinitely multiplies that multiplicity, and adds every undiscriminated shade and mode of being to those which man has discriminated or which nature contains. Essence is not something invented or instituted for a purpose ; it is something passive, anything that might be found, every quality of being ; it therefore has not the function of reducing plurality to unity for the convenience of our poor wits or economy of language. It is far more garrulous than nature, herself not laconic.

Nor have essences a metaphysical status, so as to exercise a non-natural control over nature. My doctrine lends no countenance to the human presumption that whatsoever man notices or names or loves ought to be more deeply seated in reality or more permanent than what he ignores or despises. The good is a great magnet over discourse and imagination, and therefore rightly rules the Platonic world, which is that of moral philosophy only ; but this good is itself defined and chosen by the humble animal nature of man, demanding to eat and live and love. In the realm of essence this human good has no pre-eminence,

and being an essence it has no power. The Platonic
notion that ideas were models which things imperfectly imitated expresses admirably the moral nature
of man attaining to self-knowledge and proclaiming
clearly his instinctive demands ; or possibly (if the
moralist is also a poet plastic to the wider influences
of nature) defining also the demands which non-
human creatures would make on themselves or on us
if they had life and thought. Platonic ideas, in their
widest range, express sympathy with universal life ;
they are anagrams of moral insight. Hence their
nobility, and constant appeal to minds struggling after
perfection, whether in art or in self-discipline. The
spirit, by expressing itself in them, is fortified, as the
artist is by his work taking shape before his eyes and
revealing to him his own hidden intentions and judgements never expressed. But the realm of essence is
no more limited to these few ideals chosen and projected heavenwards by the aspiration of living creatures,
than the celestial galaxy is limited to the north star.
Excellence is relative to the accidental life of nature
which selects now one essence and now another to be
the goal of some thought or endeavour. In the realm
of essence no emphasis falls on these favourite forms
which does not fall equally on every other member
of that infinite continuum. Every bad thing — bad
because false to the ideal which its own nature may
propose to it—illustrates an essence quite as accurately
as if it had been good. No essence, except temporarily
and by accident, is the goal of any natural process,
much less its motive power.

Thus the discernment of essence, while confirming
Platonic logic in the ideal status which it assigns to
the terms of discourse (and discourse includes all that
is mental in sensation and perception), destroys the
illusions of Platonism, because it shows that essences,
being non-existent and omnimodal, can exercise no

domination over matter, but themselves come to light in nature or in thought only as material exigencies may call them forth and select them.   The realm of essence is a perfect democracy, where everything that is or might be has a right of citizenship ; so that only some arbitrary existential principle — call it the predis-positions in matter or the blindness of absolute will— can be rendered responsible, in a verbal metaphysics, for things being as they are, causing them to fall now into this form and now into that, or to choose one essence rather than another to be their type and ideal. These chosen types are surrounded in the realm of essence by every monster, every unexampled being, and every vice ; no more vicious there, no more anomalous or monstrous than any other nature.   Seen against that infinite background even the star-dust of modern astronomy, with its strange rhythms and laws, and its strange fertility, seems the most curious of accidents : what a choice for existence to make, when it might have been anything else ! And as to the snug universe which the ancients, and most men in their daily thoughts, have imagined about them, presided over by its Olympian deities, or its Jewish God, or its German Will, it is not only the figment of the most laughable egotism, but even if by chance it were the actual world, it would be utterly contingent and ephemeral.

This is one hygienic effect of the discovery of essence : it is a shower-bath for the dreamy moralist, and clears Platonism of superstition.

On the other hand, the discernment of essence reinstates the Socratic analysis of knowledge, by showing that essences are indispensable terms in the perception of matters of fact, and render transitive knowledge possible. If there were no purely ideal characters present to intuition yet not existentially a part either of the mind or of the environment, nothing ulterior could ever be imagined, much less truly conceived. Every supposed instance of knowledge would be either a bit of sentience without an object, or an existing entity unrelated to any mind. But an essence given in intuition, being non-existent in itself and by no means the object at that moment intended by the animal in his alertness or pursuit, may become a description of that object. If there is to be intelligence at all, the immediate must be vehicular. It is so when animal fancy is turned to the description of things; for then passive sensibility supplies terms which are in themselves volatile and homeless, and these terms may be dispersed as names, to christen the things that receive them, carrying intelligence by its intent to its objects (objects already selected by animal endeavour) and reporting the objects to the animal mind by their appearance. What is given becomes in this manner a sign for what is sought, and a conventional description of it; and the object originally posited by faith and intent in the act of living may be ultimately more and more accurately revealed to belief and to thought. Essences are ideal terms at the command of fancy and of the senses (whose data are fancies) as words are at the command of a ready tongue. If thought arises at all, it must think something after some fashion; and the essences it evokes in intuition enable it to imagine, to assert, and perhaps truly to know something about what is not itself nor its own condition: some existing thing or removed event which would otherwise run on blindly in its own medium, at best overtaking the animal unawares, or confronting him to no purpose. But when the animate body responds to circumstances and is sensitive, in various unprecedented ways, to their variations, it acquires a whole sensuous vocabulary in which to describe them, colours, sounds, shapes, sizes, excellences, and defects being the parts of speech in its grammar. It feels hot or cold according to the season ; so that cold and heat become signs of the seasons for the spirit, the homely poetry in which the senses render the large facts and the chief influences of nature. Perhaps even the vegetative soul has her dreams, but in the animal these floating visions are clarified by watchfulness and can be compared and contrasted in their character as well as in their occasions; and they lend intelligence terms in which to think and judge. The toys of sense become the currency of commerce ; ideas, which were only echoes of facts, serve as symbols for them. Thus intuition of essences first enables the mind to say something about anything, to think of what is not given, and to be a mind at all.

A great use of the discovery of essence, then, is to justify the notions of intelligence and knowledge, otherwise self-contradictory, and to show how such transcendence of the actual is possible for the animal mind.

The notion of essence is also useful in dismissing and handing over to physical science, where it belongs, the mooted question concerning the primary and secondary qualities of matter. There is a profound but genuine problem here which no logical discrimination and no psychological analysis can affect, namely : What are the elements of matter, and by what arrangement or motion of these elements do gross bodies acquire their various properties ? The physical philosophers must tell us, if they can, how matter is composed : and as they are compelled, like the rest of us, to begin by studying the aspects and behaviour of obvious bodies, on the scale of human perception, it is but fair to give them time, or even eternity, in which to come to a conclusion. But the question of primary and secondary qualities, as mooted in modern philosophy, is a false problem. It rests on the presumption that the data of sense can be and should be constituents of the object in nature, or at least exactly like its constituents. The object in nature is, for example, bread I am eating : and the presumption of modern psychologists is that this object is, or ought to be, composed of my sensations of contact, colour, temperature, movement, and pleasure in eating it. The pleasure and the colour, however, soon prove to be reversible according to the accidents of appetite or jaundice in me, without any change in the object itself. In the act of eating (overlooked by these psychologists) I have my radical assurance of that object, know its place, and continue to testify to its identity. The bread, for animal faith, is this thing I am eating, and causing to disappear to my substantial advantage ; and although language is clumsy in expressing this assurance, which runs much deeper than language, I may paraphrase it by saying that bread is this substance I can eat and turn into my own substance ; in seizing and biting it I determine its identity and its place in nature, and in transforming it I prove its existence. If the psychological critics of experience overlooked this animal faith in fact as they do in theory, their theory itself would have no point of application, and they would not know what they were talking about, and would not really be talking about anything. Their data would have no places and no context. As it is, they continue illegitimately to posit the bread, as an animal would, and then, in their human wisdom, proceed to remove from the description of it the colour and the pleasure concerned, as being mere effects on themselves, while they identify the bread itself with the remainder of their description hypostatised : shape, weight, and hardness. But how should some data, when posited, produce others entirely different, but contemporary, or perhaps earlier ? Evidently these so-called primary qualities are simply those essences which custom or science continues to use in its description of things :

but meantime the things have evaporated, and the description of them, in no matter what terms, ought to be idle and useless. All knowledge of nature and history has become a game of thought, a laborious dream in which a dim superstition makes me believe that some trains of images are more prosperous than others.

It is because essences are not discerned that philosophers in so many ways labour the hopeless notion that there is nothing in sense which is not first in things. Either perception and knowledge (which are animal faith) are deputed to be intuition, so that things have to be composed pictorially, out of the elements of human discourse, as if their substance consisted of images pressed together like a pack of cards ; or else ideas must be explained as imports from the outer world, prolonging the qualities of things, as if the organs of sense were only holes in the skin, through which emanations of things could pass ready-made into the heart or head, and perhaps in those dark caverns could breed unnaturally together, producing a monstrous brood of dreams and errors. But, as a matter of fact, elaborate bodily mechanisms are just as requisite for seeing as for thinking, and the landscape, as a man sees it, is no less human than the universe as his philosophy constructs it—and we know how human that is. Evidences soon accumulate to prove that no quality in the object is like any datum of sense. Nothing given exists. Consider, for instance, the water which seems cold to one hand and warm to the other. Shall the water be called hot or cold ? Both, certainly, if a full description of it, in all its relations and appearances, is what is sought. But if what is sought is the substance of the water, properties shown to be relative to my organs of sense cannot be " real " qualities of that substance. Their original (for they were still expected to have originals) was accordingly placed elsewhere. Perhaps the " real " cold might be in the warm hand, and the " real " warmth in the cold one ; or in cold and hot tracts of the brain respectively ; or else " in the mind "—a substance which might endure heat and cold simultaneously in different parts of itself. Or perhaps the mind was simply the heat and the cold existing successively, each a feeling absolute in itself : but in this case a second mind would be required to observe, remember, and appropriate those existing feelings, and how should reflection reach those feelings or know at all what they were ? If they are past, how should intuition possess them now ? And if they are only the present data of intuition, need they ever have existed before, or in any form but that in which I feel them now, when I feel them no longer ?

The notion that knowledge is intuition, that it must either penetrate to the inner quality of its object or else have no object but the overt datum, has not been carried out with rigour : if it had, it might have been sooner abandoned. Rudimentary vital feelings, such as pleasure or hunger, are not supposed even by the most mythological philosophers to be drawn from external sources of the same quality. Plato in one place says of intelligence that there must surely be floods of it in the vast heavens, as there are floods of light there, whence puny man may draw his dribblet. He neglects, however, to extend this principle to pain, pleasure, or hunger. He does not argue that my paltry pains and pleasures can be but drops sucked in from some vast cosmic reservoir of these feelings, nor that my momentary hunger could never have improvised its own quality, but must be only a bit, transferred to my mortal stomach, of a divine hunger eternally gnawing the whole sky. Yet this is the principle on which many a candid idolater has supposed, and still supposes, that light, space, music, and reason, as his intuition renders them, must permeate the universe.

The illusion is childish, and when we have once discerned essence, it seems strangely idolatrous. The essences given in intuition are fetched from no original. The reason, music, space, and light of my imagination are essences existing nowhere : the intuition of them is quite as spiritual and quite as personal as my pain, pleasure, or hunger, and quite as little likely to be drawn from an imaginary store of similar substances in the world at large. They are dream-lights kindled by my fancy, like all the terms of discourse ; they do not need to be previously resident either in the object or in the organ of sense. Not existing at all, they cannot be the causes of their own appearance ; nor would introducing an existing triangle under the skin, or making the brain triangular, in the least help to display the triangle to intuition. But if some material thing called a triangle is placed before me at a suitable distance, my eyes and brain will do the rest, and the essence dear to Euclid will arise in my mind's eye. No essence would ever appear simply because many hypostatic instances of it existed in the world : a living body must create the intuition and blossom into it, evoking some spontaneous image. Sense is a faculty of calling names under provocation ; all perception and thought are cries and comments elicited from the heart of some living creature. They are original, though not novel, like the feelings of lovers : normal phases of animation in animals, whose life carries this inner flux of pictures and currents in the fancy, mixed with little and great emotions and dull bodily feelings : nothing in all this discourse being a passive copy of existences elsewhere.

On the other hand, if the so-called primary qualities, taken pictorially, are just as symbolic as the secondary ones, the secondary, taken indicatively, are just as true as the primary. They too report some particularity in the object which, being relative to me, may be of the highest importance, and being also relative to something in the constitution of the object, may be a valuable indication of its nature, like greenness in grapes. The qualities most obviously relative and reversible, like pleasant and unpleasant, good and bad, are truly qualities of things in some of their relations. They can all, by judicious criticism and redistribution, become *true* expressions of the life of nature. They have their exits and their entrances at appointed times, and they supply a perspective view, or caricature, of the world no less interesting and pungent for being purely egotistical. Artists have their place, and the animal mind is one of them.

That like knows like is a proverb, and after the manner of proverbs it is applicable on occasion, but its opposite is so too. Similar minds can understand the same things, and in that sense can understand each other : they can share and divine one another's thoughts. This is because similar organs under similar stimulation will yield similar intuitions, revealing the same essence : like knows like by dramatic sympathy and ideal unanimity. But in sensuous perception the unlike knows the unlike. Here the organ is not adjusted to a similar organ, like instruments tuned up to the same key : the adjustment is rather to heterogeneous events in the environment or remote facts on quite a different scale ; and the images that mediate this knowledge are quite unlike the events they signify. It would be grotesque to expect a flower to imitate or to resemble the soil, climate, moisture, and light, or even the seed and sap, that preside over its budding : but the flower presupposes all these agencies and is an index to them ; an index which may become a sign and a vehicle of knowledge when it is used as an index by some discursive observer.

Any given essence is normally a true sign for the object or event which occupies animal attention when that essence appears : as it is true of arsenic that it is poisonous and of pepper that it is hot, although the quality of being hot or poisonous cannot possibly be a material constituent of those substances, nor a copy of such a constituent. The environment determines the occasions on which intuitions arise, the psyche— the inherited organisation of the animal—determines their form, and ancient conditions of life on earth no doubt determined which psyches should arise and prosper ; and probably many forms of intuition, unthinkable to man, express the facts and the rhythms of nature to other animal minds. Yet all these various symbolisms and sensuous dialects may be truly significant, composing most relevant complications in nature, by which she comments on herself. To suppose that some of these comments are poetical and others literal is gratuitous. They are all presumably poetical in form (intuition being poetry in act) and all expressive in function, and addressed to the facts of nature in some human and moral perspective, as poetry is too.

The absurdity of wishing to have *intuitions of things* reaches its climax when we ask whether things, if nobody looked at them, would still look as they do. Of course they would still be what they are : but whether their intrinsic essence, whether they are looked at or not, *resembles* such essences as eyes of one sort or another might gather by looking at them, is an idle question. It is not resemblance but relevance and closeness of adaptation that render a language expressive or an expression true. We read nature as the English used to read Latin, pronouncing it like English, but understanding it very well. If all other traditions of Latin euphony had been lost, there would have been no means of discovering in what respect the English pronunciation was a distortion, although the judicious would have suspected that the Romans could not have had an Oxonian accent. So each tribe of animals, each sense, each stage of experience and science, reads the book of nature according to a phonetic system of its own, with no possibility of exchanging it for the native sounds : but this situation, though hopeless in one sense, is not unsatisfactory practically, and is innocently humorous. It adds to the variety, if not to the gaiety, of experience ; and perhaps a homely accent in knowledge, as in Latin, renders learning more savoury and familiar, and makes us more willing to read.

It is just because the images given in sense are so very original and fantastic that understanding can enlarge knowledge by correcting, combining, and discounting those appearances. Sensible qualities, like pet names, do very well at home, when no consistent or exact description of things is required, but only some familiar signal. When it comes to public business, however, more serious and legal designations have to be used, and these are what we call science. The description is not less symbolic but more accurate and minute. It may also involve—as in optics and psychology—a discovery of the images of sense as distinct from their original uses as living visions of things ; and we may then learn that our immediate experience was but a diving-board, on which we hardly knew we were standing in plunging into the world. It was indeed essentially a theoretic eminence, a place of outlook, intended to fortify and prepare us for the plunge. Accordingly the symbols of sense are most relevant to their object at the remove and on the scale on which our daily action encounters it. In science, analogies and hypotheses, if not microscopes and telescopes, supply ideas of things more immediate or more remote. Thus the warmth and the cold felt at once in the same water inform me more directly about the water in relation to my two hands, than about my temperature, my brain, or my intuitions ; and yet these things too are involved in that event and may be discovered in it by science. But science and sense, though differing in their scope, are exactly alike in their truth ; and the views taken by science, though more penetrating and extensive, are still views : ground plans, elevations, and geometric projections taking the place of snapshots. All intuitions, whether in sense or thought, are theoretic : all are appropriate renderings, on some method and on some scale, of the circumstances in which they arise, and may serve to describe those circumstances truly : but experience and tact are requisite, as in the use of any language or technique of art, in distributing our stock symbols, and fitting the image to the occasion and the word to the fact.

The notion of essence also relieves the weary philosopher of several other problems, even more scholastic and artificial, concerning sensations and ideas, particulars and universals, the abstract and the concrete. There are no such differences in essences as they are given : all are equally immediate and equally unsubstantial, equally ideal and equally complete. Nothing could be more actual and specific than some unpleasant inner feeling or sentiment, as it colours the passing moment ; yet nothing could be less descriptive of anything further, or vaguer in its significance, or more ephemeral an index to processes and events which it does not disclose but which are all its substance. And the clearest idea—say a geo-metrical sphere—and the most remote from sense (if we mean by sense the images actually supplied by the outer organs) is just such a floating presence, caught and lost again, an essence that in itself tells me nothing of its validity, nor of a world of fact to which it might apply. All these current distinctions are extraneous to essences, which are the only data of experience. The distinctions are borrowed from various ulterior existential relations subsisting between facts, some mental and some material, but none of them ever given in intuition. The mental facts, namely the intuitions to which the essences appear, may be confused by psychologists with those essences, as the material things supposed to possess those essences as qualities may be confused with them by the practical intellect, and both may be called by the same names ; a double equivocation which later enables the metaphysician, by a double hypostasis of the datum, to say that the material thing and the mental event are one and the same *given fact*. We may innocently speak of given facts, meaning those posited in previous perceptions or referred to in previous discourse : but no fact can be a given fact in the sense of being a datum of intuition. And it is entirely on relations between facts not given that those current distinctions rest. They may often express truly the relative scope of intuitions, or the manner in which they take place amongst the general events in nature or arise in the animal body : but in respect to essences, which are the only terms of actual thought, they are perfectly unmeaning.

Suppose, for instance, that I see yellow, that my eyes are open, and that there is a buttercup before me ; my intuition (not properly the essence " yellow " which is the datum) is then called a sensation. If again I see yellow with my eyes closed, the intuition is called an idea or a dream—although often in what is called an idea no yellow appears, but only words. If yet again I see yellow with my eyes open, but there is no buttercup, the intuition is called a hallucination. These various situations are curious, and worth distinguishing in optics and in medical psychology, but for the sceptical scrutiny of experience they make no difference. What can inform me, when I see yellow simply, whether my eyes are open or shut, or whether I am awake or dreaming, or what functions material buttercups may have in psycho-physical correlation, or whether there is anything physical or anything psychical in the world, or any world at all ? These notions are merely conventional, imported knowledge or imported delusion. Such extraneous circumstances, whether true or false, cannot alter in the least the essence which I have before me, nor its sort of reality, nor its status in respect to my intuition of it.

Suppose again that I am at sea and feel the ship rocking. This feeling is called external perception ; but if I feel nausea, my feeling is called internal sensation, or emotion, or introspection ; and there are sad psychologists to conclude thence that while the ship rocking is something physical, and a mere appearance, nausea is something psychical, and an absolute reality. Why this partiality in distributing metaphysical dignities amongst things equally obvious ? Each essence that appears appears just as it is, because its appearance defines it, and determines the whole being that it is or has. Nothing given is either physical or mental, in the sense of being intrinsically a thing or a thought ; it is just a quality of being. Essences (like " rocking ") which serve eventually to describe material facts are given in intuitions which are just as mental as those which supply psychological terms for describing mental discourse. On the other hand, essences (like " nausea ") used first perhaps for describing discourse, mark crises in the flux of matter just as precisely as those which are used to describe material facts directly ; because discourse goes on in animals subject to material influences. But in neither case can the intuitions—which constitute discourse and the mental sphere—be ever given in intuition.

They are posited in memory, expectation, and dramatic psychology. The rocking I feel is called physical, because the essence before me—say coloured planes crossing—serves to report and designate very much more complicated and prolonged movements in the ship and the waves ; and the nausea I also feel is called psychical, because it reports nothing (unless my medical imagination intervenes) but is endured pathetically, with a preponderating sense of time, change, and danger, as it largely consists in feeling how long this lasts, how upset I am, and how sick I am about to be.

Again, if I see yellow once, my experience is called a particular impression, and its object, yellow, is supposed to exist and to be a particular too ; but if I see yellow again, yellow has mysteriously become a universal, a general idea, and an abstraction. Yet the datum for intuition is throughout precisely the same. No essence is abstract, yet none is a particular thing or event, none is an object of belief, perception, or pursuit, having a particular position in the context of nature. Even the intuition, though it is an event, cannot become an object of pursuit or perception ; and its conventional place in history, when it has been posited and is believed to have occurred, is assigned to it only by courtesy, at the place and time of its physical support, as a wife in some countries takes her husband's name. Not the data of intuition, but the objects of animal faith, are the particulars perceived : they alone are the existing things or events to which the animal is reacting and to which he is attributing the essences which arise, as he does so, before his fancy. These data of intuition are universals ; they form the elements of such a description of the object as is at that time possible ; they are never that object itself, nor any part of it. Essences are not drawn out or abstracted from things ; they are given before the thing can be clearly perceived, since they are the terms used in perception ; but they are not given until attention is stretched upon the thing, which is posited blindly in action ; and they come as revelations, or oracles, delivered by that thing to the mind, and symbolising it there. In itself, as suspended understanding may suffer us to recognise it in reflection, each essence is a positive and complete theme : it is impossible that for experience anything should be more concrete or individual than is this exact and total appearance before me. Having never been parts of any perceived object, it is impossible that given essences should be abstracted from it. Being obvious and immediate data they cannot even have that congenital imperfection, that limp, which we might feel in a broken arch, or in the half of anything already familiar as a whole. But given essences are indeed visionary, they are unsubstantial ; and in that respect they seem strange and unearthly to an animal expecting to work amongst things without realising their appearance. Yet ghostly as his instinct may deem them, they are perfect pictures, with nothing abstract or abstruse in their specious nature. The abstract is a category posterior to intuition, and applicable only to terms, such as numbers and other symbols of mathematics, which have been intentionally substituted for other essences given earlier, by which they were suggested ; but even these technical terms are abstract only by accident and in function ; they have a concrete essence of their own, and are constitutive elements of perfectly definite structures in their own plane of being, forming patterns and running into scales there, like so much music.

Similarly, nothing given in sensation or thought is in the least vague in itself. Vagueness is an adventitious quality, which a given appearance may be said to possess in relation to an object presumed to have other determinations : as the cloud in *Hamlet* is but a vague camel or a vague weasel, but for the landscape-painter a perfectly definite cloud. The vague is merely the *too* vague for some assumed purpose ; and philosophers with a mania for accuracy, who find all discourse vague that is discourse about anything in the world of practice, are like critics of painting who should find all colours and forms vague, when they had been touched by aerial perspective, or made poetical by the rich dyes of fancy and expression. That sort of vagueness is perfection of artistic form, as the other sort of vagueness may be perfection of judgement : for knowledge lies in thinking aptly about things, not in becoming like them. If the standard of articulation in science were the articulation of existence, science would be impossible for an animal mind, and if it were possible would be useless : because nothing would be gained for thought by reproducing a mechanism without any adaptation of its scale and perspective to the nature of the thinker.

If the instincts of man were well adapted to his conditions, his thoughts, without being more accurate, would not seem confused. As it is, intuition is most vivid in the act of hunting or taking alarm, just when mistakes are probable : and any obvious essence is then precipitated upon the object, and quarrelled with and dismissed if the object does not sustain it. An essence, however evident, may even be declared absent and inconceivable, if it cannot be attributed absolutely to the substance of the object being chased or eaten. The hungry nominalist may well say to himself : " If the hues of the pheasant are no part of the bird, whence should he have fetched them ? Am I not looking at the very creature I am pursuing and hoping presently to devour ? And as my teeth and hands cannot possibly add anything to the substance they will seize upon, how should my eyes do so now ?

If therefore any alleged image can be proved to be no part of my object, I must be mistaken in supposing that I see such an image at all." This is also the argument of the primitive painter, who knowing that men have two eyes and their hands five fingers, will not admit that their image might be less complete. In this way the wand of that Queen Mab, intuition, is assimilated by a too materialistic philosophy to a tongue or an antenna, and required to reach out to the object and stir it up, exploring its intrinsic quality and structure. But it is a magic wand, and calls up only wild and ignorant visions, mischievous and gaily invented ; and if ever a philosopher dreams he has fathomed the thing before him in action, that wand is tickling his nose. Intuition cheats in enriching him, and nature who whispers all these tales in his ear is laughing at him and fondling him at the same time. It is a kindly fiction ; because the dreams she inspires are very much to his mind, and the lies she invents for his benefit are her poetic masterpiece. Practical men despise the poetry of poets, but they are well pleased with their own. They would be ashamed of amusements which might defeat their purposes, or mislead them about the issue of events ; but they embrace heartily the ingenuous fictions of the senses which they almost recognise to be fictions, and even the early myths and religions of mankind. These they find true enough for practical and moral purposes ; their playfulness is a convenient compendium for facts too hard to understand ; they are the normal poetry of observation and policy. Fancy disorganises conduct only when it expresses vice ; and then it is the vice that does the mischief, and not the fancy.

Even philosophers, when they wish to be very plain and economical, sometimes fall to denying the immediate. Fact-worship, which is an idolatry of prudence, prejudices them against their own senses, and against the mind, which is what prudence serves, if it serves anything ; and perhaps they declare themselves incapable of framing images with fewer determinations than they believe material things to possess. If a material triangle must have a perfectly defined shape (although at close quarters matter might elude such confines), or if a material house must have a particular number of bricks and a particular shade of colour at each point of its surface, a professed empiricist like Berkeley may be tempted to deny that he can have an idea of a triangle, *et cetera*, without such determinations ; whereas, however clear his visual images may have been, it is certain he never could have had, even in direct perception, an image specifying all the bricks or all the tints of *any* house, nor the exact measure of *any* angle. Berkeley himself, I suspect, was secretly intent upon essence, which in every degree of conventional determination is its own standard of completeness. But given essences have any degree of vagueness in respect to the material or mathematical objects which they may symbolise, and to which Berkeley in his hasty nominalism wished to assimilate them. He almost turned given essences into substances, to take the place of those material things which he had denied. Each essence is certainly not two contradictory essences at once ; but the definitions which render each precisely what it is lie in the realm of essence, an infinite continuum of discrete forms, not in the realm of existence. Essences, in order to appear, do not need to beg leave of what happens to exist, or to draw its portrait ; yet here the trooping essences are, in such gradations and numbers as intuition may lend them. It is not by hypostatising them as they come that their roots in matter or their scope in knowledge can be discovered.

Thus the discrimination of essence has a happy tendency to liberalise philosophy, freeing it at once from literalness and from scepticism. If all data are symbols and all experience comes in poetic terms, it follows that the human mind, both in its existence and in its quality, is a free development out of nature, a language or music the terms of which are arbitrary, like the rules and counters of a game. It follows also that the mind has no capacity and no obligation to copy the world of matter nor to survey it impartially. At the same time, it follows that the mind affords a true expression of the world, rendered in vital perspectives and in human terms, since this mind arises and changes symptomatically at certain foci of animal life ; foci which are a part of nature in dynamic correspondence with other parts, diffused widely about them ; so that, for instance, alternative systems of religion or science, if not taken literally, may equally well express the actual operation of things measured by different organs or from different centres.

CHAPTER XI

THE WATERSHED OF CRITICISM

I HAVE now reached the culminating point of my survey of evidence, and the entanglements I have left behind me and the habitable regions I am looking for lie spread out before me like opposite valleys. On the one hand I see now a sweeping reason for scepticism, over and above all particular contradictions or fancifulness of dogma. Nothing is ever present to me except some essence ; so that nothing that I possess in intuition, or actually see, is ever *there* ; it can never exist bodily, nor lie in that place or exert that power which belongs to the objects encountered in action. Therefore, if I regard my intuitions as knowledge of facts, all my experience is illusion, and life is a dream. At the same time I am now able to give a clearer meaning to this old adage ; for life would not be a dream, and all experience would not be illusion, if I abstained from believing in them. The evidence of data is only obviousness ; they give no evidence of anything else ; they are not witnesses. If I am content to recognise them for pure essences, they cannot deceive me ; they will be like works of literary fiction, more or less coherent, but without any claim to exist on their own account. If I hypostatise an essence into a fact, instinctively placing it in relations which are not given within it, I am putting my trust in animal faith, not in any evidence or implication of my

actual experience. I turn to an assumed world about
me, because I have organs for turning, just as I expect
a future to reel itself out without interruption because
I am wound up to go on myself. To such ulterior
things no manifest essence can bear any testimony.
They must justify themselves. If the ulterior fact is
some intuition elsewhere, its existence, if it happens to
exist, will justify that belief ; but the fulfilment of my
prophecy, in taking my present dream for testimony
to that ulterior experience, will be found only in the
realm of truth—a realm which is itself an object of
belief, never by any possibility of intuition, human or
divine. So too when the supposed fact is thought
of as a substance, its existence, if it is found in the
realm of nature, will justify that supposition ; but the
realm of nature is of course only another object of
belief, more remote if possible from intuition than
even the realm of truth. Intuition of essence, to which
positive experience and certitude are confined, is therefore always illusion, if we allow our hypostatising
impulse to take it for evidence of anything else.

In adopting this conclusion of so many great
philosophers, that all is illusion, I do so, however, with
two qualifications. One is emotional and moral only,
in that I do not mourn over this fatality, but on the
contrary rather prefer speculation in the realm of
essence—if it can be indulged without practical inconvenience—to alleged information about hard facts.
It does not seem to me ignominious to be a poet, if
nature has made one a poet unexpectedly. Unexpectedly nature lent us existence, and if she has
made it a condition that we should be poets, she has
not forbidden us to enjoy that art, or even to be proud
of it. The other qualification is more austere : it
consists in not allowing exceptions. I cannot admit
that some particular essence—water, fire, being, atoms,
or Brahma—is the intrinsic essence of all things, so

that if I narrow my imagination to that one intuition I shall have intuited the heart and the whole of existence. Of course I do not deny that there is water and that there is being, the former in most things on earth, and the latter in everything anywhere ; but these images or words of mine are not the things they designate, but only names for them. Desultory and partial propriety these names may have, but no metaphysical privilege. No more has the expedient of some modern critics who would take illusion as a whole and call it the universe ; for in the first place they are probably reverting to belief in discourse, as conventionally conceived, so that their scepticism is halting ; and in the second place, even if human experience could be admitted as known and vouched for, there would be an incredible arrogance in positing it as the whole of being, or as itself confined to the forms and limits which the critic assigns to it. The life of reason as I conceive it is a mere romance, and the life of nature a mere fable ; such pictures have no metaphysical value, even if as sympathetic fictions they had some psychological truth.

The doctrine of essence thus renders my scepticism invincible and complete, while reconciling me with it emotionally.

If now I turn my face in the other direction and consider the prospect open to animal faith, I see that all this insecurity and inadequacy of alleged knowledge are almost irrelevant to the natural effort of the mind to describe natural things. The discouragement we may feel in science does not come from failure ; it comes from a false conception of what would be success. Our worst difficulties arise from the assumption that knowledge of existences ought to be literal, whereas knowledge of existences has no need, no propensity, and no fitness to be literal. It is symbolic initially, when a sound, a smell, an indescribable feeling are signals to the animal of his dangers or chances ; and it fulfils its function perfectly—I mean its moral function of enlightening us about our natural good— if it remains symbolic to the end. Can anything be more evident than that religion, language, patriotism, love, science itself speak in symbols ? Given essences unify for intuition, in entirely adventitious human terms, the diffuse processes of nature ; the æsthetic image—the sound, the colour, the expanse of space, the scent, taste, and sweet or cruel pressure of bodies —wears an aspect altogether unlike the mechanisms it stands for. Sensation and thought (between which there is no essential difference) work in a conventional medium, as do literature and music. The experience of essence is direct; the expression of natural facts through that medium is indirect. But this indirection is no obstacle to expression, rather its condition ; and this vehicular manifestation of things may be know-ledge of them, which intuition of essence is not. The theatre, for all its artifices, depicts life in a sense more truly than history, because the medium has a kindred movement to that of real life, though an artificial setting and form ; and much in the same way the human medium of knowledge can perform its pertinent synthesis and make its pertinent report all the better when it frankly abandons the plane of its object and expresses in symbols what we need to know of it. The arts of expression would be impossible if they were not extensions of normal human perception. The Greeks recognised that astronomy and history were presided over by Muses, sisters of those of tragic and comic poetry ; had they been as psychological as modern reflection has become, they might have had Muses of sight, hearing, and speech. I think they honoured, if they did not express, this complementary fact also, that all the Muses, even the most playful, are witnesses to the nature of things. The arts are evidences of wisdom, and sources of it ; they include science. No Muse would be a humane influence, nor worthy of honour, if she did not studiously express the truth of nature with the liberty and grace appropriate to her special genius.

Philosophers would not have overlooked the fact that knowledge is, and ought to be, symbolical, if intuition did not exist also, giving them a taste of something which perhaps they think higher and more satisfying. Intuition, when it is placid and masterful enough to stand alone, free from anxiety or delusion about matters of fact, is a delightful exercise, like play ; it employs our imaginative faculty without warping it, and lets us live without responsibility. The playful and godlike mind of philosophers has always been fascinated by intuition ; philosophers—I mean the great ones—are the infant prodigies of reflection. They often take intuition of essence for their single ideal, and wish to impose it on the workaday thoughts of men ; they make a play-world for themselves which it is glorious to dominate, much as other men of genius, prolonging the masterfulness of childhood, continue to play at this or at that in their politics and their religion. But knowledge of existence has an entirely different method and an entirely different ideal. It is playful too, because its terms are intuitive and its grammar or logic often very subjective. Perception, theory, hypothesis are rapid, pregnant, often humorous ; they seize a fact by its skirts from some unexpected quarter, and give it a nickname which it might be surprised to hear, such as the rainbow or the Great Bear. Yet in the investigation of facts all this play of mind is merely instrumental and indicative : the intent is practical, the watchfulness earnest, the spirit humble. The mind here knows that it is at school ; and even its fancies are docile. Its nicknames for things and for their odd ways of behaving are like those which country people give to flowers ; they often pointedly describe how things look or what they do to us. The ideas we have of things are not fair portraits ; they are political caricatures made in the human interest ; but in their partial way they may be masterpieces of characterisation and insight. Above all, they are obtained by labour, by investigating what is not given, and by correcting one impression by another, drawn from the same object—a thing impossible in the intuition of essences. They therefore conduce to wisdom, and in their perpetual tentativeness have a cumulative truth.

Consider the reason why, instead of cultivating congenial intuitions, a man may be drawn to the study of nature at all. It is because things, by their impact, startle him into attention and a new thought. Such external objects interest him for what they do, not for what they are ; and knowledge of them is significant, not for the essence it displays to intuition (beautiful as this may be) but for the events it expresses or foreshadows. It matters little therefore to the pertinent knowledge of nature that the substance of things should remain recondite or unintelligible, if their movement and operation can be rightly determined on the plane of human perception. It matters little if their very existence is vouched for only by animal faith and presumption, so long as this faith posits existence where existence is, and this presumption expresses a prophetic preadaptation of animal instincts to the forces of the environment. The function of perception and natural science is, not to flatter the sense of omniscience in an absolute mind, but to dignify animal life by harmonising it, in action and in thought, with its conditions. It matters little if the news these methods can bring us of the world is fragmentary and is expressed rhetorically ; what matters is that science should be integrated with art, and that the arts should substitute the dominion of man over circumstances, as far as this is possible, for the dominion of chance.   In this there is no sacrifice of truth to utility ; there is rather a wise direction of curiosity upon things on the human scale, and within the range of art.   Speculation beyond those limits cannot be controlled, and is irresponsible ; and the symbolic terms in which it must be carried on, even at close quarters, are the best possible indications for the facts in question.   All these inadequacies and imperfections are proper to perfect signs, which should be brief and sharply distinguished.

Complete scepticism is accordingly not inconsistent with animal faith ; the admission that nothing given exists is not incompatible with belief in things not given.   I may yield to the suasion of instinct, and practise the arts with a humble confidence, without in the least disavowing the most rigorous criticism of knowledge or hypostatising any of the data of sense or fancy.   And I need not do this with a bad conscience, as Parmenides and Plato and the Indians seem to have done, when they admitted illusion or opinion as an epilogue to their tight metaphysics, on the ground that otherwise they would miss their way home.   It is precisely by *not* yielding to opinion and illusion, and by *not* delegating any favourite essences to be the substance of things, that I aspire to keep my cognitive conscience pure and my practical judgement sane ; because in order to find my way home I am by no means compelled to yield ignominiously to any animal illusion ; what guides me there is not illusion but habit ; and the intuitions which accompany habit are normal signs for the circle of objects and forces by which that habit is sustained.   The images of sense and science will not delude me if instead of hypostatising them, as those philosophers did the terms of their dialectic, I regard them as graphic symbols for home and for the way there. That such external things exist, that I exist myself, and live more or less prosperously in the midst of them, is a faith not founded on reason but precipitated in action, and in that intent, which is virtual action, involved in perception. This faith, which it would be dishonest not to confess that I share, does no violence to a sceptical analysis of experience ; on the contrary, it takes advantage of that analysis to interpret this volatile experience as all animals do and must, as a set of symbols for existences that cannot enter experience, and which, since they are not elements in knowledge, no analysis of knowledge can touch—they are in another realm of being.

I propose now to consider what objects animal faith requires me to posit, and in what order ; without for a moment forgetting that my assurance of their existence is only instinctive, and my description of their nature only symbolic. I may know them by intent, based on bodily reaction ; I know them initially as whatever confronts me, whatever it may turn out to be, just as I know the future initially as whatever is coming, without knowing what will come. That something confronts me here, now, and from a specific quarter, is in itself a momentous discovery. The aspect this thing wears, as it first attracts my attention, though it may deceive me in some particulars, can hardly fail to be, in some respects, a telling indication of its nature in its relation to me. Signs identify their objects for discourse, and show us where to look for their undiscovered qualities. Further signs, catching other aspects of the same object, may help me to lay siege to it from all sides ; but signs will never lead me into the citadel, and if its inner chambers are ever opened to me, it must be through sympathetic imagination. I might, by some happy unison between my imagination and its generative principles, intuit the essence which is actually the essence of that thing. In that case (which may often occur when the object is a sympathetic mind) knowledge of existence, without ceasing to be instinctive faith, will be as complete and adequate as knowledge can possibly be. The given essence will be the essence of the object meant ; but knowledge will remain a claim, since the intuition is not satisfied to observe the given essence passively as a disembodied essence, but instinctively affirms it to be the essence of an existence confronting me, and beyond the range of my possible apprehension. Therefore the most perfect knowledge of fact is perfect only pictorially, not evidentially, and remains subject to the end to the insecurity inseparable from animal faith, and from life itself.

Animal faith being a sort of expectation and open-mouthedness, is earlier than intuition ; intuitions come to help it out and lend it something to posit. It is more than ready to swallow any suggestion of sense or fancy ; and perhaps primitive credulity, as in a dream, makes no bones of any contradiction or incongruity in successive convictions, but yields its whole soul to every image. Faith then hangs like a pendulum at rest ; but when perplexity has caused that pendulum to swing more and more madly, it may for a moment stop quivering at a point of unstable equilibrium at the top ; and this vertical station may be likened to universal scepticism. It is a more wonderful and a more promising equilibrium than the other, because it cannot be maintained ; but before declining from the zenith and desisting from pointing vertically at zero, the pendulum of faith may hesitate for an instant which way to fall, if at that uncomfortable height it has really lost all animal momentum and all ancient prejudice. Before giving my reasons—which are but prejudices and human— for believing in events, in substances, and in the variegated truths which they involve, it may be well to have halted for breath at the apex of scepticism, and felt all the negative privileges of that position. The mere possibility of it in its purity is full of instruction; and although I have, for my own part, dwelt upon it only ironically, by a scruple of method, and intending presently to abandon it for common sense, many a greater philosopher has sought to maintain himself acrobatically at that altitude. They have not succeeded; but an impossible dwelling-place may afford, like a mountain-top, a good point of view in clear weather from which to map the land and choose a habitation.

CHAPTER XII

HUMAN beliefs and ideas (which in modern philosophy are called human knowledge) may be arranged systematically in various different series or orders. One is the *order of genesis*. The origin of beliefs and ideas, as of all events, is natural. All origins lie in the realm of matter, even when the being that is so generated is immaterial, because this creation or intrusion of the immaterial follows on material occasions and at the promptings of circumstance. It is safe to say this, although it may sound dogmatical, since an immaterial being not grafted in this way upon material events would be undiscoverable ; no place, time, or other relations in nature could be assigned to it, and even if by chance it existed it would have to exist only for its own benefit, unreported to any one else. It is accordingly in the realm of matter, in the order of events in animal life, that I must distribute human beliefs and ideas if I wish to arrange them in the order of their genesis.

Beliefs and ideas might also be surveyed in the *order of discovery*, as within the field of human grammar and thought they come to be discriminated. Such a survey would be a biography of reason, in which I should neglect the external occasions on which ideas and beliefs arise and study only the changing patterns which they form in the eye of thought, as in a kaleidoscope. What would probably come first in the order of discovery would be goods and evils ; or a romantic metaphysician might turn this experience into a fable, referring goods and evils to a transcendental will which should pronounce them (for no reason) to be such respectively. Will or moral bias is actually the background on which images of objects are gradually deciphered by an awakening intellect ; they all appear initially loaded with moral values and assigned to rival camps and quarters in the field of action. Discovery is essentially romantic ; there is less clearness in the objects that appear than there is vehemence in the assertion and choice of them. The life of reason is accordingly a subject to be treated imaginatively, and interpreted afresh by every historian with legitimate variations ; and if no theme lies nearer to the heart of man, since it is the history of his heart, none is more hopelessly the sport of apperception and of dramatic bias in the telling.

Finally, beliefs and ideas may be marshalled in the *order of evidence* ; and this is the only method that concerns me here. At any juncture in the life of reason a man may ask himself, as I am doing in this book, what he is most certain of, and what he believes only on hearsay or by some sort of suggestion or impulse of his own, which might be suspended or reversed. Alternative logics and creeds might thus suggest themselves, raised in different styles of architecture upon the bed-rock, if there is a bed-rock, of perfect certitude. I have already discovered what this bed-rock of perfect certitude is ; somewhat disconcertingly, it turns out to be in the regions of the rarest ether. I have absolute assurance of nothing save of the character of some given essence ; the rest is arbitrary belief or interpretation added by my animal impulse. The obvious leaves me helpless ; for among objects in the realm of essence I can establish

none of the distinctions which I am most concerned
to establish in daily life, such as that between true and
false, far or near, just now and long ago, once upon a
time, and in five minutes.   All these terms of course
are found there, else I could not mention them, but
they are found only as pictures ; each is present only
in essence, without any reason for choosing, asserting,
or making it effective.   The very opposite terms, if
I am only willing to think of them, lie sleeping side
by side with these which I happen first to have
come upon.   All essences and combinations of essences
are brother-shapes in an eternal landscape ; and the
more I range in that wilderness, the less reason I find
for stopping at anything, or for following any particular path.   Willingly or regretfully, if I wish to live,
I must rouse myself from this open-eyed trance into
which utter scepticism has thrown me.   I must allow
subterranean forces within me to burst forth and to
shatter that vision.   I must consent to be an animal
or a child, and to chase the fragments as if they were
things of moment.   But which fragment, and rolling
in what direction ?   I am resigned to being a dogmatist ; but at what point shall my dogmatism begin,
and by what first solicitation of nature ?

Starting, as here I should, from absolute certitude
—that is, from the obvious character of some essence—
the first object of belief suggested by that assurance
is the *identity* of this essence in various instances and
in various contexts.   This identity in divers cases is
not tautological, as identity would be if I spoke of
the identity of any essence with itself.   Identity, to be
significant, must be problematical.   I must pick up
my pebble twice, so that a juggler might without my
knowledge have substituted another pebble for it in
the interval ; and when I say confidently, *the same
pebble*, I may always be deceived.   My own thought
is not at all unlikely to play this trick on me ; it is

good at legerdemain. In attending a second time to what I call the same essence, I may really summon a different essence before me ; my memory need not retain the first intuition so precisely that its disparity from the present one can be sensible to me now. Identity of essences given at different times evidently presupposes time—an immense postulate ; and besides, it presupposes ability in thought to traverse time without confusion, so that having lived through two intuitions I may correctly distinguish them as events, whilst correctly identifying their common object. These are ambitious and highly questionable dogmas. Yet there is a circumstance in pure intuition of any essence which can insensibly lead me to those elaborate conclusions, and can lead me at the same time to posit the natural existence of myself, the possible dupe, having those intuitions and surviving them, and even the existence of my natural object, the persisting pebble, which those intuitions described unanimously.

This circumstance is closely connected with the property of essence which is most ideal and remote from existence, namely, its eternity. Eternity, taken intrinsically, has nothing to do with time, but is a form of being which time cannot usher in nor destroy ; it is always equally real, silent, and indestructible, no matter what time may do, or what time it may be. But intuition peruses eternal being in time ; consequently, so long as I am attending to an essence, this essence seems to me *to endure* ; and when, after an interval, I revert to it or to any feature of it, this feature seems to me *to be identical* with what it was. This identity and this duration are not properly predicated of essence in its own realm ; they are superfluous epithets essentially, and almost insults, because they substitute a questionable for an unquestionable subsistence in the essence. Yet the epithets are well meant, and indicate fairly enough the aspect which essences present to moving thought when it plays upon them. Intuition finds essence by watching, by exerting animal attention. Now when he watches, an animal thinks that what he watches is watching him with the same intensity and variability of attention which he is exerting ; for attention is fundamentally an animal uneasiness, fostered by the exigences of life amid other material beings that can change and jump. Stillness or constancy in any object accordingly does not seem to an animal eternity in an essence ; it seems rather a suspension of motion in a thing, a pause for breath, an ominous and awful silence. He is superstitious about the eternity of essences, as about all their other properties. This breathless and ghostly duration which he attributes to essences, treating them like living things, is his confused temporal translation of their eternity, mixing it with existence, which is the negation of eternity. Thus he assimilates it to the quasi-permanence in himself which is transfused with change ; for of course he is far from perceiving that if essences were not natively eternal and non-existent, it would be impossible for crawling existence to change from one form to another. This illusion is inevitable. The dubious and iterative duration proper to animal life, when the lungs breathe and the mind is appetitive, seems to this mind a pulsation in all being.

Moreover, in watching any image, it is often possible to observe one feature in it persisting while another disappears. The man not only says to himself, " This, and still this," but he ventures to say, " This, and again this with a variation." A variation in *this* ? Here, from the point of view of essence, is a sheer absurdity. *This* cannot change its nature, though what we have before us a moment later may be something but slightly different from *this* ; and of course the essence now brought to view can be slightly different from the one formerly in evidence only because each is eternally itself, so that the least variant from it marks and constitutes a different essence. Material categories such as existence, substance, and change, none of which are applicable to pure data, are thus insinuated by the animal intellect into contemplation. They transform intuition into belief ; and this belief, as if it would reinforce essences when they appear and annul them when they disappear, ultimately posits an imaginary shuffling of sensible existences—hypostatised essences—dancing about us as we watch the scene. Even if this hypostasis is retracted afterwards by the critic, the postulate remains that he is steadily perusing the *same essence*, or returning to reconsider it. Without this postulate it would be impossible to say or think anything on any subject. No essence could be recognised, and therefore no change could be specified. Yet this necessary belief is one impossible to prove or even to defend by argument, since all argument presupposes it. It must be accepted as a rule of the game, if you think the game worth playing.

What shall I say of the probable truth of such fundamental assumptions ? Shall I think them false, because groundless, and shall I say that they invalidate the whole edifice of natural faith which is raised upon them ? Or shall I say that the experienced security of this edifice justifies them and implies their truth ? Neither ; because the happy results and fertility of an assumption do not prove it true literally, but only prove it to be suitable, to be worth cultivating as an art and repeating as a good myth. The axioms of sanity and art must correspond *somehow* to truth, but the correspondence may be very loose and very partial. Moreover, the circumstance that even this symbolic rightness is vouched for only by an experience which would be false in all its records and memories if this assumption were false, robs such experimental tests of all logical force. Corroboration is no new argument ; if I am deceived once, I may all the more readily be deceived again. In the perspectives of experience I cannot, except in these very perspectives, reach the terms which they posit as self-existent, in order to see whether my perspectives were rightly drawn. I am in the region of belief mediated by symbols, in the region of animal faith.

CHAPTER XIII

BELIEF IN DEMONSTRATION

THE essence which is the object of intuition is probably not simple. Perhaps nothing that has a character recognisable in reflection can be utterly simple. The datum may seem purely qualitative, like a smell or like absolute Being, and yet some plurality may lurk in its very diffuseness or continuity, giving a foothold for discrimination of different moments or parts within it. Usually this inward complexity of given essences is very marked, and a chief element in their nature ; but it is not at all incompatible with the æsthetic and logical individuality which makes them terms for possible recognition and discourse. Essences, like things, may be perfectly unambiguous objects to name or to point to, and may be counted as units, without prejudice to their internal complexity. My dog is one and the same dog unmistakably, without prejudice to the possibly infinite complexity of his organism or the interpenetration of his qualities. In the same way Euclidean space is a single and definite essence ; yet its character is subject to analysis. I may say it has three dimensions, is necessarily infinite, without scale, etc. These implications, which I may enumerate successively, lie in the essence together, and lie there from the beginning, even if my intuition is slow to disentangle them, or never does so at all. The simplicity of the essence given at first was a pregnant simplicity; it had enough character to be identified with the total and unitary aspect of another essence—Euclidean space analysed—which may appear later.

Intuition therefore is a view of essence, attention fixed upon it, and not that essence itself. When I say Euclidean space has three dimensions, I am counting them; I am proceeding from one specious plane, or felt direction of motion, to another, and perhaps back again, for the sake of verification. If this operation is to be a valid survey of the essence proposed, the plane or directions specified must, so to speak, stay in their places. Each must remain itself, so that in passing from it to another, as I do in counting, I may pass to something truly different, and may be able to revert from this to the original element, and find it still there, identical with its former self. But, as I have already discovered, this self-identity of a term to which I revert cannot be given either in the first intuition of it, nor in the second. All that either intuition can yield while it endures is the nature of the datum there, with the terms and relations which are displayed there within it. Intuition can never yield the relation of its total datum to anything not given. It cannot refer to the latent at all, since its object, by definition, is just what is given immediately. To take the leap from one intuition to another, and assert that they view the same essence, or have the same intent, I must take my life in my hands and trust to animal faith. Otherwise all dialectic would be arrested.

Let me assume in the first place that I may steadily peruse the same essence, and may revert to it on occasion. Let me assume further that in so doing I may turn passive intuition into analysis, and analysis into some fresh synthesis of the elements identified and distinguished in the given essence. Intuition will thus pick up and group together, in various ways, terms which by hypothesis are identical in these various settings. It will scrutinise essences piece-meal and successively, although in their own realm they compose a simultaneous and eternal manifold. Suppose, for instance, I have reached the conclusion of a calculation, and the final equation is before me : the inner relations between its terms are parts of a given essence. Intuition, not demonstration, syn-thesises this manifold. This synthetic essence is therefore no conclusion ; it is not an answer nor a deduction ; it is not true. It is simply the pattern of terms which it is ; no one of these terms, for aught I know, having ever figured in any other equation. Thus any survey which is analytic, so that it gives foothold for demonstration, or any definition follow-ing upon such analysis, presupposes the repetition of the same essences in different contexts. This pre-supposition cannot be justified by the intuition occupy-ing the mind at any one time. No more can the assurance that a term remains the same in two successive instances and in two different contexts, nor that what is asserted by a predicate is asserted of the very subject which before had been intuited without that predicate. Explication is a process, a deduction is an event ; and although the force of logical analysis or synthesis does not depend on assuming that fact, but rather on ignoring it, this fact may be deduced from faith in the validity of demonstration, which would lapse if this fact were denied. The validity of demonstration is accordingly a matter of faith only, depending on the assumption of matters of fact incapable of demonstra-tion. I must believe that I noted the terms of the argument separately and successively if I am to assert anything in identifying them or pronouncing them equivalent, or if the conclusion in which they appear now is to be relevant in any way to the premises in which they appeared originally.

The force of dialectic, then, lies in identifying terms in isolation with the same terms in relation ; so that even an analytic judgement is synthetic. To say, for instance, that in " extended colour " " extension " is involved is analysis ; yet to identify the element of extension abstracted from the first essence with the second essence as a whole, is synthesis ; and it is far from inconceivable that this synthesis should be erroneous. In the identification of an essence given in one intuition with something given in another intuition in a superadded context, there is a postulate that in transcendent intent I am hitting a hidden target. It is not two similar intuitions taken existentially that are identified ; they are not only admittedly distinct numerically and as events in the world, but they have, by hypothesis, different total data before them. It is mind, a spiritual counterpart of attitude and action, that intends in both cases to consider the same essence. There is repetition posited ; and repetition, if actual, involves adventitious differences accruing to a term that remains individually identical. There is a difference in the setting of the same essence here and its setting there. In judgement, accordingly, there is more than intuition ; there is assumed discourse, involving time, transcendent reference, and various adventitious surveys of identical objects. Thus if I wish to believe that any demonstration whatsoever is significant or correct, I must assume (what I can never demonstrate) that there is an active intelligence at work, capable of reverting to an old idea like the dog returning to his vomit : an operation utterly extraneous to the timeless identity of each element recovered.

In other words, demonstration is an event, even when the thing demonstrated is not an event. Without adventitious choice of some starting-point, without selective and cumulative advance, and without recapitulation, there would be no dialectic. Premises and conclusions would all be static and separate terms ; the dialectical nerve of their relation would not be laid bare and brought to intuition. I should know nothing about essence, in the sense of possessing such sciences of it as mathematics or rhetoric, if the argument were not adventitious to the subject-matter, casting the light of intuition now along this path and now along that in a field posited as static, so as to enlarge and confirm my apprehension of it ; for if I lost at one end all that I gained at the other, my progress would not enrich apprehension, nor ever twice mean the same thing. Dialectic therefore is a two-edged sword : on the one hand, if valid, it involves a realm of essence, independent of it, over which it may range ; and on the other hand it involves its own temporal and progressive existence ; since it is a name for the fact that some part of that realm of essence has been chosen for perusal, considered at leisure, folded upon itself, as it were, and recognised as having this or that articulation. Even pure in- tuition shares (as I shall try to show presently) this spiritual existence, distinct from the logical or æsthetic being proper to the essences it apprehends ; intuition itself can hardly be prolonged without winking or re-survey. But this coming and going of attention, in flashes and in varied assaults, is even more conspicuous in dialectic ; and the validity and advance of insight in such cases depends on the essences in hand being constant, in spite of the pulsations of attention upon them and the variety of relations disclosed successively.

Thus belief in the existence of mental discourse (which is a sort of experience), whilst of course not demonstrable in itself, is involved in the validity of any demonstration ; and I come to the interesting insight that dialectic would lose all its force if I renounced my instinctive faith in my ability to pick up old meanings, to think consecutively, to correct myself without changing my subject-matter, and in fine to discourse and to live rationally. Challenge this faith, and demonstration collapses into the illusion that a demonstration has been made. If I confine myself to the given essence without admitting discourse about it, I exclude all analysis of that essence, or even examination of it. I must simply stare at it, in a blank and timeless æsthetic trance. If this does not happen, the reason is not dialectical. No logic could drive me from the obvious, unless I read omens in it which are not there. The reason for my proclivity to play with ideas, to lose them and catch them, and pride myself on my ability to keep them circling without confusion in the air, is a vital reason. This logic is a fly-wheel in my puffing engine ; it is not logic at all. The animal life which underlies discourse is concerned to discharge its predetermined responses, which are but few, whenever an occasion presents itself which will at all do ; and all such occasions it calls the same. It claps some recurrent name on different objects, which is one source of error or of perpetual inaccuracy in its knowledge of things ; but even before that, in identifying the various instances of that name, alleging the essence present now to be the same present before, it runs a risk of error and may slip into self-contradiction. Is the round square an essence ? Certainly ; but not in the geometry of Euclid, because in his geometry the square is one essence and the circle another, definitely and irreparably distinct from it. The round square is an essence of comic discourse, actualised when, having confused names, definitions and ideas, a fumbling or an impudent mind sets about to identify two incompatibles ; and this attempt is no more impossible to a mind—which is subject to animal vapours—than it is impossible for such a mind to look for a lost word. The psyche has the lost word in store, as it has the intuitions of the circle and the square ; but the loss of memory or the confusion of ideas may arise notwithstanding, because the movement in discourse which should culminate in those intuitions may be intercepted mechanically, and arrested at a stage where the name is not yet recovered, or where the words circle and square have fused their associations and are striving to terminate in the intuition of both as one. Such stammerings and contradictions make evident the physical basis of thought and the remote level from which it turns to its ideal object, like the moth to the star ; but this physical basis is really just as requisite for correcting a logical error as for falling into it. Thus dialectic, which in intent and deliverance does not trespass beyond the realm of essence, but only defines some fragment of the same, yet in fact, if it is to be cogent, must presuppose time, change, and the persistence of meanings in progressive discourse.

Belief in demonstration, when it is admitted, has inversely some steadying influence on belief in matters of fact. When poetic idealists cry that life is a dream, they are indulging in a hyperbole, if they still venture to compare one illusion with another in beauty or in duration. Poetry, like demonstration, would not be possible if intuition of essences could not be sustained and repeated in various contexts. The poet could not otherwise express cumulative passions nor develop particular themes. But life is no dream, if it justifies dialectic ; because dialectic explores various parts of the realm of essence — where everything is steadfast, distinct, and imperishable — with a continuous and coherent intent, and reaches valid insight into their structure ; and this amount of wakefulness and sanity the dialectical or poetic mind would have in any case, even in the absence of a material world, of all moral interests, and of any life except the life of discourse itself.

Nevertheless, if discourse were always a pellucid apprehension of essential relations, its existence would be little noted ; only a very scrupulous philosopher would insist on it, in view of the selective order and direction of survey which discourse adds to its subject-matter. There is, however, a much louder witness to the fact that discourse exists and is no part of essence, but rather a function of animal life ; and this witness is error. Thought becomes obvious when things betray it ; as they cannot have been false, something else must have been so, and this something else, which we call thought, must have existed and must have had a different status from that of the thing it falsified. Error thus awakens even the laziest philosophy from the dream of supposing that its own meanderings are nothing but strands in the texture of its object.

I have now, by the mere consideration of the way in which essence presents itself, managed to snatch from the jaws of scepticism one belief familiar to me before I encountered that romantic dragon ; namely, belief in the existence of discourse, or of mind thinking. But be it observed that I have so far seen reason for reinstating this belief only in a very attenuated form. Thought here means nothing more than the fact that some essence is contemplated, and discourse means only that this essence is approached and surveyed repeatedly or piecemeal, with partiality, succession, and possible confusion in describing it. Save for this distinction of intuition from the essence intuited, I have as yet no object before me that claims existence or solicits belief. The whole datum is still simply an essence ; but by the mere study of that datum, when this study is reflected upon and admitted, I have reintroduced a belief which relieves me of what was most obnoxious to the flesh in my radical scepticism. I have found that even when no change is perceived in the image before me, my discourse changes its phases and makes progress in surveying it; so that in discourse I now admit a sphere of events in which real variations are occurring. I may now assert, when I perceive a motion, that this intuition of change is *true*; that is, that it has actually followed upon the intuition of a static first term, from which my attention has passed to this intuition of change; and this I may now assert without confusing the essences given successively, or trying, like animal perception, to knead one concrete thing out of their incompatible natures. The existence of changing things or events in nature I may still deny or doubt or ignore; in the object I shall, with perfect clearness, see only an essence, and if this happens to be the essence of change, and to present the image of some motion, that theme will seem to me as determinate, as ideal and as unchanging as any other, and as little prone to lapse into any different theme. Any motion seen will be but a fixed image of motion. Actual flux and actual existence will have their appropriate and sufficient seat in my thought; I shall conceive and believe, when I reflect on my rapt contemplations, that I have been ruminating, and passing from one to another; but these objects will be only the several essences, the several images or tunes or stories, each always itself, which my mind picks up or invents or reconsiders.

CHAPTER XIV

ESSENCE AND INTUITION

To believe nothing and live immersed in intuition might be the privilege of a disembodied spirit ; and if a man could share it he would not only be relieved from doubt but would, in one dimension, lose nothing in the scope of his experience, since the realm of essence, which would still be open to him, is absolutely infinite, and contains images of all the events that any existing world could enact, or that all possible worlds could enact together. Yet all this variety and richness would form a mosaic, a marble effigy of life, or chronicle of ancient wars. The pangs and horrors would be there, as well as the beauties, but each would burn in its eternal place, balancing all the rest, and no anxious eye would glance hurriedly from one to the other, wondering what the next might be. The spirit that actually breathes in man is an animal spirit, transitive like the material endeavours which it expresses ; it has a material station and accidental point of view, and a fevered preference for one alternative issue over another. It thirsts for news ; and this curiosity, which it borrows of course from the insecurity and instinctive anxiety of the animal whose spirit it is, is strangely self-contradictory ; because the further it ranges in the service of animal will, the more the spectacle it discloses rebukes that animal will and tends to neutralise it. It would indeed not be spirit at all if it did not essentially tend to discount its accidental point of view, and to exchange the material station to which it finds itself unaccountably attached in its birth. In so far as it is spirit, and is not called back by its animal allegiance to pleasures and ambitions which pure spirit could not share (since they imply ignorance), it accordingly tends to withdraw from preoccupation with animal life, from the bias of time and place, and from all thought of existence. In so doing, far from perishing, it seems to acquire a more intense, luminous, and placid being. Since the roots of spirit, at least in man, are in matter, this would seem to be an illusion ; yet the experience is normal, and no illusion need attach to it, if once the nature of intuition is understood.

At the vanishing-point of scepticism, which is also the acme of life, intuition is absorbed in its object. For this reason, philosophers capable of intense contemplation—Aristotle, for instance, at those points where his thought becomes, as it were, internal to spirit—have generally asserted that in the end essence and the contemplation of essence are identical. Certainly the intuition of essence is oblivious of itself, and cognisant of essence only, to which it adds nothing whatever internally, either in character or in intensity ; because the intensity of a thunder-clap is the chief part of its essence, and so the peculiar intolerableness of each sort of pain, or transitiveness of each sort of pleasure. If in fact when any such essence is given there had been nothing prior to this intuition, nothing beside it existentially, and nothing to follow upon it, this obliviousness to the intuition itself, as distinct from the given essence, would not be an oversight ; it would be rather an absence of illusion. For it would then have been an illusion to suppose, as I should in calling the presence of that essence an intuition of it, that a soul with a history and with other adventitious qualities had come to contemplate that essence at one moment in its career. There would really be the essence only, with no relations other than those perfectly irreversible internal ones to other essences which define it in its own realm. Those very high numbers, for instance, which nobody has ever thought of specifically, have no other relations than those which they have eternally in the series of whole numbers ; they have no place in any man's life. So too those many forms of torment for which nature does not provide the requisite instrument, and which even hell has neglected to exemplify ; they remain essences only, of which fortunately there is no intuition. Evidently the being of such numbers or such torments is constituted by their essence only, and has not attained to existence. Yet it is this essential being alone that, if there was intuition of those numbers or those torments, would be revealed in intuition ; for no external adventitious relations, such as the intuition has in the life of some soul, would be presented within it, if (as I assume) nothing but these essences was then given.

It is therefore inevitable that minds singly absorbed in the contemplation of any essence should attribute the presence and force of that essence to its own nature, which alone is visible, and not to their intuition, which is invisible. Thought as it sinks into its object rises in its deliverance out of the sphere of contingency and change, and loses itself in that object, sublimated into an essence. This sublimation is no loss ; it is merely absence of distraction. It is the perfect fruition and fulfilment of that experience. In this manner I can understand why Aristotle could call the realm of essence, or that part of it which he had considered, a deity, and could declare sublimely that its inalienable being was an eternal life. More strictly, it would have been an eternal actualisation of cognitive life only; animal life would have ceased, because animal life requires us to pick up and drop the essences we consider, and to attribute temporal as well as eternal relations to them; in other words, to regard them not as essences but as things. But though cognitive life begins with this attention to practical exigences and is kindled by them, yet its ideal is sacrificial; it aspires to see each thing clearly and to see all things together, that is to say, under the form of eternity, and as sheer essences given in intuition. To cease to live temporally is intellectually to be saved; it is $\dot{\alpha}\theta\alpha\nu\alpha\tau\dot{\iota}\zeta\epsilon\iota\nu$, to fade or to brighten into the truth, and to become eternal. It is the inmost aim and highest achievement of cognition to cease to be knowledge for a self, to abolish the bias and transcend the point of view by which knowledge establishes its perspectives, so that all things may be present equally, and the truth may be all in all.

All this comes about, however, only subjectively, in that vital and poetic effort of the mind to understand which begins with a candid self-forgetfulness and ends in a passionate self-surrender. Seen from outside, as it takes place psychologically, the matter wears an entirely different aspect. In reality, essence and the intuition of essence can never be identical. If all animal predicaments were resolved, there would be no organ and no occasion for intuition; and intuition ceasing, no essences would appear. Certainly they would not be abolished by that accident in their own sphere, and each would be what it would have seemed if intuition of it had arisen; but they would all be merely logical or æsthetic themes unrehearsed, as remote as possible from life or from the intense splendour of divinity. Essence without intuition would be not merely non-existent (as it always is), but what is worse, it would be the object of no contemplation, the goal of no effort, the secret or implicit ideal of no life. It would be valueless. All that joy and sense of liberation which pure objectivity brings to the mind would be entirely absent ; and essence would lose all its dignity if life lost its precarious existence.

I believe that Aristotle, and even more mystical spokesmen of the spirit, would not have ignored this circumstance if they had not taken so narrow a view of essence. They see it only through some peep-hole of morals, grammar, or physics ; the small part of that infinite realm which thus becomes visible they take for the whole ; or if they feel some uneasiness at the obvious partiality of this survey, they rather blot out and blur the part before them, lest it seem arbitrary, instead of imagining it filled out with all the rest that, in the realm of essence, cannot help surrounding it. Even Spinoza, who so clearly defines the realm of essence as an infinite number of kinds of being, each having an infinite number of variations, calls this infinity of being *substance* ; as if at once to weight it all with existence (a horrible possibility) and to obliterate its internal distinctions ; but distinction, infinitely minute and indelible distinction of everything from everything else, is what essence means. Yet people suppose that whatever is non-existent is nothing—a stupid positivism, like that of saying that the past is nothing, or the future nothing, or everything nothing of which I happen to be ignorant. If people reflected that the non-existent, as Leibniz says, is infinite, that it is everything, that it is the realm of essence, they would be more cautious in regarding essence as something selected, superior in itself, and worthy of eternal contemplation. They would not conceive it as the power or worth in things actual, but rather as the form of everything and anything.

Value accrues to any part of the realm of essence by virtue of the interest which somebody takes in it, as being the part relevant to his own life. If the organ of this life comes to perfect operation, it will reach intuition of that relevant part of essence. This intuition will be vital in the highest degree. It will be absorbed in its object. It will be unmindful of any possibility of lapse in that object, or defection on its own part ; it will not be aware of itself, of time, or of circumstances. But this intuition will continue to exist, and to exist in time, and the pulsations of its existence will hardly go on without some oscillation, and probably a quick evanescence. So the intuition will be an utterly different thing from the essence intuited : it will be something existent and probably momentary ; it will glow and fade ; it will be perhaps delightful ; that is, no essences will appear to it which are not suffused with a general tint of interest and beauty. The life of the psyche, which rises to this intuition, determines all the characters of the essence evoked, and among them its moral quality. But as pure intuition is life at its best, when there is least rasping and thumping in its music, a prejudice or presumption arises that *any* essence is beautiful and life-enhancing. This platonic adoration of essence is undeserved. The realm of essence is dead, and the intuition of far the greater part of it would be deadly to any living creature.

The contemplation of so much of essence as is relevant to a particular life is what Aristotle called the entelechy or perfect fruition of that life. If the cosmos were a single animal, as the ancients supposed, and had an aim and a life which, like human life, could be fulfilled in the contemplation of certain essences, then a life like that of Aristotle's God would be involved in the perfection of nature, if this perfection was ever attained. Or if, with Aristotle, we suppose that the cosmos has always been in perfect equilibrium, then a happy intuition of all relevant

essence on the part of the cosmos would actually exist
and would be that sustained, ecstatic, divine life which
Aristotle speaks of. Yet even then the cosmic intuition
of essence would not be the essence it beheld. The
intuition would be a natural fact, by accident perpetual and necessarily selective ; because the cosmos
might stop turning at any moment, and certainly the
music of those spheres, even while they rolled well,
would not be every sort and any sort of noise, nor
even of music. A different cosmos would have had,
or might elsewhere be having, a different happiness.
Each, however, would be a divine life, as the ancients
conceived divinity. It would have such a natural
basis as any life must have, and the consequent warmth
and moral colour ; for natural operations lend these
values to the visions in which they rest. The love of
certain special essences which animates existence is
an expression of the direction which the movement
of existence happens to have. If the cosmos were a
perfect animal—and in its unknown secular pulsations
it may possibly be one—the cosmic intellect in act
would not be the whole of the realm of essence, nor
any part of it. It would be the intuition of so much
of essence as that cosmos had for its goal.

The external and naturalistic point of view from
which all this appears is one I have not yet justified
critically : I have anticipated it for the sake of rendering the conception of essence perfectly unambiguous.
But if we start from the realm of essence, which
demands no belief, we may at once find conclusive
reasons for believing that sundry intuitions of parts
of it exist in fact. One reason is the selectiveness of
discourse. All essences are always at hand, ready to
be thought of, if any one has the wit to do so. But my
discourse takes something up first, and then, even if
it is purely dialectical, passes to some implication or
complement of that idea ; and it never exhausts its

themes. It traverses the realm of essence as, in a mosque, some ray of light from some high aperture might shoot across the sombre carpets : it is a brief, narrow, shifting, oblique illumination of something vast and rich. The fact that intuition has a direction is an added proof of its existential character, and of its complete diversity in nature from the essences it lights up. Life begins unaccountably and moves irreversably : when it is prosperous and intelligent, it accumulates its experience of things in a personal perspective, largely alien to the things themselves. When the objects surveyed are essences, no one can be prior to any other in their own sphere : they do not arise at all, and lie in no order of precedence. When one essence includes another as number two includes number one, it is as easy and as proper to reach one by dividing two as to reach two by repeating one. In themselves essences have no genesis ; and to repeat one would be impossible if duality were not begged at the start, as well as unity, to institute the possibility of repetition. In seizing upon any particular essence first, discourse is guided by an irrational fatality. Some chance bit is what first occurs to the mind : I run up against this or that, for no logical reason. This arbitrary assault of intuition upon essence is evidence that something not essence, which I call intuition, has come into play. Thus all discourse, even if it traces ideal implications, is itself contingent to them, and in its existence irrational. Animal life is involved in the perusal of essence, just as animal faith is involved in the trust I put in demonstration. If I aspired to be a disembodied spirit, I ought to envisage all essences equally and at once—a monstrous requirement. If I aspire instead to dwell in the presence only of the pertinent, the beautiful, and the good, I confess that I am but a natural creature, directed on a small circle of interests and perfections ;

and that my intuition in particular exercises an adventitious choice, and has a private method, in its survey of essence.

The first existence, then, of which a sceptic who finds himself in the presence of random essences may gather reasonable proof, is the existence of the intuition to which those essences are manifest. This is of course not the object which the animal mind first posits and believes in. The existence of things is assumed by animals in action and expectation before intuition supplies any description of what the thing is that confronts them in a certain quarter. But animals are not sceptics, and a long experience must intervene before the problem arises which I am here considering, namely, whether anything need be posited and believed in at all. And I reply that it is not inevitable, if I am willing and able to look passively on the essences that may happen to be given : but that if I consider what they are, and how they appear, I see that this appearance is an accident to them ; that the principle of it is a contribution from my side, which I call intuition. The difference between essence and intuition, though men may have discovered it late, then seems to me profound and certain. They belong to two different realms of being.

CHAPTER XV

BELIEF IN EXPERIENCE

I HAVE now agreed to believe that discourse is a contingent survey of essence, partial, recurrent, and personal, with an arbitrary starting-point and an arbitrary direction of progress. It picks up this essence or that for no reason that it can assign. However dialectical the structure of the theme considered may be, so that its various parts seem to imply one another, the fact that this theme rather than any other is being considered is a brute fact : and my discourse as a whole is a sheer accident, initiated, if initiated at all, by some ambushed power, not only in its existence, but in its duration, direction, and scope.

Nevertheless this fatality does not raise any problem in that discourse itself, because it occasions no surprise. Problems are created after discourse is in full swing, by contradictory presumptions or aching voids arising within it. There are no problems in nature, and none in the realm of essence. Existence—the most inexplicable of surds—is itself no problem in its own eyes : it takes itself blandly for granted, so long as it is prosperous. This is a healthy dulness on its part, because if there is no reason why a particular fact should exist rather than any other, or none at all, there is also no reason why it should not exist. The philosopher who has learned to make nature the standard of naturalness will not wonder at it. He will repeat on a large scale that act of ready submission to fate which every new - born intuition performs spontaneously. It does not protest against its sudden existence. It is not surprised at the undeserved favour that has fallen to its share. It modestly and wisely forgets itself and notes only the obvious, profoundly self-justified essence which appears before it. That this essence might just as well, or might far better, have been replaced by some other is not a suggestion to be possibly gathered from that essence itself. Nor is the psyche (the ambushed power from which the intuition actually comes) less self-satisfied and at peace. The psyche, too, takes her own idiosyncrasy for granted, singular and highly determinate as this is, and extraordinarily censorious concerning all other things. Her nature seems to her by right everlasting, and that to which it is the obvious duty of all other things to adjust themselves. God, too, if we refer these agreeable fatalities ultimately to his decrees, is conceived in like manner never to wonder why he exists although evidently nothing could have previously demanded his existence, or prepared the way for it, or made it intelligible. Nevertheless the mortal psyche perhaps thinks she sees the secret even of that, because it was necessary that God should exist in order to make her own existence perfectly safe, legitimate, and happy for ever. This assurance is needed, because there are unfortunately some circumstances that might suggest the opposite.

Before turning to these circumstances, it may be well to observe that actual discourse, as distinguished from the internal dialectic of essences, may have any degree of looseness ; that is, the terms which it takes up in succession may have nothing to do with one another essentially. There is no added paradox in this : what is groundless and irrational in its inception may well be groundless and irrational in its procedure, and an appearance that has no reason for arising has no reason for not yielding to any other appearance, or to vacancy. And yet sometimes the course of appearances does produce wonder and discontent. How can this be? If I am not surprised at beginning to exist, or at finding something before me, since present being cannot contain any presumption or contradiction against itself, so it would seem that I should not be surprised at any changes in existence, however radical and complete. Often, indeed, I am not surprised, but follow the development of discourse, as in a dream, with perfect acquiescence, or even with a distinct premonition of what is coming, and eagerness that it should come. If I were a pure spirit, or even an open mind, this ought to be always the case. However different essences may be, they cannot in their own realm exclude or contradict one another; there, infinite diversity provokes no conflict and imposes no alternatives, and the being of anything, far from impeding that of other things, seems positively to invite and to require it, somewhat as every part of Euclidean space, far from denying the other parts, implies them. Irrelevance is, as it were, mere distance; and there is nothing strange or evil in quickness of thought, that should jump from one essence to another altogether dissimilar to it, or even contrary.

And yet I cannot prolong or intensify discourse without soon coming upon what I call interruption, confusion, doubt, or contradiction. An impulse to select, to pursue, and to reject specific essences insinuates itself into discourse. Why this animosity or this impatience? I do not disparage, nor subordinate, nor remove the circle from the realm of essence, when I think of the square and say it is no circle. Why then should I be angry if I find the one rather than the other? Evidently my discourse here is not pure contemplation. Of course, no essence is any other essence ; but a clear spirit would not call any two essences incompatible. Their diversity is part of their being ; they *are* because, each being eternally itself, the two are eternally different. If they are incompatible, I must ask : Incompatible for what purpose ? Even in calling them contradictory, I am surreptitiously speaking for some hidden interest, which cannot put up with them both. There is an inertia or prior direction somewhere, in the region of what I call myself, that demands one of them, and rejects the other for the innocent crime of not being that one. The incongruous essence appearing offends me because I am wedded to an old one, and to its close relations. I will tolerate nothing but what I meant should come, what fills my niche, and falls in with my undertaking.

Irrelevance, incongruity, and contradiction are accordingly possible in discourse only because discourse is not a play of essences but a play of attention upon them ; which attention is no impartial exercise of spirit but a manifestation of interest, intent, preference, and preoccupation. A hidden life is at work. If I deny this, because my scepticism eschews everything hidden, I must consistently abandon all dialectic and revert to undirected dreaming, without comments on my dream intended to be veridical : because if the least comment on my dreams were veridical I must begin at once to reject, in my comments, all the essences suggesting themselves which deviate from that particular dream I mean to describe. Meaning, which is my guide in discriminating one suggestion from another as being the right one, springs from beneath the surface ; it is a nether influence. It is a witness to my psychic life going on beneath, which can be disturbed by the intrusion of one event, or furthered by another ; and this subterranean impulse breaks out into judgements about the rightness and wrongness of essences—utterly absurd and unmeaning judgements if the essences were considered simply in themselves. If I feel that they clash, if I make a stumbling-block of their irrelevance or diversity, I prove that I am discoursing about them for an ulterior purpose, in the service of some alien interest. I am stringing my pearls ; therefore I require them to be of a particular quality. I am a collector, not a poet ; and what concerns me, even in the purest dialectic or the most desultory dream, is not to explore essence, but to gather *experience*. The psyche below is busy selecting her food, fortifying her cave, and discriminating her friends from her enemies ; and in these meanderings of mine over the realm of essence, in spite of myself, I am only her scout.

By experience I understand a fund of wisdom gathered by living. I call it a fund of wisdom, rather than merely memory or discursive ideation, because experience accrues precisely when discrimination amongst given essences is keenest, when only the relevant is retained or perhaps noticed, and when the psyche sagaciously interprets data as omens favourable or unfavourable to her interests, as perilous or inviting, and, if she goes wrong, allows the event to correct her interpretation. I think it mere mockery to use the word experience for what is not learning or gathering knowledge of facts ; if experience taught me nothing it would not be experience, but reverie. Experience accordingly presupposes intent and intelligence, and it also implies, as will appear presently, a natural world in which it is possible to learn to live better by practising the arts.

Intuition is an event, although it reveals only an essence ; and in like manner discourse is an experience, even when its deliverance is mere dialectic. It is an experience for two reasons : first, because it is guided unawares by the efforts of the psyche to explore, not the realm of essence, but the world that controls her fortunes ; and secondly, because the essences unrolled before it, apparently at random and for no reason, really convey knowledge ; in reality they are manifestations to the psyche of that surrounding world which it concerns her to react upon wisely. Discourse is hers ; and it is full of the names—since images not auditory may be names also—which she gives to her friends and enemies, and of her ingenious imaginations concerning their ways. However original the terms of discourse may be, under the control of the psyche and her environment they fall into certain rhythms ; they run into familiar sequences ; they become virtual and available knowledge of things, persons, nature, and the gods. Imagination would be very insecure and inconstant in these constructions, and they would not become automatic habits in discourse, if instinct within and nature without did not control the process of discourse, and dictate its occasions. So controlled, discourse becomes experience.

That discourse is secretly an experience, and may be turned into knowledge, becomes particularly evident when it is interrupted by *shocks*. Not only may an essence suddenly present itself which was not the essence I expected or should have welcomed, but the whole placid tenor of my thoughts may be arrested or overwhelmed. I may suffer a sort of momentary and conscious death, in that I survive to feel the extinction of all that made up my universe, and to face a blank, or a precipice. When in my placid discourse one thing seemed to contradict another, they were but rival images in the same field, and I had but to choose between them, and proceed with the argument. Shock contradicts nothing, but uproots the whole experience. The lights go out on the stage, and discourse loses its momentum.

In the sense of contradiction there is probably some element of shock. The purest æsthetic or logical contemplation hardly goes on without a throbbing accompaniment of interest, haste, reversals, and satisfactions ; but these dramatic notes are merged in the counterpoint of the themes surveyed, and I think, prove, and enjoy without noticing that I do so. But when a clap of thunder deafens me, or a flash of lightning at once dazzles and blinds me, the fact that something has *happened* is far more obvious to me than just what it is that has occurred ; and there are perhaps shocks internal to the psyche in which the tension of the event reaches a maximum, whilst the nature of it remains so obscure that perhaps my only sense of it is a question, a gasp, or a recoil. The feeling present in such a case is, with but little further qualification, the sheer feeling of experience.

Now experience of the most brutal and dumbest sort may be theoretically described, and described exhaustively, in terms of the successive intuition of essences ; for loudness, dazzlingness, pain, or terror are essences or elements of essences like any other data ; and when such essences are present, all is present that it is possible ever to feel in that direction, and with any degree of intensity. Utter blankness, intolerable strain, shrieking despair, are just the essences they are, and they are unrolled and revealed to intuition like any other essences. But such intuitions, being those proper to the most brutal and rudimentary life, have a suasion in them out of all proportion to their articulation, or rather, we might almost say, inversely proportional to it ; as if the more an experience meant the less it cried out, and the more it cried out the less it meant. The purest discourse is (without noticing it) an experience, and the blindest experience (also without noticing it) is a discourse, since we should not call it experience if it contained no sense of passage, no experiential perspective ; but in proportion as shock cancels discourse and obliterates its own background, experience becomes mere experience, and inarticulate.

In brute experience, or shock, I have not only a clear indication, for my ulterior reflection, that I exist, but a most imperious summons at that very moment to *believe* in my existence. Discourse, as I first disentangled the evidence for it from the pure intuition of essence, seemed to be a progressive observation of the permanent — studious attention perusing and registering the essential mutual relations of given terms. But now, when shock interrupts me, discourse suffers violence. The subject-matter itself takes up arms ; one object leaves me in the lurch, while another, quite irrelevantly, assaults me. And since my discourse witnesses and records this revolution, I must now assert it to be a permanent knowledge of the changing.

Shocks *come* : if they did not *come*, if I had not pre-existed, if I had never been anything more than the intuition of this shock, then this shock would not be a shock in fact, but only the illusion of a shock, only the essence of shock speciously persuading me that something had happened, when in fact nothing had occurred. If the sense of shock does not deceive me, I must have passed from a state in which the shock was not yet, into the state in which the shock first startled me ; and I must since have passed from that startled state into another, in which my intuition covers synthetically the coming, the nature, and the subsidence of that shock ; so that I am aware how startled I was, without being startled afresh now. A wonderful and ambiguous presence of the absent and persistence of the receding, which is called *memory*. My objects have receded, yet I continue to consider them. They are no longer essences, but facts, and my consideration is not intuition of something given but faith in something absent, and a persistent indication of it as still the same object, although my image of it is constantly changing, is perhaps intermittent, and probably grows fainter, vaguer, and more erroneous at every instant.

Experience of shock, if not utterly delusive, accordingly establishes the validity of memory and of transitive knowledge. It establishes realism. If it be true that I have ever had any experience, I must not only have existed unawares in order to gather it, but I am justified in explicitly asserting a whole realm of existence, in which one event may contain realistic knowledge of another. Experience, even conceived most critically as a series of shocks overtaking one another and retained in memory, involves a world of independent existences deployed in an existing medium. Belief in experience is belief in nature, however vaguely nature may as yet be conceived, and every empiricist is a naturalist in principle, however hesitant his naturalism may be in practice.

Nevertheless shock, like any other datum, intrinsically presents an essence only, and *might* be nothing more ; but in that case the dogmatic suasion of it (which alone lends interest to so blank an experience) would be an illusion. The intuition would be what it is, but it would be nobody's intuition, and it would mean nothing. For I should not be a self, if that intuition made up my whole being, so that it involved no change in my condition, but was perhaps itself the whole universe. Shock will not suffer me, while it lasts, to entertain any such hypothesis. It is itself the most positive, if the blindest, of beliefs ; it loudly proclaims an event ; so that if by chance the change which I feel were merely a feeling within the unity of apperception, shock would be an illusion, in the only sense in which this can be said of any intuition :

it would incite me to a false belief that something like the given essence existed. If the change has really occurred, and not merely been imagined, shock is not only intuition of change, but trouble in a process of change enveloping that intuition. I am right in positing a desultory experience in which this intuition is an incident. I am not a spectator watching this cataract, but a part of the water precipitated over the edge. Thus if being shocked was, as perhaps it ought to be, the first sensation in life, it proclaimed the existence of a previous state without sensation. Unless it is an illusion, which I cannot admit while I feel it, it implies variation in a voluminous vegetative life in which the sense of surprise is a true indication of novelty.

Before I had noticed shock, or consented to accept its witness, I had already admitted, on dialectical grounds, that discourse was a process ; but now that I observe how shocks, more or less violent, interrupt discourse at every moment, I can call discourse experience. For now I see that in endeavouring to trace dialectical relations discourse is not itself dialectical. Sheer chance decides whether it shall pursue faithfully the theme it may have picked out, as sheer chance decided that it should pick up that theme in particular. In my theoretical bewilderment and helplessness before this absolute contingency of all themes and all data, I am steadied only by animal presumptions, habits, expectations, or omens, all of which my sceptical reflection must condemn as utterly arbitrary. I can only say that I am the sport of an unfathomable destiny ; that in these shocks that fall upon me thick and fast, and in the calmer stretches between them, miscellaneous essences are revealed to me, most of them gratuitous and mutually irrelevant ; and that if the current of them did not carry me, somewhat congenially, into a vortex of work and play,

I should be condemned for ever to blank watching and to sheer wonder. The very belief in experience is a suggestion of instinct, not of experience itself. The steadfastness of my nature, doggedly retaining its prejudices and assuming its power, supplies and imposes a routine upon my experience which is far from existing in my direct intuitions, very shifty in their quality (even when signs of the same external object) and much mixed with dream. Even the naturalist has to make up by analogy and presumption (which perhaps he calls induction) the enormous spaces between and beyond his actual observations.

Belief in experience is the beginning of that bold instinctive art, more plastic than the instinct of most animals, by which man has raised himself to his earthly eminence : it opens the gates of nature to him, both within him and without, and enables him to transmute his apprehension, at first merely æsthetic, into mathematical science. This is so great a step that most minds cannot take it. They stumble, and remain entangled in poetry and in gnomic wisdom. Science and reasonable virtue, which plunge their roots in the soil of nature, are to this day only partially welcome or understood. Although they bring freedom in the end, the approach to them seems sacrificial, and many prefer to live in the glamour of intuition, not having the courage to believe in experience.

CHAPTER XVI

BELIEF IN THE SELF

EXPERIENCE, when the shocks that punctuate it are reacted upon instinctively, imposes belief in something far more recondite than mental discourse, namely, a person or self; and not merely such a transcendental ego as is requisite intrinsically for any intuition, nor such a flux of sentience as discourse itself constitutes, but a substantial being preceding *all* the vicissitudes of experience, and serving as an instrument to produce them, or a soil out of which they grow.

Shock is the great argument of common sense for the existence of material things, because common sense does not need to distinguish the order of evidence from the order of genesis. If I know already that a tile has fallen on my head, my sore head is a proof to me that the tile was real; but if I start from the pain itself in all innocence, I cannot draw any inference from it about tiles or the laws of gravity. By common sense experience is conceived as the effect which the impact of external things makes on a man when he is able to retain and remember it. As a matter of fact, of course, shocks usually have an external origin, although in dreams, madness, apparitions, and in disease generally, their cause is sometimes internal. But all question concerning the source of a shock is vain for the sceptic; he knows nothing of sources;

he is asking, not whence shocks come, but to what beliefs they should lead. In the criticism of knowledge the *argumentum baculaneum* is accordingly ridiculous, and fit only for the backs of those who use it. Why, if I am a spirit beholding essences, should I not feel shocks? Why are not novelties and surprises as likely themes for my entertainment as the analysis or synthesis of some theorem or of some picture? All essences are grist for the mill of intuition, and any order or disorder, any quality of noise or violence, is equally appropriate in an experience which, for all I know or as yet believe, is absolute and groundless. And I call it experience, not because it discloses anything about the environment which produced it, but because it is composed of a series of shocks, which I survey and remember.

If, however, consenting to listen to the voice of nature, I ask myself what a shock can signify, and of what it brings me most unequivocal evidence, the least hazardous answer will be: evidence of prepossessions on my part. What shock proves, if it proves anything, is that I have a nature to which all events and all developments are not equally welcome. How could any apparition surprise or alarm me, or how could interruption of any sort overtake me, unless I was somehow running on in a certain direction, with a specific rhythm? Had I not such a positive nature, the existence of material things and their most violent impact upon one another, shattering the world to atoms, would leave me a placid observer of their movement; whereas a definite nature in me, even if disturbed only by cross-currents or by absolute accidents within my own being, would justify my sense of surprise and horror. A self, then, not a material world, is the first object which I should posit if I wish the experience of shock to enlarge my dogmas in the strict order of evidence.

But what sort of a self ? In one sense, the existence of intuition is tantamount to that of a self, though of a merely formal and transparent one, pure spirit. A self somewhat more concrete is involved in discourse, when intuition has been deployed into a successive survey of constant ideal objects, since here the self not only sees, but adds an adventitious order to the themes it rehearses ; traversing them in various directions, with varying completeness, and suspending or picking up the consideration of them at will ; so that the self involved in discourse is a thinking mind. Now that I am consenting to build further dogmas on the sentiment of shock, and to treat it, not as an essence groundlessly revealed to me, but as signifying something pertinent to the alarm or surprise with which it fills me, I must thicken and substantialise the self I believe in, recognising in it a nature that accepts or rejects events, a nature having a movement of its own, far deeper, more continuous and more biassed than a discoursing mind : the self posited by the sense of shock is a living psyche.

This is a most obscure subterranean object ; I am venturing into the nether world. It is alarming and yet salutary to notice how near to radical scepticism are the gates of Hades. I shall have occasion later to consider what the psyche is physically, when I have learned more about the world in which she figures ; she has some stake in it, since she welcomes or strives against sundry events. So anxious a being must have but precarious conditions of existence, and yet some native adaptation to them, since she manages to exist at all. Here I need admit only this : that the pure spirit involved in any intuition of essence is in my case repeatedly and somewhat consecutively actualised in a running mental discourse ; that, further, it is employed in remembering, loving, and hating, so that it almost seems to spring like a wild beast upon its visions, as upon its prey, and to gnaw and digest them into its own substance. Spirit, as I shall soon find, is no substance, and has no interests ; all this absurd animal violence may still be nothing but a dream ; and the fact, now agreed upon, that discourse is going on, may suffice to dispose of these passionate movements. Music, which is ethereal in its being and, in the objective direction, terminates in pure essence, nevertheless in its play with pure essence is full of trepidation, haste, terror, potentiality, and sweetness. If mere sound can carry such a load, why should not discourse do likewise, in which images of many other sorts come trooping across the field of intuition ? This is no idle doubt, since the whole Buddhist system is built on accepting it as a dogma ; and transcendentalism, though it talks much of the self, denies, or ought to deny, its existence, and the existence of anything ; the transcendental self is pure spirit, incoherently identified with the principle of change, preference, and destiny which this philosophy calls Will, but which in truth, as I shall find, is matter. The Buddhists too, in denying the self, are obliged to introduce an ambiguous equivalent in the heritage of guilt, ignorance, and illusion which they call Karma. These are ulterior mystifications, which I mention here only lest I should proceed to posit the natural psyche without a due sense of the risks I am taking. The natural psyche, being a habit of matter, is to be described and investigated from without, scientifically, by a behaviourist psychology ; but the critical approach to it from within, as a postulate of animal faith, is extremely difficult and fraught with danger. Literary psychology, to which I am here confined, is at home only in the sentiments and ideas of the adult mind, as language has expressed them : the deeper it tries to go, the vaguer its notions ; and it soon loses itself in the dark altogether. I cannot hope to discover, therefore, what precisely this psyche is, this self of mine, the existence of which is so indubitable to my active and passionate nature. The evidence for it in shock hardly goes beyond the instinctive assertion that I existed before, that I am a principle of steady life, welcoming or rejecting events, that I am a nucleus of active interests and passions. It will be easy to graft upon these passions and interests the mental discourse which I had previously asserted to be going on, and which made up, in this critical reconstruction of belief, my first notion of myself. And yet here is one of the dangers of my investigation, because mental discourse is not, and cannot be, a self nor a psyche. It is all surface ; it neither precedes, nor survives, nor guides, nor posits its data ; it merely notes and remembers them. Discourse is a most superficial function of the self ; and if by the self I was tempted to understand a series of ideas, I should be merely reverting sceptically to that stage of philosophic denudation in which I found myself, before I had consented to accept the evidence of shock in favour of my own existence. I, if I exist, am not an idea, nor am I the fact that several ideas may exist, one of which remembers the other. If I exist, I am a living creature to whom ideas are incidents, like aeroplanes in the sky ; they pass over, more or less followed by the eye, more or less listened to, recognised, or remembered ; but the self slumbers and breathes below, a mysterious natural organism, full of dark yet definite potentialities ; so that different events will awake it to quite disproportionate activities. The self is a fountain of joy, folly, and sorrow, a waxing and waning, stupid and dreaming creature, in the midst of a vast natural world, of which it catches but a few transient and odd perspectives.

CHAPTER XVII

THE COGNITIVE CLAIMS OF MEMORY

BELIEF in memory is implicit in the very rudiments of mind ; mind and memory are indeed names for almost the same thing, since memory furnishes most of the resources of a mind at all developed, and nothing is ever in the mind but may reappear in memory, if the psyche can fall again for a moment into her old paces. Mind and memory alike imply cognisance taken of outlying things, or knowledge. When the things known are events within the past experience of the psyche, spontaneously imagined, knowledge is called memory ; it is called mind or intelligence when they are past, present, or future events in the environment at large, no matter by what means they are suggested or reported. Memory itself must report facts or events in the natural world, if it is to be knowledge and to deserve the name of memory. An intuition by chance repeating an intuition that had occurred earlier would not be memory or knowledge of that earlier event. There must be belief in its previous occurrence, with some indication of its original locus.

Intuition without memory must be assumed to have existed in the beginning, but such intuition regards essence only. Not being directed by memory upon the past, nor by animal faith upon the future or upon external things, pure intuition exercises no sagacity, no transitive intelligence, and does not think.

It is merely the light of awareness lending actuality to some essence. When identity and duration come to be attributed to this essence, memory begins to make its claims felt, although indirectly. When I call an essence identical I imply that I have considered it twice, and that I possess a true memory of my past intuition, since I know it presented this very essence. Similarly, when I call an essence the same, but without distinguishing my two intuitions of it, which may be continuous, I posit the truth of memory unawares ; for this sensation of living on, of having lived up to the present, is a primary memory. It sets up a temporal perspective, believing firmly in its recessional character ; parts of the specious present are interpreted as survivals of a receding present, a present that can never return, but the vision of which I have not wholly lost. The perspective is not taken to be specious only, but a true memorial of facts past and gone.

Memory deploys all the items of its inventory at some distance, yet sees them directly, by a present glance. It makes no difference to the directness of this knowledge how great the distance of the object may be in the direction of the past. So also in foresight : I foresee my death as directly as I do my dinner, not necessarily more vaguely, and far more certainly. Memory and prophecy do in time what perception does in space ; here too the given essence is projected upon an object remote from the living psyche which is the organ of the intuition and of the projection. The object is indeed not remote from the *mind*, if by mind I understand the intellectual energy of memory, prophecy, or perception reaching to that object, and positing it there in intent ; but it is remote from the psyche, from the material agent, from me here and now. A little less or a little more interval of time or space—and there is always an interval—does not render less ocular and immediate the description of a removed event by the essences it brings before me. I see a peewit in the sky as directly as I see the watch in my hand, and I hear his note as easily as I do the ticking of the watch against my ear. So I remember the Scotch kilt I wore when a child as directly as the umbrella I carried this morning. The difficulty in extending the range of knowledge, is physical only ; I may be near-sighted ; and the mechanism of memory may break down, or may be choked with parasitic fancies as it grows old.

In memory it is sometimes possible to reproduce almost exactly some earlier scene or experience. If the psyche happens to run through the same process twice—and being material she is compacted of habits —she will twice have exactly the same intuition ; but this precise repetition of the past, far from constituting a perfect memory, excludes memory. The sentiment of pastness, the receding perspective in which memory places its data, will be wanting ; and this perfect recovery of experience will not be remembrance. Nor is any fulness or precision in the image of the past necessary to the truth of memory. The nerve of recollection lies elsewhere, in the projection of the given essence—which may be vague or purely verbal— to a precise point or nucleus of relations in the natural past. Memory is genuine if the events it designates actually took place, and conformed to the description, however brief and abstract, which I give of them. Pictorial fulness and emotional reversion to the past are not important, and they are found most often at unimportant points. Healthy memory excludes them, and for two reasons. The bodily reaction to the old environment is now hardly possible, and certainly not appropriate ; and therefore, even if the neurogram in the psyche could spring again into perfect life, it would bring a dream into being, an interruption to life in the present, rather than a sober memory filling the present appropriately with a long perspective. The second reason is that the neurogram is likely to have been modified by the accidents of nutrition and waste intervening, so that the old movement cannot really be repeated, and the essence called up will not really be the original one. That it may *seem* to be the original, in its very life, is nothing to the purpose. How, if vivid, should it not seem so, when no other memory exists to control it ? But if I can control it by circumstantial evidence, I usually find that this specious recovery of past experience is a cheap illusion. If the reversion to the past seems complete, it is not because the facts are remembered accurately, but because some subtle influence fills me with a sentiment wholly foreign to my present circumstances, and redolent of a remote past ; and that dramatic shift seems to lift all the details of the picture out of the perspective of memory into the foreground of the present. It is the fancy that comes forward, producing a waking dream, not the memory that sinks back into an old experience. The scent of a cedar chest in which old finery is kept may carry me back vividly to my earliest childhood ; but the images that now seem to live again will be creatures of my present sophisticated and literary fancy ; I shall see them romantically, not with the eyes of a child. I may truly recover knowledge of long-forgotten facts, but I shall not re-enact a long-past experience. And what need is there ? A miraculous identity may be felt emotionally even when the two descriptions of the identical thing differ in *every* sensible term, as happens in metaphors, in myths, in myself as body and as mind, in idolatry, or in the doctrine—which expresses a mystical experience—of transubstantiation. In such cases the vital reaction, the deeper readjustment of the psyche, to the two appearances is the same ;

therefore I feel that the thing appearing in the two ways is identical, that the one is *really* the other, however diverse the two sets of symbols may be.

I have already accepted the belief in memory ; indeed, without accepting it I could not have taken the first step forward from the most speechless scepticism. But since such acceptance is an act of faith, and asserts transitive or realistic knowledge, I will pause to consider somewhat more explicitly what the cognitive claims of memory are, on which all human beliefs are reared.

The paradox of knowing the absent is posited in the past tenses of the verb ; it is the paradox of knowledge itself, since intuition of essence is not properly called knowledge ; it is imagination, since the only object present is then non-existent and the description of it, being creative, is infallible. The claim to knowledge everybody understands perfectly when he makes it, which he does whenever he perceives, remembers, or believes anything ; but if we wish to paraphrase this claim reflectively, we may perhaps say that in it attention professes to fall on an object explicitly at a distance, being framed by other nearer objects (though at some distance themselves) upon which attention falls only virtually. If this foreground or frame were absent altogether, I should live in the pictured past thinking it present ; memory would overleap its memorial office and become a dream. It would cease to be liable to error, being no longer a report about anything else ; but it would become an idle entertainment, which a moralist might call an illusion, on the ground that its images were irrelevant to the practice of rational life, and its emotions wasted. But it would not misrepresent anything, since in ceasing to be a memory it would have abandoned all cognitive claims.

A frame or foreground is accordingly indispensable

to the projection which renders a present image a vision of some past fact : I must stand here to point there. Yet if my present station were explicitly perceived, if the whole immediate datum were focussed equally in thought, the picture would seem flat and the perspective merely painted upon it, as upon a cheap drop-curtain in a theatre. It would destroy the claim and, if you like, the illusion of memory to remember that I am remembering ; for then I should be considering myself only, and only the present, whereas in living remembrance I am self-forgetful, and live in the present thinking only of the past, and observe the past without supposing that I am living in it. My recollections, my *souvenirs*, are only essences which I read as I should the characters on this page, not viewing them contemplatively in their own category as forms present in their entirety, but accepting them readily (as in all knowledge) as messengers, as signs for existences of which they furnish but an imperfect description, for which I am perhaps hopeful of substituting a better view. In lapsing into the past I seem to myself to be entering a realm of shadows ; and a chief part of my wakefulness, which prevents me from actually dreaming that I am living in that other world, is precisely this eagerness of mine to see better, to remember all, to recover the past as it really was ; and the elusive and treacherous character of such images as come to me troubles me seriously, as a mist distorting and shutting off the truth. My heart, as it were, is fixed on that removed reality, and I know that my eyes see it but imperfectly. Yet if my heart had intuition now of what that reality once was, recollection would be superfluous, since I should possess all it could bring me before it brought it ; and on the other hand, if my heart did not know the reality, how could I reject, criticise, or approve the images that professed to restore its forgotten aspects ?

Obviously what I am calling the heart, which is the psyche, is blind in herself : imagination is her only light, her only language ; but she is a prior principle of choice and judgement and action in the dark ; so that when the light shines in that darkness, she comprehends it, and feels at once whether the ray falls on the object towards which she was groping, or on some irrelevant thing. The psyche, in the case of memory, contains all the seeds, all the involutions and latent habits, which the past left there in passing ; any one of these may be released freely, or only irritated and summoned to activity without being sufficiently fed, or only to be at once thwarted and contradicted ; and the *sentiment* of this prosperous or mutilated rendering of experience, when memory proffers its images, enables the psyche to judge these images to be true or false, adequate or inadequate, without possessing any other images with which to compare them.

This felt imperfection of memory is no obstacle to the directness of such knowledge as it does afford. Memory, however vague, transports me to the intended scene ; I walk by its wavering light through those ancient chambers ; I see again (incorrectly, no doubt) what occurred there. But if many a detail once obvious is thereby lost or misplaced, memory may see the chief features of the past in a truer perspective than that in which experience placed them originally. The ghostliness of memory carries this compensation with it, comparable to the breadth of sympathy that compensates old age for the loss of vivaciousness ; memory is a reconstruction, not a relapse. The view which the opened chest creates in me now of my family history may be truer than any I had when a child. My perceptions when a child were themselves descriptions, naïve, disjointed, limited. In reproducing my past perceptions, my dreaming memory does not regard those perceptions — perceptions being spiritual facts, can become objects of intent only. Memory regards the same objects (essences or things) which the past perceptions regarded. But the soil in which these intuitions now grow has been tilled and watered, and, even if a little exhausted, it may yield a fairer description of those ancient incidents than existed before, more voluminous, better knit, more knowing. Memory has fundamentally the same function as history and science — to review things more intelligently than they were ever viewed. Mind would never rise out of the most helpless animal routine if it could not forget in remembering, and could not substitute a moral perspective for the infinite flatness of physical experience. That much drops out is a blessing ; that something creeps in, by way of idealisation, hyperbole, and legend, is not an unmixed evil. In spite of this admixture of fiction, memory, legend, and science achieve a true intellectual dominion over the flux of events ; and they add a poetic life and rhythm of their own, like the senses.

This possibility of dominion proves that the images and the apperception involved in remembering are fresh images and a fresh apperception. It shows also that the later station in time of the act of remembering in no way annuls the directness of the knowledge involved, nor cuts it off from its object ; on the contrary, the object being posited and chosen by the psyche before any images or any apperception arise, these are free to describe that object in any way they can, bringing all later resources of the mind to illustrate it, and thereby perhaps describing it far more truly than the senses revealed it when it was present.

Here an important detail has come into view which at first sight might seem paradoxical, but only because the paucity of language obliges us often to use the same word for very different things. Thus it seems natural to say that a man may remember his own experience, and can remember nothing else ; and yet it is not his *experience* that he commonly remembers at all, but the usual object of his memory is the object of his former experience, the events or the situation in which his earlier experience occurred. Experience is intuition, it is discourse interspersed with shocks and recapitulated ; but intuition, actual experience, is not an object of any possible intuition or experience, being, as I have said above, a spiritual fact. Its existence can be discovered only by moral imagination, and posited dramatically, as the experience proper to spirit under certain real or imaginary circumstances. And this is true of my own past or future, no less than of the experience of others. When I remember I do not *look at* my past experience, any more than when I think of a friend's misfortunes I look at his thoughts. I imagine them ; or rather I imagine something of my own manufacture, as if I were writing a novel, and I attribute this intuited experience to myself in the past, or to the other person. Naturally, I can impute only such feelings as my present psyche can evoke ; and she, although creative, creates automatically and in accordance with patterns fixed by habit or instinct ; so that it is true, in a loose way, that I can remember or conceive only what I have experienced ; but this is not because my experience itself remains within me, and can be re-observed. Such a notion needs but to be made clear to be made ridiculous. Living intuition cannot be preserved ; and even while it lives, it cannot be found. It is spiritual.

Recollection is accordingly incipient dreaming ; it views the same objects as the experience did which it rehearses, since the memory arises by a renewal of the very process in the psyche by which that experience was created originally. The psyche, in so far as she is occupied with that dream, does not know that it is a memory, nor that its objects are remote and perhaps no longer exist ; she posits them with all the confidence of action, as in any other dream. Yet in normal memory the illusion is controlled and corrected, and the experience actually given, with all its posited objects, is relegated to the past ; because this time it is framed in another experience, with more obstinate objects and an environment to which the body is adjusted, incompatible with the remembered environment. Hence the shadowy, vaporous, unreal aspect of the remembered past : images chase one another through it, as they chase one another sometimes in a cinema, or as in a dream what was just now a white-capped wave may become a horse galloping. Meantime reason rides the storm of seething incipient fancies, anchored in the outer senses by the steady pull of the instincts which bind it to the present world.

Experience cannot be remembered, a perception cannot be perceived nor re-perceived. This fact explains both the directness of memory (since it regards the same objects, the same environment, as the old experience, and repeats the same emotions), and also the ghostliness of memory and of all imagination (since the beliefs and emotions evoked are irrelevant to the present world, and inhibited by peremptory present reactions).

There is a great difference conventionally between memory and fancy, between history and fiction, and the two things diverge widely in their physical significance, one regarding events in nature and the other imaginary scenes ; nevertheless psychologically they are clearly akin. It is only by an ulterior control that we can distinguish which sort of fancy is memory and which sort of fiction is historical. This control, for the immediate past, is exercised by habit and sensation.

The immediate past is continuous with the present ; I believe that I remember, and do not merely imagine, the street in which I live, because I am ready to walk out into it confidently, and by raising my eyes can see it out of the window. It is an object continuous with the recurrent objects of my present faith. When the past is more remote, this control, while the same in principle, is less directly exercised ; it is mainly the *habit* of memory that testifies to the truth of memory. I believe I remember, and do not merely imagine, what I have always said I remembered ; just as we believe events to be historical and not invented, when historians have always repeated them. It is consequently very easy for a fiction, once incorporated in what, because of our practical habits, we regard as real events, to pass for a fact for ever. Autobiographies and religions (even when not systematically recast by the fancy, as they usually are) contain many such involuntary confusions. *Vice versa*, a lively fiction spontaneously takes the form of a history or a memory. Although no junction with genuine memory or history may be attempted in *Robinson Crusoe* at the beginning or at the end, many a real fact may be woven into the narrative, to add to its verisimilitude, and absorb, as it were, the fancied details into the romantic medley of things commonly believed. " Once upon a time," says the story - teller, in order vaguely to graft his imaginary events on to the tree of memory ; and in the *Thousand and One Nights* we are transported to one of the cities amongst cities, or to an island amongst the isles of the sea ; whereby the fiction grows more arresting, or the real world more marvellous and large.

Criticism of memory and history is a ticklish and often a comic matter, because only fancy can be employed to do it ; and we judge the authority of records and the reports of our past experience by the criterion of what, at the present moment, can exercise a decided suasion over our belief, and create a living illusion. But the principle by which we trust memory at all is always the same, and deeply paradoxical. How can a flux be observed at all ? If flux there be, the earlier part is gone when the latter part appears : how then can the relation, the passage, be observed ? And where is the observation ? If it occupies each instant in turn, how can it bridge them ? If it stands outside, how can it touch any of them ? In any case the observation would seem to be out of the flux which it imagines, but does not undergo : for if its being is instantaneous, there is no flux in it ; and if it is comprehensive, and contemporary with all the instants surveyed, again it endures no change. Indeed, analytically, it is obvious that a sense of change, falling necessarily under a unity of apperception, transcends *that* change, however changeful may be the conditions of its own genesis : mind, by its very character as mind, is timeless. Is time, then, merely a picture of time, and can it be nothing else ? And is flux, which is an essential quality of existence, only a mere appearance, and essentially incapable of existing in fact ?

There is danger here of an enormous illusion, into which I think the most redoubtable metaphysicians have fallen. We must admit that spirit is not in time, that the perception of flux (or of anything else) is not a flux, but a synthetic glance and a single intuition of relation, of form, of quality. The seen is everywhere a universal, the seeing is everywhere supernatural. But this admission is far from involving a denial of flux—a denial, that is, of the deliverance of this very spirit to which we are assigning such pompous prerogatives. The one prerogative which we must assume spirit to possess—because we claim it in exercising spirit at all—is that it *understands*, that it tells truly something about something. Its own conditions of being, that it must be immaterial, timeless, synthetic, intuitive, do not preclude it, if it is truly intelligent, from revealing things differently constituted from itself : much less can it prevent these non-spiritual things from existing. What madness is this, because we may at last discern the spirituality of spirit, to deny that there could ever have been anything for spirit to discern ? Why stultify the very faculty we are discovering that we possess ? Why tumble in this way head over heels from our little eminence, and reduce ourselves to speechlessness in wonder at our capacity to speak ? This supernatural status and supertemporal scope of spirit are not prerogatives ; they are deprivations ; they are sacrificial conditions, from the point of view of natural existence, to which any faculty must submit, if it is to understand. Of course understanding is itself an achievement (though not all philosophers esteem it highly), but it must be bought at a price : at the price of escaping into a fourth dimension, of not being that which we understand. So when the flux, in its rumble and perpetual superposition of movements, remembers that it flows, it is not arrested materially ; but the sense that what flows through it at this instant has come from afar, that it has taken a fresh shape, and is hurrying to new transformations, has itself eluded that fate : for this sense, as distinguished from the psyche that exercises it, is tangential to the flux it surveys, neither instantaneous nor prolonged, but simply intelligent. How far into the past or future its glance may reach, is a matter of accident, and of the range of adjustments at that moment in the psyche. But spirit is virtually omniscient : barriers of space and time do not shut it in ; they are but the boundary-stones of field and field in its landscape. It is ready to survey all time and all existence if, by establishing some electric connection with its seat, time and existence will consent to report themselves to it. For spirit has no interests, no curiosity, no animal impatience ; and as it arises only when and where nature calls it forth, so it surveys only what nature happens to spread before it.

CHAPTER XVIII

KNOWLEDGE IS FAITH MEDIATED BY SYMBOLS

IN the claims of memory I have a typical instance of
what is called knowledge. In remembering I believe
that I am taking cognisance not of a given essence but
of a remote existence, so that, being myself here and
now, I can consider and describe something going
on at another place and time. This leap, which
renders knowledge essentially faith, may come to
seem paradoxical or impossible like the leap of physical
being from place to place or from form to form which
is called motion or change, and which some philosophers
deny, as they deny knowledge. Is there such a leap
in knowing? Am I really here and now when I
apprehend some remote thing? Certainly, if by
myself I understand the psyche within my body,
which directs my outer organs, reacts on external
things, and shapes the history and character of the
individual animal that bears my name. In this sense
I am a physical being in the midst of nature, and my
knowledge is a name for the effects which surrounding
things have upon me, in so far as I am quickened by
them, and readjusted to them. I am certainly confined
at each moment to a limited space and time, but may
be quickened by the influence of things at any distance,
and may be readjusting myself to them. For the
naturalist there is accordingly no paradox in the leap

of knowledge other than the general marvel of material interaction and animal life.

If by myself, however, I meant pure spirit, or the light of attention by which essences appear and intuitions are rendered actual, it would not be true that I am confined or even situated in a particular place and time, nor that in considering things remote from my body, my thoughts are taking any unnatural leap. The marvel, from the point of view of spirit, is rather that it should need to be planted at all in the sensorium of some living animal, and that, being rooted there, it should take that accidental station for its point of view in surveying all nature, and should dignify one momentary phase of that animal life with the titles of the Here and the Now. It is only spirit, be it observed, that can do this. In themselves all the points of space-time are equally central and palpitating, and every phase of every psyche is a focus for actual readjustments to the whole universe. How then can the spirit, which would seem to be the principle of universality and justice, take up its station in each of these atoms and fight its battles for it, and prostitute its own light in the service of that desperate blindness ? Can reason do nothing better than supply the eloquence of prejudice ? Such are the puzzles which spirit might find, I will not say in the leap of knowledge, but in the fatality which links the spirit to a material organ so that, in order to reach other things, it is obliged to leap ; or rather can never reach other things, because it is tethered to its starting-point, except by its intent in leaping, and cannot even discover the stepping-stone on which it stands because its whole life is the act of leaping away from it. There is no reason, therefore, in so far as knowledge is an apanage of spirit, why knowledge should not bathe all time and all existence in an equal light, and see everything as it is, with an equal sympathy and immediacy.

The problem for the spirit is how it could ever come to pick out one body or another for its cynosure and for its instrument, as if it could not see save through such a little eye-glass, and in such a violent perspective. This problem, I think, has a ready answer, but it is not one that spirit could ever find of itself, without a long and docile apprenticeship in the school of animal faith. This answer is that spirit, with knowledge and all its other prerogatives, is intrinsically and altogether a function of animal life ; so that if it were not lodged in some body and expressive of its rhythms and relations, spirit would not exist at all. But this solution, even when spirit is humble enough to accept it, always seems to it a little disappointing and satirical.

Spirit, therefore, has no need to leap in order to know, because in its range as spirit it is omnipresent and omnimodal. Events which are past or future in relation to the phase of the psyche which spirit expresses in a particular instance, or events which are remote from that psyche in space, are not for that reason remote from spirit, or out of its cognitive range : they are merely hidden, or placed in a particular perspective for the moment, like the features of a landscape by the hedges and turns of a road. Just as all essences are equally near to spirit, and equally fit and easy to contemplate, if only a psyche with an affinity to those essences happens to arise ; so all existing things, past, future, or infinitely distant, are equally within the range of knowledge, if only a psyche happens to be directed upon them, and to choose terms, however poor or fantastic, in which to describe them. In choosing these terms the psyche creates spirit, for they are essences given in intuition ; and in directing her action or endeavour, backward or forward, upon those remote events, she creates intent in the spirit, so that the given essences become descriptions of the things with which the psyche is then busied.

But how, I may ask, can intent distinguish its hidden object, so that an image, distorted or faithful, may be truly or falsely projected *there*, or used to describe *it* ?   How does the spirit divine that there is such an object, or where it lies ?   And how can it appeal to a thing which is hidden, the object of mere intent, as to a touchstone or standard for its various descriptions of that object, and say to them, as they suggest themselves in turn : You are too vague, You are absurd, You are better, You are absolutely right ?

I answer that it does so by animal presumption, positing whatsoever object instinct is materially pre-disposed to cope with, as in hunger, love, fighting, or the expectation of a future.   But before developing this reply, let me make one observation.   Since intuition of essence is not knowledge, knowledge can never lie in an overt comparison of one datum with another datum given at the same time ; even in pure dialectic, the comparison is with a datum *believed* to have been given formerly.   If both terms were simply given they would compose a complex essence, without the least signification.   Only when one of the terms is indicated by intent, without being given exhaust-ively, can the other term serve to define the first more fully, or be linked with it in an assertion which is not mere tautology.   An object of faith—and know-ledge is one species of faith—can never, even in the most direct perception, come within the circle of intuition.   Intuition of things is a contradiction in terms.   If philosophers wish to abstain from faith, and reduce themselves to intuition of the obvious, they are free to do so, but they will thereby renounce all knowledge, and live on passive illusions.   No fact, not even the fact that these illusions exist, would ever be, or would ever have been, anything but the false idea that they had existed.   There would be nothing but the realm of essence, without any intuition of any part of it, nor of the whole : so that we should be driven back to a nihilism which only silence and death could express consistently ; since the least actual assertion of it, by existing, would contradict it.

Even such acquaintance with the realm of essence as constitutes some science or recognisable art—like mathematics or music—lies in intending and positing great stretches of essence not now given, so that the essences now given acquire significance and become pregnant, to my vital feeling, with a thousand things which they do not present actually, but which I know where to look for eventually, and how to await. Suppose a moment ago I heard a clap of thunder, loud and prolonged, but that the physical shock has subsided and I am conscious of repose and silence. I may find some difficulty, although the thing was so recent, in *rehearsing* even now the exact volume, tone, and rumblings of that sound ; yet I *know* the theme perfectly, in the sense that when it thunders again, I can say with assurance whether the second crash was longer, louder, or differently modulated. In such a case I have no longer an intuition of the first thunderclap, but a memory of it which is knowledge ; and I can define on occasion, up to a certain point and not without some error, the essence given in that particular past intuition. Thus even pure essences can become objects of intent and of tentative knowledge when they are not present in intuition but are approached and posited indirectly, as the essences given on another particular occasion or signified by some particular word. The word or the occasion are natural facts, and my knowledge is focussed upon them in the first instance by ordinary perception or conception of nature : and the essence I hope to recover is elicited gradually, imaginatively, perhaps incorrectly, at the suggestion of those assumed facts, according to my quickness of wit, or my familiarity with the conventions of that art or science. In this way it becomes possible and necessary to learn about essences as if they were things, not initially by a spontaneous and complete intuition, but by coaxing the mind until possibly, at the end, it beholds them clearly. This is the sort of intuition which is mediated by language and by works of fine art ; also by logic and mathematics, as they are learned from teachers and out of books. It is not happy intuition of some casual datum : it is laborious recovery, up to a certain point, of the *sort* of essence somebody else may have intuited. Whereas intuition, which reveals an essence directly, is not knowledge, because it has no ulterior object, the designation of some essence by some sign does convey knowledge, to an intelligent pupil, of what that essence was. Obviously such divination of essences present elsewhere, so that they become present here also, in so far as it is knowledge, is trebly faith. Faith first in the document, as a genuine natural fact and not a vapid fancy of my own ; for instance, belief that there is a book called the Bible, really handed down from the ancient Jews and the early Christians, and that I have not merely dreamt of such a book. Faith then in the significance of that document, that it means some essence which it is not ; in this instance, belief that the sacred writers were not merely speaking with tongues but were signifying some intelligible points in history and philosophy. Faith finally in my success in interpreting that document correctly, so that the essences it suggests to me now are the very essences it expressed originally : in other words, the belief that when I read the Bible I understand it as it was meant, and not fantastically.

I revert now to the question how it is possible to posit an object which is not a datum, and how without knowing positively what this object is I can make it the criterion of truth in my ideas. How can I test the accuracy of descriptions by referring them to a subject-matter which is not only out of view now but which probably has never been more than an object of intent, an event which even while it was occurring was described by me only in terms native to my fancy ? If I know a man only by reputation, how should I judge if the reputation is deserved ? If I know things only by representations, are not the representations the only things I know ?

This challenge is fundamental, and so long as the assumptions which it makes are not challenged in turn, it drives critics of knowledge inexorably to scepticism of a dogmatic sort, I mean to the assertion that the very notion of knowledge is absurd. One assumption is that knowledge should be intuition : but I have already come to the conclusion that intuition is not knowledge. So long as a knowledge is demanded that shall be intuition, the issue can only be laughter or despair ; for if I attain intuition, I have only a phantom object, and if I spurn that and turn to the facts, I have renounced intuition. This assumption alone suffices, therefore, to disprove the possibility of knowledge. But in case the force of this disproof escaped us, another assumption is at hand to despatch the business, namely, the assumption that in a true description—if we grant knowledge by description—the terms should be identical with the constituents of the object, so that the idea should *look like* the thing that it knows. This assumption is derived from the other, or is a timid form of it : for it is supposed that I know by intuiting my idea, and that unless that idea resembled the object I wish to know, I could not even by courtesy be said to have discovered the latter. But the intuition of an idea, let me repeat, is not knowledge ; and if a thing resembling that idea happened to exist, my intuition would still not be knowledge of it, but contemplation of the idea only.

Plato and many other philosophers, being in love with intuition (for which alone they were perhaps designed by nature), have identified science with certitude, and consequently entirely condemned what I call knowledge (which is a form of animal faith) or relegated it to an inferior position, as something merely necessary for life. I myself have no passionate attachment to existence, and value this world for the intuitions it can suggest, rather than for the wilderness of facts that compose it. To turn away from it may be the deepest wisdom in the end. What better than to blow out the candle, and to bed ! But at noon this pleasure is premature. I can always hold it in reserve, and perhaps nihilism is a system—the simplest of all —on which we shall all agree in the end. But I seem to see very clearly now that in doing so we should all be missing the truth : not indeed by any false assertion, such as may separate us from the truth now, but by dumb ignorance—a dumb ignorance which, when proposed as a solution to actual doubts, is the most radical of errors, since it ignores and virtually denies the pressure of those doubts, and their living presence. Accordingly, so long as I remain awake and the light burning, that total dogmatic scepticism is evidently an impossible attitude. It requires me to deny what I assert, not to mean what I mean, and (in the sense in which seeing is believing) not to believe what I see. If I wish, therefore, to formulate in any way my actual claim to knowledge—a claim which life, and in particular memory, imposes upon me—I must revise the premisses of this nihilism. For I have been led to it not by any accidental error, but by the logic of the assumption that knowledge should be intuition of fact. It is this presumption that must be revoked.

Knowledge is no such thing. It is not intramental

nor internal to experience. Not only does it not require me to compare two given terms and to find them similar or identical, but it positively excludes any intuitive possession of its object. Intuition subsists beneath knowledge, as vegetative life subsists beneath animal life, and within it. Intuition may also supervene upon knowledge, when all I have learned of the universe, and all my concern for it, turn to a playful or a hypnotising phantom ; and any poet or philosopher, like any flower, is free to prefer intuition to knowledge. But in preferring intuition he prefers ignorance. Knowledge is knowledge because it has compulsory objects that pre-exist. It is incidental to the predicaments and labour of life : also to its masterful explorations and satirical moods. It is reflected from events as light is reflected from bodies. It expresses in discourse the modified habits of an active being, plastic to experience, and capable of readjusting its organic attitude to other things on the same material plane of being with itself. The place and the pertinent functions of these several things are indicated by the very attitude of the animal who notices them ; this attitude, physical and practical, determines the object of intent, which discourse is about.

When the proverbial child cries for the moon, is the object of his desire doubtful ? He points at it unmistakably ; yet the psychologist (not to speak of the child himself) would have some difficulty in recovering exactly the sensations and images, the gathering demands and fumbling efforts, that traverse the child's mind while he points. Fortunately all this fluid sentience, even if it could be described, is irrelevant to the question ; for the child's sensuous experience is not his object. If it were, he would have attained it. What his object is, his fixed gaze and outstretched arm declare unequivocally. His elders may say that he doesn't know what he wants, which is probably true of them also : that is, he has only a ridiculously false and inconstant idea of what the moon may be in itself. But his attention is arrested in a particular direction, his appetition flows the same way ; and if he may be said to know anything, he knows there is something there which he would like to reach, which he would like to know better. He is a little philosopher ; and his knowledge, if less diversified and congealed, is exactly like science.

The attitude of his body in pointing to the moon, and his tears, fill full his little mind, which not only reverberates to this physical passion, but probably observes it : and this felt attitude *identifies the object* of his desire and knowledge *in the physical world*. It determines what particular thing, in the same space and time with the child's body, was the object of that particular passion. If the object which the body is after is identified, that which the soul is after is identified too : no one, I suppose, would carry dualism so far as to assert that when the mouth waters at the sight of one particular plum, the soul may be yearning for quite another.

The same bodily attitude of the child *identifies the object in the discourse of an observer*. In perceiving what his senses are excited by, and which way his endeavour is turned, I can see that the object of his desire is the moon, which I too am looking at. That I am looking at the same moon as he can be proved by a little triangulation : our glances converge upon it. If the child has reached the inquisitive age and asks " What is that ? " I understand what he means by " that " and am able to reply sapiently " That is the moon," only because our respective bodies, in one common space, are discoverably turned towards one material object, which is stimulating them simultaneously. Knowledge of discourse in other people, or of myself at other times, is what I call literary psychology. It is, or may be, in its texture, the most literal and adequate sort of knowledge of which a mind is capable. If I am a lover of children, and a good psycho-analyst, I may feel for a moment exactly as the child feels in looking at the moon : and I may know that I know his feeling, and very likely he too will know that I know it, and we shall become fast friends. But this rare adequacy of knowledge, attained by dramatic sympathy, goes out to an object which in its existence is known very indirectly : because poets and religious visionaries feel this sort of sympathy with all sorts of imaginary persons, of whose existence and thoughts they have only intuition, not knowledge. If I ask for evidence that such an object exists, and is not an *alter ego* of my private invention, I must appeal to my faith in nature, and to my conventional assumption that this child and I are animals of the same species, in the same habitat, looking at the same moon, and likely to have the same feelings : and finally the psychology of the tribe and the crowd may enable me half to understand how we know that we have the same feelings at once, when we actually share them.

The attitude of the child's body also *identifies the object for him, in his own subsequent discourse.* He is not likely to forget a moon that he cried for. When in stretching his hand towards it he found he could not touch it, he learned that this bright good was not within his grasp, and he made a beginning in the experience of life. He also made a beginning in science, since he then added the absolutely true predicate " out of reach " to the rather questionable predicates " bright " and " good " (and perhaps " edible ") with which his first glimpse had supplied him. That active and mysterious thing, co-ordinate with himself, since it lay in the same world with his body, and affected it—the thing that attracted his hand, was evidently the very thing that eluded it. His failure would have had no meaning and would have taught him nothing—that is, would not have corrected his instinctive reactions—if the object he saw and the object he failed to reach had not been identical ; and certainly that object was not brightness nor goodness nor excitements in his brain or psyche, for these are not things he could ever have attempted or expected to touch. It is only things on the scale of the human senses and in the field of those instinctive reactions which sensation calls forth, that can be the primary objects of human knowledge : no other things can be discriminated at first by an animal mind, or can interest it, or can be meant and believed in by it. It is these instinctive reactions that select the objects of attention, designate their locus, and impose faith in their existence. But these reactions may be modified by experience, and the description the mind gives of the objects reacted upon can be revised, or the objects themselves discarded, and others discerned instead. Thus the child's instinct to touch the moon was as spontaneous and as confident at first as his instinct to look at it ; and the object of both efforts was the same, because the same external agency aroused them, and with them the very heterogeneous sensations of light and of disappointment. These various terms of sense or of discourse, by which the child described the object under whose attractions and rebuffs he was living, were merely symbols to him, like words. An animal naturally has as many signs for an object as he has sensations or emotions in its presence. These signs are miscellaneous essences— sights, sounds, smells, contacts, tears, provocations— and they are alternative or supplementary to one another, like words in different languages. The most diverse senses, such as smell and sight, if summoned to the same point in the environment, and guiding a single action, will report upon a single object. Even when one sense brings all the news I have, its reports will change from moment to moment with the distance, variation, or suspension of the connection between the object and my body : and this without any relevant change in the object itself. Nay, often the very transformation of the sensation bears witness that the object is unchanged ; as music and laughter, over-heard as I pass a tavern, are felt and known to continue unabated, and to be no merriment of mine, just because they fade from my ears as I move away.

The object of knowledge being that designated in this way by my bodily attitude, the æsthetic qualities I attribute to it will depend on the particular sense it happens to affect at the moment, or on the sweep and nature of the reaction which it then calls forth on my part. This diversity in signs and descriptions for a single thing is a normal diversity. Diversity, when it is not contradiction, irritates only unreasonably dogmatic people ; they are offended with nature for having a rich vocabulary, and sometimes speaking a language, or employing a syntax, which they never heard at home. It is an innocent prejudice, and it yields easily in a generous mind to pleasure at the wealth of alternatives which animal life affords. Even such contradictions as may arise in the description of things, and may truly demand a solution, reside in the implication of the terms, not in their sensuous or rhetorical diversity : they become contradictory only when they assign to the object contrary movements or contrary effects, not when they merely exhibit its various appearances. Looking at the moon, one man may call it simply a light in the sky ; another, prone to dreaming awake, may call it a virgin goddess ; a more observant person, remembering that this luminary is given to waxing and waning, may call it the crescent ;

and a fourth, a full-fledged astronomer, may say (taking the æsthetic essence before him merely for a sign) that it is an extinct and opaque spheroidal satellite of the earth, reflecting the light of the sun from a part of its surface. All these descriptions envisage the same object—otherwise no relevance, conflict, or progress could obtain among them. What that object is in its complete constitution and history will never be known by man; but that this object exists in a known space and time and has traceable physical relations with all other physical objects is a fact posited from the beginning; it was posited by the child when he pointed, and by me when I saw him point. If it did not so exist and (as sometimes happens) he and I were suffering from a hallucination, in thinking we were pointing at the moon we should be discoverably pointing at vacancy: exploration would eventually satisfy us of that fact, and any by-stander would vouch for it. But if in pointing at it we were pointing to it, its identity would be fixed without more ado; disputes and discoveries concerning it would be pertinent and soluble, no matter what diversity there might be in the ideal essences—light, crescent, goddess, or satellite—which we used as rival descriptions of it while we pointed.

I find that the discrimination of essence brings a wonderful clearness into this subject. All data and descriptions—light, crescent, goddess, or satellite—are equally essences, terms of human discourse, in-existent in themselves. What exists in any instance, besides the moon and our various reactions upon it, is some intuition, expressing those reactions, evoking that essence, and lending it a specious actuality. The terms of astronomy are essences no less human and visionary than those of mythology; but they are the fruit of a better focussed, more chastened, and more prolonged attention turned upon what actually occurs;

that is, they are kept closer to animal faith, and freer
from pictorial elements and the infusion of reverie.
In myth, on the contrary, intuition wanders idly and
uncontrolled ; it makes epicycles, as it were, upon the
reflex arc of perception ; the moonbeams bewitch
some sleeping Endymion, and he dreams of a swift
huntress in heaven. Myth is nevertheless a relevant
fancy, and genuinely expressive ; only instead of being
guided by a perpetual fresh study of the object posited
by animal faith and encountered in action, it runs into
marginal comments, personal associations, and rhetorical asides ; so that even if based originally on perception, it is built upon principles internal to human
discourse, as are grammar, rhyme, music, and morals.
It may be admirable as an expression of these principles,
and yet be egregiously false if asserted of the object,
without discounting the human medium in which it
has taken form. Diana is an exquisite symbol for the
moon, and for one sort of human loveliness ; but she
must not be credited with any existence over and above
that of the moon, and of sundry short-skirted Dorian
maidens. She is not other than they : she is an
image of them, the best part of their essence distilled
in a poet's mind. So with the description of the
moon given by astronomers, which is not less fascinating ; this, too, is no added object, but only a new
image for the moon known even to the child and me.
The space, matter, gravitation, time, and laws of
motion conceived by astronomers are essences only,
and mere symbols for the use of animal faith, when
very enlightened : I mean in so far as they are alleged
to constitute knowledge of a world which I must bow
to and encounter in action ; for if astronomy is content
to be a mathematical exercise without any truth, an
object of pure intuition, its terms and its laws will, of
course, be ultimate realities, apart from what happens
to exist : realities in the realm of essence. In the

description of the natural world, however, they are mere symbols, mediating animal faith. Science at any moment may recast or correct its conceptions (as it is doing now) giving them a different colour ; and the nerve of truth in them will be laid bare and made taut in proportion as the sensuous and rhetorical vesture of these notions is stripped off, and the dynamic relations of events, as found and posited by material exploration, are nakedly recorded.

Knowledge accordingly is belief : belief in a world of events, and especially of those parts of it which are near the self, tempting or threatening it. This belief is native to animals, and precedes all deliberate use of intuitions as signs or descriptions of things ; as I turn my head to see who is there, before I see who it is. Furthermore, knowledge is true belief. It is such an enlightening of the self by intuitions arising there, that what the self imagines and asserts of the collateral thing, with which it wrestles in action, is actually true of that thing. Truth in such presumptions or conceptions does not imply adequacy, nor a pictorial identity between the essence in intuition and the constitution of the object. Discourse is a language, not a mirror. The images in sense are parts of discourse, not parts of nature : they are the babble of our innocent organs under the stimulus of things ; but these spontaneous images, like the sounds of the voice, may acquire the function of names ; they may become signs, if discourse is intelligent and can recapitulate its phases, for the things sought or encountered in the world. The truth which discourse can achieve is truth in its own terms, appropriate description : it is no incorporation or reproduction of the object in the mind. The mind notices and intends ; it cannot incorporate or reproduce anything not an intention or an intuition. Its objects are no part of itself even when they are essences, much less when they are things. It thinks the essences, with that sort of immediate and self-forgetful attention which I have been calling intuition ; and if it is animated, as it usually is, by some ulterior interest or pursuit, it takes the essences before it for messages, signs, or emanations sent forth to it from those objects of animal faith ; and they become its evidences and its description for those objects. Therefore any degree of inadequacy and originality is tolerable in discourse, or even requisite, when the constitution of the objects which the animal encounters is out of scale with his organs, or quite heterogeneous from his possible images. A sensation or a theory, no matter how arbitrary its terms (and all language is perfectly arbitrary), will be true of the object, if it expresses some true relation in which that object stands to the self, so that these terms are not misleading as signs, however poetical they may be as sounds or as pictures.

Finally, knowledge is true belief grounded in experience, I mean, controlled by outer facts. It is not true by accident ; it is not shot into the air on the chance that there may be something it may hit. It arises by a movement of the self sympathetic or responsive to surrounding beings, so that these beings become its intended objects, and at the same time an appropriate correspondence tends to be established between these objects and the beliefs generated under their influence.

In regard to the original articles of the animal creed—that there is a world, that there is a future, that things sought can be found, and things seen can be eaten—no guarantee can possibly be offered. I am sure these dogmas are often false ; and perhaps the event will some day falsify them all, and they will lapse altogether. But while life lasts, in one form or another this faith must endure. It is the initial expression of animal vitality in the sphere of mind,

the first announcement that anything is going on.
It is involved in any pang of hunger, of fear, or of love.
It launches the adventure of knowledge. The object
of this tentative knowledge is things in general, whatsoever may be at work (as I am) to disturb me or
awake my attention. The effort of knowledge is to
discover what sort of world this disturbing world
happens to be. Progress in knowledge lies open in
various directions, now in the scope of its survey, now
in its accuracy, now in its depth of local penetration.
The ideal of knowledge is to become natural science :
if it trespasses beyond that, it relapses into intuition,
and ceases to be knowledge.

CHAPTER XIX

BELIEF IN SUBSTANCE

ALL knowledge, being faith in an object posited and partially described, is belief in substance, in the etymological sense of this word ; it is belief in a thing or event subsisting in its own plane, and waiting for the light of knowledge to explore it eventually, and perhaps name or define it. In this way my whole past lies waiting for memory to review it, if I have this faculty ; and the whole future of the world in the same manner is spread out for prophecy, scientific or visionary, to predict falsely or truly. Yet the future and the past are not ordinarily called substances ; probably because the same material substance is assumed to run through both. Nevertheless, from the point of view of knowledge, every event, even if wholly psychological or phenomenal, is a substance. It is a self-existing fact, open to description from the point of view of other events, if in the bosom of these other events there is such plasticity and intent as are requisite for perception, prophecy, or memory.

When modern philosophers deny material substance, they make substances out of the sensations or ideas which they regard as ultimate facts. It is impossible to eliminate belief in substance so long as belief in existence is retained. A mistrust in existence, and therefore in substance, is not unphilosophical ; but modern philosophers have not given full expression to this sceptical scruple. They have seldom been disinterested critics, but often advocates of some metaphysic that allured them, and whose rivals they wished to destroy. They deny substance in favour of phenomena, which are hypostatised essences, because phenomena are individually wholly open to intuition ; but they forget that no phenomenon can intuit another, and that if it contains knowledge of that other, it must be animated by intent, and besides existing itself substantially must recognise its object as another substance, indifferent in its own being to the cognisance which other substances may take of it. In other words, although each phenomenon in passing is an object of intuition, all absent phenomena, and all their relations, are objects of faith ; and this faith must be mediated by some feature in the present phenomenon which faith assumes to be a sign of the existence of other phenomena elsewhere, and of their order. So that in so far as the instinctive claims and transcendent scope of knowledge are concerned, phenomenalism fully retains the belief in substance. In order to get rid of this belief, which is certainly obnoxious to the sceptic, a disinterested critic would need to discard all claims to knowledge, and to deny his own existence and that of all absent phenomena.

For my own part, having admitted discourse (which involves time and existences deployed in time, but synthesised in retrospect), and having admitted shocks that interrupt discourse and lead it to regard itself as an experience, and having even admitted that such experience involves a self beneath discourse, with an existence and movement of its own—I need not be deterred by any *a priori* objections from believing in substance of any sort. For me it will be simply a question of good sense and circumstantial evidence how many substances I admit, and of what sort.

In the genesis of human knowledge (which I am

not attempting to trace here) the substance first posited is doubtless matter, some alluring or threatening or tormenting thing. The ego, as Fichte tells us, unaware of itself, posits a non-ego, and then by reflection posits itself as the agent in that positing, or as the patient which the activity posited in the non-ego posits in its turn. But all this positing would be mere folly, unless it was an intelligent discovery of antecedent facts. Why should a non-existent ego be troubled with the delirious duty of positing anything at all? And, if nothing else exists, what difference could it make what sort of a world the ego posited, or whether it posited a thousand inconsequential worlds, at once or in succession? Fichte, however, was far from sharing that absolute freedom in madness which he attributes to the creative ego; he had a very tight tense mind, and posited a very tense tight world. His myths about the birth of knowledge (or rather of systematic imagination) out of unconscious egos, acts, and positings concealed some modest truths about nature. The actual datum has a background, and Fichte was too wise to ignore so tremendous a fact. Romantic philosophy, like romantic poetry, has its profound ways of recognising its own folly, and so turning it into tragic wisdom. As a matter of fact, the active ego is an animal living in a material world; both the ego and the non-ego exist substantially before acquiring this relation of positing and being posited. The instinct and ability to posit objects, and the occasion for doing so, are incidents in the development of animal life. Positing is a symptom of sensibility in an organism to the presence of other substances in its environment. The sceptic, like the sick man, is intent on the symptom; and positing is his name for felt plasticity in his animal responses. It is not a bad name; because plasticity, though it may seem a passive thing, is really a spontaneous quality.

If the substance of the ego were not alive, it would not leap to meet its opportunities, it would not develop new organs to serve its old necessities, and it would not kindle itself to intuition of essences, nor concern itself to regard those essences as appearances of the substances with which it was wrestling. The whole life of imagination and knowledge comes from within, from the restlessness, eagerness, curiosity, and terror of the animal bent on hunting, feeding, and breeding ; and the throb of being which he experiences at any moment is not proper to the datum in his mind's eye —a purely fantastic essence—but to himself. It is out of his organism or its central part, the psyche, that this datum has been bred. The living substance within him being bent, in the first instance, on pursuing or avoiding some agency in its environment, it projects whatever (in consequence of its reactions) reaches its consciousness into the locus whence it feels the stimulus to come, and it thus frames its description or knowledge of objects. In this way the ego really and sagaciously posits the non-ego : not absolutely, as Fichte imagined, nor by a gratuitous fiat, but on occasion and for the best of reasons, when the non-ego in its might shakes the ego out of its primitive somnolence.

Belief in substance is accordingly identical with the claim to knowledge, and so fundamental that no evidence can be adduced for it which does not presuppose it. In recognising any appearance as a witness to substance and in admitting (or even in rejecting) the validity of such testimony, I have already made a substance of the appearance ; and if I admit other phenomena as well, I have placed that substance in a world of substances having a substantial unity. It is not to external pressure, through evidence or argument, that faith in substance is due. If the sceptic cannot find it in himself, he will never find it.

I for one will honour him in his sincerity and in his solitude. But I will not honour him, nor think him a philosopher, if he is a sceptic only histrionically, in the wretched controversies of the schools, and believes in substance again when off the stage. I am not concerned about make-believe philosophies, but about my actual beliefs. It is only out of his own mouth, or rather out of his own heart, that I should care to convince the sceptic. Scepticism, if it could be sincere, would be the best of philosophies. But I suspect that other sceptics, as well as I, always believe in substance, and that their denial of it is sheer sophistry and the weaving of verbal arguments in which their most familiar and massive convictions are ignored.

It might seem ignominious to believe something on compulsion, because I can't help believing it ; when reason awakes in a man it asks for reasons for every-thing. Yet this demand is unreasonable : there cannot be a reason for everything. It is mere auto-matic habit in the philosopher to make this demand, as it is in the common man not to make it. When once I have admitted the facts of nature, and taken for granted the character of animal life, and the in-carnation of spirit in this animal life, then indeed many excellent reasons for the belief in substance will appear ; and not only reasons for using the category of substance, and positing substance of some vague ambient sort, but reasons for believing in a substance rather elaborately defined and scientifically describable in many of its habits and properties. But I am not yet ready for that. Lest that investigation, when undertaken, should ignore its foundations or be impatient of its limits, I must insist here that trust in knowledge, and belief in anything to know, are merely instinctive and, in a manner, pathological. If philo-sophy were something prior to convention rather than (as it is) only convention made consistent and deliberate, philosophy ought to reject belief in substance and in knowledge, and to entrench itself in the sheer confession and analysis of this belief, as of all others, without assenting to any of them. But I have found that criticism has no first principle, that analysis involves belief in discourse, and that belief in discourse involves belief in substance ; so that any pretensions which criticism might set up to being more profound than common sense would be false pretensions. Criticism is only an exercise of reflective fancy, on the plane of literary psychology, an afterimage of that faith in nature which it denies ; and in dwelling on criticism as if it were more than a subjective perspective or play of logical optics, I should be renouncing all serious philosophy. Philosophy is nothing if not honest ; and the critical attitude, when it refuses to rest at some point upon vulgar faith, inhibits all belief, denies all claims to knowledge, and becomes dishonest ; because it itself claims to know.

Does the process of experience, now that I trust my memory to report it truly, or does the existence of the self, now that I admit its substantial, dynamic, and obscure life underlying discourse, require me to posit any other substances ? Certainly it does. Experience, for animal faith, begins by reporting what is not experience ; and the life of the self, if I accept its endeavours as significant, implies an equally substantial, dynamic, ill-reported world around it, in whose movements it is implicated. In conveying this feeling, as in all else, experience *might* be pure illusion ; but if I reject this initial and fundamental suasion of my cognitive life, it will be hard to find anything better to put in its place. I am unwilling to do myself so much useless violence as to deny the validity of primary memory, and assert that I have never, in fact, had any experience at all ; and I should be doing myself even greater violence if I denied the validity of perception, and asserted that a thunder-clap, for instance, was only a musical chord, with no formidable event of any sort going on behind the sound. To be startled is to be aware that something sudden and mysterious has occurred not far from me in space. The thunder-clap is felt to be an event in the self and in the not-self, even before its nature as a sound—its æsthetic quality for the self—is recognised at all ; I first know I am shaken horribly, and then note how loud and rumbling is the voice of the god that shakes me. That first feeling of something violent and resistless happening in the world at large, is accompanied by a hardly less primitive sense of something gently seething within me, a smouldering life which that alien energy blows upon and causes to start into flame.

If this be not the inmost texture of experience, I do not know what experience is. To me experience has not a string of sensations for its objects ; what it brings me is not at all a picture-gallery of clear images, with nothing before, behind, or between them. What such a ridiculous psychology (made apparently by studying the dictionary and not by studying the mind) calls hypotheses, intellectual fictions, or tendencies to feign, is the solid body of experience, on which what it calls sensations or ideas hang like flimsy garments or trinkets, or play like a shifting light and shade. Experience brings belief in substance (as alertness) *before* it brings intuition of essences ; it is appetition *before* it is description. Of course sensation would precede idea, if by sensation we understood contact with matter, and by idea pure reverie about ideal things ; but if idea means expectation, or consciousness having intent, and if sensation means æsthetic contemplation of data without belief, then idea precedes sensation : because an animal is aware that something is happening long before he can say to himself what that something is, or what it looks like. The ultimate datum to which a sceptic may retreat, when he suspends all life and opinion, some essence, pure and non-existent and out of all relation to minds, bodies, or events—surely that is not the stuff out of which experience is woven : it is but the pattern or picture, the æsthetic image, which the tapestry may ultimately offer to the gazing eye, incurious of origins, and contemptuous of substance. The radical stuff of experience is much rather breathlessness, or pulsation, or as Locke said (correcting himself) a certain uneasiness ; a lingering thrill, the resonance of that much-struck bell which I call my body, the continual assault of some masked enemy, masked perhaps in beauty, or of some strange sympathetic influence, like the cries and motions of other creatures ; and also the hastening and rising of some impulse in me in response. Experience, at its very inception, is a revelation of *things* ; and these things, before they are otherwise distinguished, are distinguishable into a here and a there, a now and a then, nature and myself in the midst of nature.

It is a mere prejudice of literary psychology, which uses the grammar of adult discourse, like a mythology, in which to render primitive experience—it is a mere prejudice to suppose that experience has only such categories as colour, sound, touch, and smell. These essences are distinguished eventually because the senses that present them can be separated at will, the element each happens to furnish being thus flashed on or cut off, like an electric light : but far more primitive in animal experience are such dichotomies as good and bad, near and far, coming and going, fast and slow, just now and very soon. The first thing experience reports is the existence of something, merely as existence, the weight, strain, danger, and lapse of being. If any one should tell me that this is an abstraction, I should reply that it would seem an abstraction to a parrot, who used human words without having human experience, but it is no abstraction to a man, whose language utters imperfectly, and by a superadded articulation, the life within him. Aristotle, who so often seems merely grammatical, was not merely grammatical when he chose substance to be the first of his categories. He was far more profoundly psychological in this than the British and German psychologists who discard the notion of substance because it is not the datum of any separate sense. None of the separate data of sense, which are only essences, would figure at all in an experience, or would become terms in knowledge, if a prior interest and faith did not apprehend them. Animal watchfulness, lying in wait for the signals of the special senses, lends them their significance, sets them in their places, and retains them, as descriptions of things, and as symbols in its own ulterior discourse.

This animal watchfulness carries the category of substance with it, asserts existence most vehemently, and in apprehension seizes and throws on the dark screen of substance every essence it may descry. To grope, to blink, to dodge a blow, or to return it, is to have very radical and specific experiences, but probably without one assignable image of the outer senses. Yet a nameless essence, the sense of a moving existence, is there most intensely present ; and a man would be a shameless, because an insincere, sceptic, who should maintain that this experience exists *in vacuo*, and does not express, as it feels it does, the operation of a missile flying, and the reaction of a body threatened or hit : motions in substance anterior to the experience, and rich in properties and powers which no experience will ever fathom.

Belief in substance, taken transcendentally, as a critic of knowledge must take it, is the most irrational, animal, and primitive of beliefs : it is the voice of hunger. But when, as I must, I have yielded to this presumption, and proceeded to explore the world, I shall find in its constitution the most beautiful justification for my initial faith, and the proof of its secret rationality. This corroboration will not have any logical force, since it will be only pragmatic, based on begging the question, and perhaps only a bribe offered by fortune to confirm my illusions. The force of the corroboration will be merely moral, showing me how appropriate and harmonious with the nature of things such a blind belief was on my part. How else should the truth have been revealed to me at all ? Truth and blindness, in such a case, are correlatives, since I am a sensitive creature surrounded by a universe utterly out of scale with myself : I must, therefore, address it questioningly but trustfully, and it must reply to me in my own terms, in symbols and parables, that only gradually enlarge my childish perceptions. It is as if Substance said to Knowledge : My child, there is a great world for thee to conquer, but it is a vast, an ancient, and a recalcitrant world. It yields wonderful treasures to courage, when courage is guided by art and respects the limits set to it by nature. I should not have been so cruel as to give thee birth, if there had been nothing for thee to master ; but having first prepared the field, I set in thy heart the love of adventure.

CHAPTER XX

ON SOME OBJECTIONS TO BELIEF IN SUBSTANCE

ACCORDING to those philosophers who look for the foundations of the universe in their own minds, substance is but a dead and fantastic thing—a ghost or abstracted shadow of many sensations, impossibly fused and objectified. These philosophers, in their intense introspection, try to catch thought alive, and the nearer they come to doing so, the more unstable and unsubstantial they find it to be. It exists only in the act of dominating or positing or meaning something ; and before this something can be specified exhaustively, something else has taken its place, the limits of vision having expanded or its centre shifted. Such self-observation may be profound, or at least sincere, although what is true of life in one animal or at one moment might well be false of life in another instance, and mere nonsense to a different mind. In myself, I find experience so volatile that no insistence on its unsubstantial flux, maniacally creative, seems to me exaggerated. But before such observations of life in the quick can be turned into arguments against the existence of substance, three assumptions must be made silently, all three of which are false : first, that thought observes itself ; secondly, that if thought is itself in flux it can observe nothing permanent ; and lastly, that if direct observation offered no illustration of the permanent, nothing permanent could exist in fact, or could be reasonably believed to exist.

In the first place, living thought is so far from observing itself, that some philosophers deny its existence, and the others find the greatest difficulty in distinguishing it from its various objects. The terms of pure thought, in which observation is couched and in which it rests, I have found to be not thoughts but essences ; and the objects of thought, when thought relapses into its animal form of belief, are again not thoughts but things. If later I contrast the order, rate, and natural locus of discourse with the movement of events in general which discourse is considering, I may begin to understand what a curious thing discourse is, and to have assurance of its existence. The introspection into which I may ultimately plunge, when I seem to be creating the world as I think it, is a violently artificial exercise, in which the wheels of life are reversed ; and the knowledge I thus gain of my imaginative operations would itself be sheer raving, creating a dream about dreaming, unless these operations were domiciled in a natural being, and expressed his history and vulgar situation in the natural world ; so that my eventual description, or rather dramatic reconstruction, of my own experience, is one of the latest forms of my knowledge, and its object one of the most derivative and insecure. It is a theme for literary psychology, of which transcendental self-consciousness, or autobiography, is one variety.

In the second place, permanence rather than change is native to the prime objects of thought. The only data observable directly are essences absolutely immutable in their nature, even if the one observed happens to be the essence of change ; since even this, so long as it is present at all, presents change and nothing but change for ever. Attention of course is continually drawn from one essence to another ; but this inconstancy in intuition could not be noticed, and could not actually exist, if the essence which drops out of view and that which succeeds it were not different, and each, therefore, always itself. Furthermore, granting that an animal mind is probably always changing in some respect, it by no means follows that no essence can be retained for more than one instant under the light of attention. On the contrary, change that was complete, and that substituted one totally new object for another totally destroyed, would afford no inkling of its own existence: only the permanent would ever appear to the mind. What happens is that some detail changes in a field that does not change, and for that reason the new element attracts attention, surprise, or joy. To hold something fast, to watch, to stare, to wait and lie low in the presence of a felt incubus, are primitive experiences ; and the length of crawling time through which a strain endures is a conspicuous feature in sensation, especially in pain. This sense of duration doubtless involves the sense of something changing at the same time—of something coming or continuing to come as it threatened or as it was demanded—of some pulse of feeling recurring and mounting towards increased potency or increased fatigue. Yet in all this setting of cumulative change (which is but a perspective in the fancy) there often shines a fixed focus of interest ; and the sense of something which lasts, and which remains itself whether I approach or elude it, is one of the first and loudest notes of awareness. Perhaps, when my mood is clear and musical, there is some permanent essence clearly revealed that arouses my curiosity and wonder ; or when the stream runs thick and turbid, the obscure life of the psyche itself rises to the surface, and yields the primary criterion of happiness and naturalness in events. In either case in mastering, recognising, and positing what I find or what I want, I know the beginnings of speculative joy and of participation in eternity. The flux touches the eternal at the top of every wave. Whatever thwarts this achievement, or disturbs the deep rhythms of the life slumbering beneath, seems illegitimate ; and until acquisitive or sexual impulses are aroused, the dozing animal counts on a perpetual well-being, and any change seems to it as hateful as it is incredible.

In this way change itself, when it is rhythmic and regular, wears to intuition the form of sustained being. The life of the body, by its latent operation, sets a measure and scale for the duration of any passing vision. There is an ever-present background felt as permanent, myself always myself ; and there is a large identity in the universe also, familiar and limited in spite of its agitation, like a cage full of birds. Everything seems to be more or less prolonged ; comfort, digestive warmth, the past still simmering, the brooding potentiality of things to come, shaping themselves in fancy before they have occurred. Both sleep and watchfulness are long drawn out, so is the very sense of movement. Though change be everywhere, it remains everywhere strange and radically unwelcome : for even when, as in destructive passion or impatience, it is imperatively sought, it is sought as an escape from an uncomfortable posture, in the hope of restoring a steady life, and resting in safety.

Thus the notion of permanence behind change—which is a chief element in the notion of substance—is trebly rooted in experience ; because every essence that appears is eternally what it is ; because many congenial images and feelings appear lastingly ; and because whatever interrupts the even flow and luxurious monotony of organic life is odious to the primeval animal.

In the third place, even if direct experience did not illustrate the permanent, the order of events when reflected on would suggest and impose a belief in it. I reserve for another occasion all discussion of the laws of nature or of the constant quantities of matter or energy : the most ordinary recognition of things being as they were, and remaining always at hand, posits their substantial nature. Suppose all intuition was instantaneous ; and in one sense it may be said always to be so, because specious durations have no common scale, and the most prolonged may be treated as a single moment, as the dome of St. Peter's may be seen through a keyhole. Instantaneous intuition, when suspended, may be suspended only for a moment, and instantly recovered, as when I blink. Such brief interruptions to perception are bridged over in primary memory, and do not break the specious identity and continuity of the object. It does not follow, however, that the interruption is not felt. On the contrary, it is felt and resented just because beneath it the object is sensibly continuous. There is a stock optical experiment in which a pencil is made to cross the field of vision between the eye and a book, without ever hiding any part of the page. What binocular vision does in that instance, the persistence of impressions does in the case of an intermittent stimulus. The interruption is startling and obvious, but the continuity of the object is obvious too. This experience may be repeated on a larger scale. The psyche, being surrounded by substances, is adapted to them, and does not suspend her adjustments or her beliefs whenever her sensations are interrupted. Children recognise and identify things and persons more readily than they distinguish them. As intuition is addressed to terms in discourse which are eternal in their nature, though the intuition of them is desultory, so faith and art are addressed to *habits* in substance, which without arresting the perpetual and pervasive flux of experience (nor perhaps that of substance itself) manifest its dynamic permanence ; and, of course, it is on its dynamic side, not pictorially or intuitively, that substance is conceived, posited, measured, and trusted.

Hence the discovery, big with scientific consequences, that an existing thing may endure unchanged, although my experience of it be intermittent. The object of these recurrent observations is not conceived, as a sophistical psychology would have it, by feigning that the *observations* are not discrete. Every one knows, when he shuts and opens his eyes, that his vision has been interrupted ; the interruption is the point of the game. The notion that the thing persists was there from the beginning ; until I blinked, I had found it persisting, and I find it persisting still after I open my eyes again. In considering the fortunes of the object posited, I simply discard the interruption, as voluntary and due to a change in myself which I can repeat at will. In spontaneous thought I never confuse the changes which the thing may undergo in its own being with the variations in my attention nor (when I have a little experience) with shifts in my perspectives. I therefore recognise it to be permanent in relation to my intermittent glimpses of it ; and this without in the least confusing or fusing my different views, or supposing them to be other than discrete and perhaps instantaneous.

On the same principle, as education advances, a thing which stimulates different senses at once or successively is easily recognised to be the same object ; and this, again, is done without in the least fusing or confusing colour with hardness or sound with shape. And with the growth of the arts and of experience of the world, the persisting and continuous engine of nature is clearly conceived as the common object which all my senses and all my theories describe in their special languages at their several awakenings.

That the syllables are broken does not make their messages conflicting ; on the contrary, they supplement one another's blindness, and correct one another's exuberance. Substance was their common object from the beginning, faith in substance not being a consequence of reasoning about appearances, but an implication of action, and a conviction native to hunger, fear, feeding, and fighting ; as an aid and guide to which the organs of the outer senses are developed, and rapidly paint their various symbols in the mind. The euphony and syntax of sense, far from disproving the existence of substance, arise and change in the act of expressing its movement, and especially the responsive organisation of that part of it which is myself.

So much for the objections to the belief in substance which may be raised from the point of view of self-consciousness, when this is regarded as the principle of knowledge or even of universal existence, neither of which it is.

Objections to the belief in substance may also come from a different quarter (or one ostensibly different), in the name of critical sense and economy in the interpretation of appearances. Suppose, the empiricist may say, that your substance exists : how does it help you to explain anything ? You never have seen, and you never will see, anything but appearances. If you trust your memory (as it is reasonable to do, since you must, if you are to play the game of discourse at all) you may assume that appearances have come in a certain order ; and if you trust expectation (for the same bad reason) you may assume that they will come in somewhat the same order in future. These assumptions are not founded on any proof or on any real probability, but it is intelligible that you should make them, because the mind can hardly be asked to discredit its vistas, when it has nothing else by which to criticise them. But why should you interpolate amongst appearances, or posit behind them, something that you can never find ? That seems a gratuitous fiction, and at best a hypostasis of grammar and names. You want a substance because you use substantives, or because your verbal logic talks in subjects and predicates.

But let us grant, the empiricist will go on, that your substance is possible, since everything is possible where ignorance is complete. In what terms can you conceive it, save in terms of appearance ? Or if you say it exists unconceived, or is inconceivable, it will simply encumber your philosophy with a metaphysical world, in addition to the given one, and with the hopeless problem of relating the two.

These empirical objections to the belief in substance might in strictness be ruled out, since (in so far as they deny substance) they rest on the same romantic view of self-consciousness as the source of knowledge and being as do the transcendental objections just considered. Empiricism, however, has the advantage of being less resolute in folly. Such terms as appearance, phenomenon, given fact (meaning given essence *plus* thing posited), and perception (meaning intuition *plus* belief) are all used sophistically to cover the muddles of introspection. They are not analysed critically, but are allowed to retain in solution many of the assumptions of common sense. The essence given is confused with the intuition of it which is not given, but which common sense knows is implicated. This intuition is then confused with the belief, prompted by animal impulse and, for analysis, utterly gratuitous, that a thing or event exists definable by the essence given. This belief finally is confused with the existence of its object, which it merely posits and cannot witness. This object, in psychological idealism, is some ulterior intuition or (as it is called by common sense, which assumes a material object producing it) some ulterior perception. But it is utterly impossible that one perception should perceive another, and it is improper to call an intuition a perception when it has no existing object.

In consequence of this halting criticism of immediate experience, empiricism admits the existence of many feelings or ideas deployed in time and referred to in memory and in social intercourse ; and in admitting this (let me repeat) it admits substance in principle. Such a flux of feelings or ideas is a permanent hidden substance for purposes of knowledge, even if each of them, being a momentary life, might not be called by that name. Each feeling or idea is substantial, however, in respect to any memory or theory, contained in some other moment, which may refer to it ; and this memory or theory is an appearance of that substantial but remote fact.

Let us suppose that David Hume, in spite of his corpulence, was nothing but a train of ideas. Some of these composed his philosophy, and I, when I endeavour to learn what it was, create in my own mind a fresh train of ideas which refer to those in the mind of Hume : and for me his opinions are a substance of which my apprehension is an appearance. My apprehension, in this case, is conceived to be an apprehension of a matter of fact, namely, the substance of Hume at some date ; and in studying his philosophy I am learning nothing but history. This is an implication of empiricism, but is not true to the facts. For when I try to conceive the philosophy of Hume I am not considering any particular ideas which may have constituted Hume at one moment of his career ; I am considering an *essence*, his total system, as it would appear when the *essences* present in his various reflective moments are collated ; and, therefore, I am really studying and learning a system of philosophy, not the presumable condition of a dead man's mind at various historical moments.

If empiricists were a little more sceptical, they would perceive that in admitting knowledge of historical facts they have admitted the principle that the beliefs they call ideas may report the existence of natural substances. If the substance of this world is a flux, and even a flux of feelings, it is none the less substantial, like the fire of Heraclitus, and the existing object of such ideas as may describe it. But this reasonable faith is obscured by the confusions I mentioned above. The empiricist forgets that he is asserting the existence of outlying facts, because he half identifies them with the living fact of his present belief in them : and, further, because he identifies this living fact, his belief now, with the essence which it is attributing to those remote existences. He thinks he believes only what he sees, but he is much better at believing than at seeing.

Apart from this unconscious admission of the existence of substances, the empirical objections to substance in the singular express a distrust of metaphysics with which I sympathise, and they show a love of home truths which deserves to be satisfied.

In the first place, the substance in which I am proposing to believe is not metaphysical but physical substance. It is the varied stuff of the world which I meet in action—the wood of this tree I am felling, the wind that is stirring its branches, the flesh and bones of the man who is jumping out of the way. Belief in substance is not imported into animal perception by language or by philosophy, but is the soul of animal perception from the beginning, and the perpetual deliverance of animal experience. Later, as animal attention is clarified, and animal experience progresses, the description of these obvious substances may be refined : the tree, the wind, and the man may reveal their elements and genesis to more patient observation, and the first aspect they wore may be found to be a fused and composite appearance of many elaborate processes within them. But the more diffused substances in operation which I shall then come upon will be simply the constituents of the tree, the wind, and the man ; they will be just as truly (though more calculably) the realities I confront and may use in action. They will be just as open to perception, although instruments or hypotheses may be required to extend the accidental range of my senses in observing them ; and they will be just as much substances and not essences, that is, objects of belief posited in action, not images given in intuition. My notions of substance will therefore be subject to error, and capable of reform : I may arrive at the belief that earth, air, water, and fire are the substances in all things ; later I may discover that fire is not a substance, but a form of motion ; for earth, air, and water I may come to substitute the four or five score elements of chemistry, or more or less ; and I may remain in doubt whether light and space and ether are substances or not. But all these opinions would be equally fantastic, and equally devoid of truth or falsehood, if there were no substance before me in the first instance which I was attempting to describe.

By a substance I understand what modern philosophers often call an " independent object "—a most unfortunate phrase, because precisely at the moment when a substance or an essence becomes my object, by becoming the theme of my discourse, it ceases to be independent of me in that capacity : and when this happens, before the cognitive relation between me and my object is established, a dynamic relation has probably arisen between the substance of that object and the substance of myself, causing me to make that intrusive substance the object of my attention. When a thing becomes my object it becomes dependent on me ideally, for being known, and I am probably, directly or indirectly, dependent on it materially, for having been led to know it. What is independent of knowledge is substance, in that it has a place, movement, origin, and destiny of its own, no matter what I may think or fail to think about it. This self-existence is what the name object jeopardises, and what the name substance indicates and asserts.

If abuses of language were not inevitable, I should be tempted to urge philosophers to revert to the etymological and scholastic sense of the words object and objective, making them refer to whatever is placed before the mind, as a target to be aimed at by attention. Objective would then mean present to imagination ; and things would become objects of thought in the same incidental way in which they become objects of desire. But I will content myself with returning in my own person to the correct use of the word substance for whatever is self-existent, and with bestowing the term object on occasion upon any substance, essence, event, or truth, when it becomes incidentally the theme of discourse.

Substances are called things when found cut up into fragments which move together and are recognisable individually ; and things are called substances when their diffuse and qualitative existence is thought of rather than their spatial limits. Flour is a substance and a loaf of bread is a thing ; but there is nothing metaphysical about flour, nor is there any difference of physical status between a thing and the substance of it.

But is not the *materia prima* of Aristotle metaphysical ? Is not the substance of Spinoza metaphysical ? Are not souls and Platonic Ideas, which are also reputed to be substances, perfectly metaphysical ?

Of course : and I shall have occasion, when

surveying the realm of matter, to show that these and other metaphysical entities are only nominal essences, and cannot be the substance of anything.

I think these explanations will suggest to the reader a sufficient answer to the other points raised by the empiricists against belief in substance. Substance does not reduplicate natural objects, but is identical with them. What it might be said to reduplicate (or rather to back up and to render significant) would be given essences. Certainly known substances, and other known objects, require to be posited by animal faith on occasion of intuitions, as that which these intuitions report. But there is hardly any reduplication here. Such representation as there is, is probably quite heterogeneous in aspect from its original, and even when—as in memory or a historical romance— some specious similarity is presumed, it is a highly selective and idealised reproduction, in a wholly different medium from the represented facts, and possessing utterly different functions and conditions of being. Nature in being discovered is not reproduced, but acquires a new dimension, and is extraordinarily enriched. Matters are ludicrously reversed if it is imagined that a pure spirit contemplating essences could *invent* a body and a world of matter surrounding it ; the body exists first, and in reacting on its environment kindles intuitions expressive of its vicissitudes ; and the commentary is like that which any language or chronicle or graphic art creates by existing. Substance is the speaker and substance is the theme ; intuition is only the act of speaking or hearing, and the given essence is the audible word. Substance is on the same plane of being as trees and houses, but, like trees and houses, it is on an entirely different plane of being from the immediate terms of experience (which are essences) and from experience itself (which is spirit thinking).

As to the reproach that substance, because it is not an appearance presented exhaustively, must remain unconceived and inconceivable, it rests on a false ideal of human knowledge. Intuition of essence is not knowledge, but fancy and mental sport : and if logic and mathematics are called sciences, they are such only as expansions of given hypotheses according to given rules may be sciences, as there is a science of chess. They are not *true* nor human, except in the special form in which actual discourse and actual bodies happen to illustrate them. A preference for dialectic over knowledge of fact (which is knowledge of substance) may manifest a poetical and superior spirit, as might a preference for music over conversation ; but it would be vain and suicidal for human knowledge to transfer that ideal to the general interpretation of experience. Substance being the object set before me in action, pursuit, and investigation cannot be antecedently in my possession, either materially or intellectually ; it confronts me as something challenging respect and demanding study ; and its intrinsic essence must remain always problematical, since I approach it only from the outside and experimentally. The essences by which it is revealed to me, and the hypotheses I frame about its nature, are so many provocations for me to manipulate and examine it, and to call it by various humorous names, expressive to me of its strange habits. My natural curiosity, if I am a healthy young animal, will prompt me to do this eagerly, and to turn my first luminous impressions into triumphant dogmas ; but to pure spirit, when that awakes, all this faith and knowingness will seem childish.

To pure spirit substance and all its ways must remain always dark, alien, and impertinent. From the transcendental point of view, which is that of spirit, substance is an unattainable goal, or object-as-such, being posited, not possessed. Only essences please this jealous lover of light, and seem to it sufficient; it hates faith, existence, doubt, anything ulterior. Substance and truth offend it by their unnecessary claims ; it would gladly brush them aside as superstitious obsessions. What ghostly thing, it says to itself, is this Speaker behind the voice, this Meaning behind the vision, this dark Substance behind the fair appearance ? Substance interrupts and besets the spirit in its innocence, and in its mad play ; one substance, which it calls the flesh, torments it from below, and a kindred substance, which it calls matter, prods, crushes, and threatens it from without. God also, another substance, looms before it, commanding and forbidding ; and he is terrible in his wrath and obscurity, until it learns his ways. Yet, as religion shows, it is possible for the spirit to be tamed and chastened. The fear of substance may be the beginning of wisdom ; and accustomed to the steady dispensations of that power, the spirit may grow pious and modest, and happy to be incarnate. God will then become in its eyes a source of protection and comfort and daily bread, as all substance is to those who learn how to live with it. When the lessons of experience are thus accepted, and spirit is domesticated in the world, the belief in substance explains everything ; because *if* substance exists, a perpetual dependence in point of destiny, and a perpetual inadequacy in knowledge are clearly inevitable, and soon come to seem proper and even fortunate.

As knowledge advances, my conception of substance becomes a map in which my body is one of the islets charted : the relations of myself to everything else may be expressed there in their true proportions, and I shall cease to be an egotist. In the symbolic terms which my map affords, I can then plan and test my actions (which otherwise I should perform without knowing it) and trace the course of other events ; but I am myself a substance, moving in the plane of universal substance, not on the plane of my map ; for neither I nor the rest of substance belong to the realm of pictures, nor exist on that scale and in that flat dimension. How we exist and what we are substantially must accordingly remain a problem to the end ; even if by chance I should ever hit upon the essence of substance, nothing could test or maintain that miraculous moment of clairvoyance. The only sphere in which clairvoyance is normal is the sphere of mental discourse, one part of which may survey another in the very terms in which the other unrolled itself in act ; as I may faithfully rehearse my own past or future thinkings, or those of men of my own mind. The probability of such clairvoyance diminishes as the similarity of structure and substance between me and the other creature diminishes ; and it vanishes altogether where life dies down ; so that in respect to inorganic substance I am indeed reduced to arbitrary symbols, at which that substance, if it could know them, would laugh. Yet for my purposes in studying inorganic substance (which is not interesting to me in itself) these symbols do very well : they arise on occasion of substantial events, and therefore appear in the same historical sequence ; so that in surveying the order of my symbols I learn the order of real events, though my pictures certainly are not portraits of their substance. Yet even the pictorial quality of these symbols expresses true variations and variety in the substance of myself : it falls and rises with my life. For this reason the map I draw of the universe in my fancy, when I grow studious, becomes a truer and truer map, rendering the movement of substance within and without me with increasing precision, though always in an original notation, native to my senses and intellect.

False ideals of knowledge are also involved in the contention that the hypothesis of substance does not help to explain appearances, and even renders appearances inexplicable. What is explanation ? In dialectic it is the utterance, in further words or images, of relations and terms implied in a given essence : it is the explication of meanings. But facts have no meaning in that sense. Essences implied ideally in their essences need never become facts too : otherwise the whole realm of essence would have to exist in act, and it would be impossible so much as to begin the survey of that horrible infinitude, for lack of any principle of emphasis to give me a starting-point, and create a particular perspective. No : facts are surds, they exemplify fragments of the realm of essence chosen for no reason : for if a will or reason choosing anything (say the good) were admitted, that will or reason would itself be a groundless fact, and an absolute accident. Existence (as the least insight into essence shows) is necessarily irrational and inexplicable. It cannot, therefore, contain any principle of explanation *a priori* ; and substance, as I understand the term, being what exists in itself, it must be also (to borrow the rest of Spinoza's definition of it) what is understood through itself, that is, by taking its own accidental nature as the standard for all explanations. If substance were some metaphysical principle, some dialectical or moral force, it might be expected to " explain " existence as a whole ; but it ought not then to be called a substance ; at best it would be a harmony or music which things somehow made. Such a harmony would not exist in things bodily and individually, rendering their essences existential, but would supervene upon them and float through them, like those principles which certain moody metaphysicians have dreamt of, as solving the riddle of the universe, and have called Sin, Will, Duty, the Good, or the Idea. Substance, as I understand the word, is nothing of that sort. It is not metaphysical, but simply whatever the physical substance may be which is found in things or between them. It therefore cannot "explain" these things, since they are its parts or instances, and it is simply their substance. They have one, since they may be cut up, ground into powder, dissolved into gases, or caused to condense again before our eyes; and if they are living things, we may observe them devouring and generating one another, the flux of substance evidently running through them, and taking on recurrent forms. When these habits of nature are taken (as they should be taken) as the true principle of explanation, the belief in substance does become a great means of understanding events. It helps me to explain their place, date, quality, and quantity, so that I am able to expect or even to produce them, when the right substances are at hand. If they were detached facts, not forms regularly taken on by enduring and pervasive substances, there would be no knowing when, where, of what sort, or in what numbers they would not assault me; and my life would not seem life in a tractable world, but an inexplicable nightmare.

I shall be thought a silly philosopher to mention this, as if it were not obvious; but why do so many wise philosophers ignore it, and defend systems which contradict it?

Finally, even if, in a moment of candour, the friend of phenomena was inclined to allow that substance, so understood, was neither metaphysical nor undiscoverable nor useless for explaining events, he might still urge that the belief in substance creates an insoluble difficulty, because opposite to substance appearance rises at once like a ghost; and how shall this ghost be laid or what room shall be found for it in the world of substance which we have posited?

In other words, substance, by hypothesis, is the source of appearances : but how, remaining substance, can it ever produce them ?

Here again the objection arises out of false demands. As at first substance was condemned on the ground that knowledge should possess its object as intuition does its data (a demand which would rob knowledge of all transitive force), so now substance is condemned on the ground that causation should be dialectical and that reality should be uniform, so that if substance exists nothing should exist except substance. Whence these absurd postulates ? In the first place, reality (since it includes the realm of essence) is infinitely omnimodal ; and even when reduced to existence it may certainly take on as many dimensions and as many varieties as it likes. Substance is not more real than appearance, nor appearance more real than essence, but only differently real. When the word reality is used invidiously or eulogistically, it is merely in view of the special sort of reality which the speaker expects or desires to find in a particular instance. So when the starving gymnosophist takes a rope for a serpent, he misses the reality of that, which is lifeless matter ; when the tourist gazing at an Arabic scroll calls it a frieze, he misses the reality of that, which is a pious sentiment ; and when the millionaire buys a picture for its antiquity and its reputation, he misses the reality of that, which is a composition. When substance is asserted, appearance is not denied ; its actuality is not diminished, but a significance is added to it which, as a bare datum, it could not have.

In the second place, in so far as causation is not sheer magic imputed by laying a superstitious emphasis on those phases which interest me most in the flux of things, causation is the order of generation in nature : whatsoever grows out of a certain conjunction in things, and only out of that conjunction, may be said to be caused by it. Nothing that happens is groundless, since whatever antecedents it actually has are adequate to produce it. Yet all that happens is marvellous, because like existence itself it is unfathomable, and, if we abstract from our familiarity with it, almost incredible. But the antecedents, the consequents, and the connection between them are equally remarkable in this respect, and equally perspicuous. The schoolboy will be delighted to learn how the refraction of the sun's rays paints the rainbow on a shower, or on the spray of the waves ; the farmer will perfectly understand that chickens are hatched from eggs ; and I for one (though other philosophers are less fortunate) can perceive clearly that when animals react upon things in certain ways these things appear to them in certain forms ; and the fact that they appear does not seem to me (so simple am I) to militate against their substantial existence.

Certainly neither the awakening of intuition, nor the character of the essences that appear, can be deduced dialectically from the state of the substance which produces them ; but dialectic traces the implication of one essence in another and can never issue from the eternal world. It is perfectly impotent to express, much less to explain, any change or any existence. If dialectic ruled the world, all implications would always have been realised, no movement would have been possible, and the very discourse that pursues dialectic would have been congealed and identified from the beginning with the essence which it describes. Existence, change, life, appearance, must be understood to be unintelligible : on any other assumption the philosopher might as well tear his hair and go mad at once. But when that assumption has been duly made, and dialectic has been relegated to an innocuous dignity, the blossoming of substance into appearance becomes the most amiable of mysteries.

If instead of admitting this evident and familiar kindling of mind in nature, which makes the charm of childhood, of morning, and of spring, I supposed that mind could animate no material body, and that the flame of spirit could rise from no natural hearth, I should not have a more intelligible world on my hands, but only a very miserable and ghostly one. I should be foolishly shutting myself up in myopic ignorance of that great world which is not mine nor like me, although I belong to it and feed on it unawares. Why should I think it philosophical to be so unintelligent, or to assert that appearances are the only possible realities, when these appearances themselves do their very best to inform me of the opposite ? For though the poor things can't be actually more than they are, they arrange themselves and troop together in such a manner that, if I make the least beginning in understanding them, I gather that they are voices of self-evolving things, on the same plane of reality as myself. Indeed, without such a background to lend them a subterranean influence over my own being, they would be unmeaning creations, and every transition from one to another of them would be arbitrary. If I am told that appearances are but loosely and unintelligibly bound to substance, I may reply that without substance appearances would be far more loosely and unintelligibly bound to one another. Appearances are at least conventional transcripts of facts ; they are expressions of substance which may serve as signs of its movements ; but what relation, moral or habitual, would each appearance, if taken absolutely and not as significant of things, retain to the other appearances that in dreaming or waking might follow upon it ? None whatever : it is only in its organs and its objects that experience touches anything continuous or measurable and possesses a background on which to piece together the broken segments of its own orbit. That substance should be capable of attaining to expression in appearance is a proof that substance is fertile, not that it is superfluous. On the contrary, it is certain that if I knew the essence of substance, and if I made nature the standard of natural necessity, the emergence of appearance in the form and on the occasions in which it emerges would seem to me necessary and inevitable.

CHAPTER XXI

SUBLIMATIONS OF ANIMAL FAITH

ANIMAL faith, being an expression of hunger, pursuit, shock, or fear, is directed upon *things* ; that is, it assumes the existence of alien self-developing beings, independent of knowledge, but capable of being affected by action. While things are running on in the dark, they may be suddenly seized, appropriated, or destroyed. In other words, animal faith posits substances, and indicates their locus in the field of action of which the animal occupies the centre. Being faith in action and inspired by action, it logically pre-supposes that the agent is a substance himself, that can act on other things and be affected by them ; although temporally the substantial existence of the self may not be posited until later, as one of the things in the world of things. Meantime in this animal faith, and even in the choice of one essence rather than another to be presented to intuition, spirit suffers violence, since spirit is inherently addressed to every-thing impartially and is always, in its own principle, ready to be omniscient and just. For by spirit I understand simply the pure light or actuality of thought, common to all intuitions, in which essences are bathed if they are given. At first, as we see in children, spirit is carried away by the joy of doing or seeing anything ; it adopts any passion unquestion-ingly, not being a respecter of persons nor at all squeamish ; it is innocently happy in accepting any task and watching any world, if the body welcomes it. Ultimately, however, the spirit may come to wonder why it regards all things from the point of view of one body in particular, which seems to have no pre-rogative over the others in their common realm. Justice and charity will then seem to lie in rescinding this illegitimate pre-eminence of one's own body : and it may come to be an ideal of the spirit, not only to extend its view over all time and all existence, but to exchange its accidental point of view for every other, and adopt every insight and every interest : an effort which, by a curious irony, might end in abolishing all interests and all views.

Such moral enlightenment is dangerous to animal life, and incidentally to the animal faith on which the recognition of existing things hangs in the first place. If the qualms and ambitions of spirit prevailed in any-body altogether, as they tend to do in the saint and even in the philosopher, he would not be able to halt at the just sympathy by which, preserving animal faith, he would admit and respect the natural interests of others as he does his own. He would be hurried on to rebel against these natural interests in himself, would call them vain or sinful, since the spirit of itself could never justify them, and would initiate some discipline, mortifying the body and transfiguring the passions, so as to free himself from that ignominy and bondage. He would not succeed : but for speculative purposes I will suppose for a moment that he succeeded. What would occur ? He would be happier fasting than eating, freezing than loving. Not sharing the impulses of his body, he would regard it as a ridiculous mechanism ; and the bodies of others would be ridiculous mechanisms too, with which he could feel no sympathy. His sympathy, if it survived at all, would be sublimated into pity for the spirits chained to those bodies by their sin and ignorance, and perhaps not even struggling to be free, but suffering in those prisons perpetual pain and dishonour. He might aspire to save the spirit in others as in himself; but hardened to his own animal vicissitudes he would be steeled to theirs (a result even easier to accomplish), and would be all scorn and lamentations for the life of the world.

I suspend all consideration of this moral issue, and revert to the variations which animal faith may undergo during this long and always imperfect transformation.

Things when they are posited are known to be substances. It would be impossible for a child to be frightened without implicitly believing in a substance at hand; and it would be impossible for him to attempt to frighten other people (as children like to do in play) without implicitly assuming that he is a substance himself. But though his assurance of substance, in both cases is complete, his knowledge of it is superficial. In conceiving his own nature especially, he begins building at the wrong end, from the weather-cock down, not from the foundations up. Although in action he identifies himself with his body, as also in vanity and all the passions, yet when he asks himself deliberately *what* he is, he may be tempted to say that he is his thoughts. Or, less analytically, he may feel that he is a soul, a living spiritual power, a deep will at work in his body and in the world; and though what he posits in other things is primarily their physical presence, he will conceive this substance of theirs, particularly when they are animals, in the same moral terms in which he conceives himself. He will imagine them to be souls, passionate powers, wills guiding events. He will not think people spirits to the exclusion of their bodies, but will conceive their persons confusedly, as souls inhabiting and using bodies, or as bodies breaking out into some thought or passion which, once existing, agitates and governs the body that bred it.

Such a thought or passion, while evidently animating the body and expressing its situation, does not exactly lie within the body ; to localise it there with any literalness or precision is absurd ; and a man feels in his own case that his thoughts and passions *come* into his heart, that they are influences visiting him, perhaps demons or obsessions. He thinks they may pass from one man to another, or perhaps exist suspended and ambient, in the form of gods or mighty laws. Hence the notion of spiritual substances ; a self-contradictory notion at bottom, because substance is a material and spirit is an entelechy, or perfection of function realised ; so that (if I may parody Aristotle), if a candle were a living being, wax would be its substance and light its spirit. Nevertheless, in the history of philosophy, and even in current discourse, the notion of spiritual substance was unavoidable. In the haste of practical life, I count the lights without counting the candles. Feelings and thoughts pass for the principles of action ; I inevitably stop there, and conceive my enemy as an evil purpose, and my contradictor as a false thought. And it is in these imagined thoughts and purposes that I lodge the power which, in action, I am contending with : although I should be truly contending with ghosts, and trying to drive essences out of the realm of essence (where each is immovable) if I did not oppose that power or defeat that purpose in the precise places and bodies in which it operates. The spirit can be confused with substance only when it is spirit incarnate. Animal faith could hardly light on such metaphysical objects unless it was called forth by a material influence, to which animal faith is the natural response ; but the mind has but vague notions of what a material influence can be, and therefore attributes the substantiality of which it is intimately aware to hybrid essences floating before it : hence superstition, myth, metaphysics, and the materialisation of words.

It is a task for natural philosophy to remove these ghosts, by discovering the true movement of that living substance on which animal faith *means* to be directed, the substance on which the animal depends and on which he can act. But the human mind naturally breathes its own atmosphere of myth and dialectic, and evidence of fact pierces this atmosphere with difficulty, only after much experience of error. Gradually the wiser heads see that all substances fall together into one system called nature ; and then various metaphysical substances, which at first seem to inhabit or compose nature, are discovered to be modes of the single familiar substance called matter. The second Book of *Realms of Being* will be devoted to this subject ; meantime, I will here draw up a list of the chief false substances which human faith may rest on when the characteristic human veil of words and pictures hides the modes of matter which actually confront the human race in action, and which there- fore, throughout, are the *intended* object of its faith.

1. *Souls*.—These are essentially moral forces, that is, passions or interests not necessarily self-conscious, conceived as magically ruling animal bodies and dictating their acts.

This notion fuses three different things, belonging to three distinct realms of being. The first is a mode of matter, the inherited mechanism and life of the body, which I am calling the psyche. This is a true dynamic unit, forming and using the outer organs of the body, a system of habits relatively complete and self-centred ; but it is only the fine quick organisation within the material animal, and not a different thing. This is the original soul which savages conceive as leaving the body in sleep or death, itself a tenuous body of similar aspect and powers ; because they feel that bodily life and action have a principle which is not visible on the surface, and yet they have no means of conceiving this principle except as an image or ghost of that very body which it is needed to control. Were wandering souls and ghosts more often met with and studied, the question of the true souls of these creatures would present itself anew : for nothing would be found on the surface of a ghost to explain its words or its motions, and it would soon be observed to give up the ghost in its turn. Even in spirit-land the judicious would have recourse in the end to a behaviourist psychology. For at the other extreme of human philosophising, the material psyche re-appears. Observation can trace back motions only to other motions, and outward actions to activities hidden within, but essentially no less observable ; so that the mechanism of the body and its habits are really the only conceivable mainspring of its behaviour. The soul again becomes a subtler body within the body : only that instead of a shadow of the whole man, even as in life he stood, it is a prodigious net-work of nerves and tissues, growing in each generation out of a seed.

Habit, though it is a mode of matter, has a unity or rhythm which reappears in many different in-stances : it is a form not of matter but of behaviour. Matter makes a vortex which reproduces itself, and plays as a unit amongst the other vortices near it ; and the eye can follow the pleasing figures of the dance, without discerning the atoms or the laws that compose it. Now the habits of animals exercise a strong influence, sympathetic or antipathetic, over the kindred observer. He feels what those habits seek ; he reads them as purposes, as tendencies, as efforts hostile or friendly to the free play of his own habits. The soul agitating those bodies is therefore in his eyes more than another ghostly body, which might quit them ; it is a passion or a will which is expressed there. And this unit of discourse, which if actual belongs to the realm of truth, he regards superstitiously as a substance and a power. He fancies that he himself is a will and a power reacting upon other wills and powers : as if these habits or relations could be prior to the terms that compose them, or could create those terms. It is this element in the notion of souls that becomes predominant in the belief in gods and in devils. Something subjective and moral, the dramatic value which habits in nature have for the observer, is projected by him, and conceived as a metaphysical power creating those habits. Passions, in men, are often arrested on words. They are often arrested, as in poetic love, upon images. And yet the magic of images and words is vicarious : they would be empty, did not subtle material influences flow through them, and hide behind them, rendering them exciting to the material soul of the observer, who in his poetic ecstasy may think he is living in a pure world of discourse.

Finally, in the notion of souls there is a projection of mental discourse : this, when it really exists in animals, is a mode of spirit. Animal life sometimes reaches its entelechy in a stream of intuitions, expressive of its modifications by the presence of other bodies, or by the ferments of its own blood. These modes of spirit are in themselves intangible, unobservable, volatile, and fugitive ; and if anything actual, about which truth and error may arise, may be called unsubstantial, they are as unsubstantial as possible. But as they arise in the operations of substance, and are read into these operations when a sympathetic being observes them, they seem to be a part of what is observed. But they are in quite another dimension of being, in the realm of spirit ;

and spirit, or the intuitions in which it exists, is not a part of the substance on which animal faith is directed, nor a mode of it, nor a natural substance at all. It cannot by any possibility be met with in action, perceived, fought with, nor (if we consider it from within, in its own being) can it be lodged anywhere in space nor even in time. It belongs to nature only by its individual outlook and moral relevance : and we may say of it only by courtesy that it lodges in the place and time which its organ occupies and in the world which, by affecting that organ, enters into its specious perspectives. When a man believes in another man's thoughts and feelings, his faith is moral, not animal. Such a spiritual dimension in the substances on which he is reacting can be revealed to him only by dramatic imagination ; only his instant sympathy can shape, or can correct, his notion of them. In origin, these tertiary qualities of bodies, imputed to them by literary psychology (which is an exercise of dramatic insight) are as superstitious and mythical as the purposes and powers of magical metaphysics ; but the intuitions assigned to other people are *possible* existences, as those metaphysical chimeras are not ; and when the creature that imputes the intuitions and the one that has them are the same, or closely akin and close together, he may be absolutely clairvoyant in imputing them. The mind as conceived by literary psychology, or as represented by dramatic historians, is hypothetical discourse, composed of what this psychology calls sensations, ideas, and emotions. It *may* exist, or may have existed, very much as conceived ; it would be a substance if idealism were true ; but in fact it is a translation into moral terms, rapid, summary, and prophetic, of an animal life going on very laboriously and persistently in the dark ; and this animal life is itself no special substance, but a special mode or vortex in the general substance of nature.

2. *Master-types*, *or Platonic Ideas.*—This is an assimilation of substances to their names. Words and grammar are professedly notes indicating the identities and relations of things ; but in practice everything, in being expressed, is conventionalised. The terms of discourse mark only the forms which things wear on the average, or at their best, or approximately ; and in discourse these conventional terms soon acquire their own identity and relations, and form a pattern quite different from that of their objects. Philosophers, who necessarily employ language, are like naturalists who should study zoology only in a farmyard : the jungle would disconcert them. An argumentative and dialectical mind trusts its verbal logic : but a logic, however cogent in itself, is always of problematical application to facts, since it describes only one possible world out of an infinite number, and (unless it is secretly founded on observation) is not likely to describe the actual one. The logicians themselves, when men of open mind, notice this fact and lament it ; and they bear the actual world a great grudge for showing so little fidelity to their principles. It is false, they are convinced, to its true nature, to the ideal it ought to realise, to the function which you see at every turn that it is endeavouring to fulfil. So that the dialectician can easily become an idealist of the Platonic type, by conceiving that the substance of things is not the moving matter that to-day is one thing and to-morrow another, and that never is anything perfectly, but that this matter is only what the voice is to a song, or a book to its message or spirit—a treacherous and subordinate vehicle of expression ; whereas the true object to look for, the source of the applicability of words to facts at all, is the eternal nature which an actual thing may illustrate : so that the form of things and not their matter is their true substance or οὐσία.

This substantiation of ideals, besides leaning on language, leans on a sort of pragmatism or utilitarianism. Things are called beds if people may sleep well upon them, and bridles if they serve to rein in a horse : this function is their essence, in so far as they are beds or bridles at all, and they are excellent in proportion to the perfection with which they fulfil this function. And here an ascetic and supernaturalistic motive begins to play a part in Platonism. For since the substance and excellence of things lie *merely* in their moral essence, or in the fulfilment of the function designated by their names, all superfluous ornaments, all variations, all hybrid combinations are monstrous. Things should have only the barely necessary matter in them, and that wholly obedient to the mastering form. What am I saying ? Need things have any matter in them at all ? What could be more ideal than the idea itself, or more perfect than the function exercised by magic, and without an instrument ? Away, then, with all material embodiments of ideas, even if these embodiments seem perfect for a moment. Being material, they will be treacherous and unstable : there will be some alloy of imperfection in them, some unreality. Fly, then, to the heaven of ideas, absolute and eternal, as the realm of essence contains them. There at last you will find the substance which in this world of phenomena you sought in vain. Things are only appearances ; in minding and loving them, and thinking they can wound us, we are befooled ; for the only bread that can feed the soul is celestial, and the only death that can overtake her is moral disintegration and the darkness of merely existing without loyalty to what she ought to be.

This is good ethics : not because our ideal is our substance nor because our soul in heaven is our true self, but because life is a harmony in material motions, reproducing themselves, and happiness is a consciousness of this harmony ; so that substance would have no value and its formations no name but for the choice they make of some eternal essence to embody, and the purity with which they manifest it. But the flux of substance is by no means limited to producing but one type of perfection, or one circle of types. The infinite is open to all variations ; and any particular idea is so far from being the substance of things, that it acquires its ideal prerogative, as a goal of aspiration, only when substance has blindly chosen it as a practicable harmony tending to establish itself and to recur in the local motions of that substance ; and nowhere else, and not for a moment longer, does any eternal essence possess any authority, express any aspiration, or even seem to exercise any power.

3. *Phenomena.*—When master-types were regarded as the true objects of knowledge, the instances of these types found in the natural world were called their appearances or phenomena ; but they were not conceived to be unsubstantial images, thrown off by the celestial type impartially into all parts of space, like rays from a luminary. Phenomena were understood to be existences, confined to particular places and times ; indeed, in contrast to the superior sort of being possessed by the types in heaven, these phenomena were existences *par excellence* : and it was to them that the philosophy of Heraclitus, that admirable description of existence, continued to apply. That phenomena appeared was therefore not the doing of the types alone : these, from their eternal seats, rained down influence and, as it were, a perpetual invitation to things to imitate and to mirror them ; but before this invitation could be accepted, or this influence gathered and obeyed, matter must exist variously distributed and predisposed ; so that of all the Ideas, equally radiating virtue, here one and there another might find expression, and that imperfectly and for a time only.

Phenomena, then, for Platonism, are simply things : and they are called appearances not because they are supposed not to exist except in the mind, but because they are believed to be copies of an original in heaven far more ideal and akin to the mind than themselves : and also perhaps because they are so unstable and indefinable, that they elude our exact knowledge and betray our affections.

Phenomena, however, were supposed to be revealed to us by sense, whereas thought revealed their types : and this way of putting things has led to a shift in the meaning of the word phenomenon, so that in modern times it has been confused with what is called an idea in the mind. Sense would not reveal phenomena in nature (where Plato supposed them to arise) if sense meant passive intuition. It would then reveal essences only : that is, just what Plato found thought to reveal : only that being merely æsthetic intuition, and not thought about nature and politics and moral life, the essences revealed would not be Platonic Ideas ; for these were only such essences as expressed the categories of Greek speech, the perfections of animals, or the other forms of the good. But sense, as opposed to dialectic, meant for the ancients animal perception and faith : it included understanding, sagacity, and a belief in matter : indeed, common speech identified immersion in sense with materialism. Modern philosophers have conceived sense passively, as mere sensation or feeling or vision of inert ideas : and the word phenomenon has sometimes been attracted into the same subjective vortex, and has come to mean a datum of intuition. So that phenomenalism suggests less a belief in the phenomena of nature than a disbelief in them, and a reduction of all natural events to images in particular minds.

The other, and proper, meaning of phenomenon seems to be retained by the positivists, who deprecate metaphysics, and even literary psychology, and wish to be satisfied with the data of science. But why use the word phenomenon for an event or an existence that is substantial, and manifests nothing deeper ? Is it because another substance, not internal to those events and existences, is supposed to exist somewhere and to be unknowable ? Or is it because the laws of nature, raised to a magical authority, are made manifest or phenomenal in the facts ? Or is it because the positivists are at heart rather afraid of the psychological critics of knowledge, and by calling things and events phenomena think that they may pass for critics themselves, no less prudent and scientific than if they talked of immediate experience or of ideas in the mind ? If so, it is a sorry expedient and a poor defence. If phenomena are essences given in intuition they are not the objects nor the themes of science, nor the facts or events in nature : and essences, such as the absolutely unprejudiced and unpractical mind may behold them, are the last things on which a positivist should pin his faith. As to immediate experience, conceived as an existing process or life, and as to ideas in the mind, they are names for discourse—the theme of just that literary psychology which the positivist disdains. And if phenomena are simply things, as they were to Plato, the positivist (who does not regard things as weak efforts of nature to realise divine Ideas) should not call them phenomena, but substances ; unless indeed he is a metaphysician without knowing it, and believes in some unknowable substance which is not in things.

4. *Truth.*—Memory presents many a scene which is not substantial, as is the world before me now : yet this *now* is fleeting, and the unsubstantiality which vitiates the past is in the act of invading the present. Is not the pre-eminence of the present, then, an illusion, and is not the reality that panorama which

all those presents would present when equalised and seen under the form of eternity ? Is not the invidious actuality of any part of things a mere appearance, and is not the substance of them all merely their truth ?

This suggestion of memory is reinforced by the suggestions of doubt, of disputation, and of information by hearsay. In our perplexities we seem always to be appealing to a metaphysical plenum or standard, which we call the truth : there all facts are not only evident, but judicial : they settle our quarrels : they correct our ignorance : they vindicate our faith. To the discoursing mind, therefore, present things and material forces may come to seem of little consequence, negligible and unsubstantial in comparison with the truth which remains immovable, while things pass before it like clouds across the constellations.

This is legitimate tragedy : the truth is the realm of being to which the earnest intellect is addressed. The senses and passions may feed on matter, and fancy may sport in the wilderness of essence : to the earnest intellect the one exercise seems instrumental and the other wasteful : what concerns it is the truth. But why is mere experience though it may fall short of truth, relevant to truth, and helpful in discovering it ? And why is play of fancy, or definition of mere essences, not an avenue to truth ? Because the truth, if not a substance, is a luminous shadow or penumbra which substance, by its existence and movements, casts on the field of essence : so that unless a substance existed which was more physical than truth, truth itself would have no nucleus, and would fade into identity with the infinite essence of the non-existent. The truth, however nobly it may loom before the scientific intellect, is ontologically something secondary. Its eternity is but the wake of the ship of time, a furrow which matter must plough upon the face of essence. Truth must have a subject-matter, it must be the truth about something : and it is the character of this moving object, lending truth and definition to the truth itself, that is substantial and fundamental in the universe. A sign that truth is simply fact, though described under the form of eternity, is the heat and haste of men in asserting what they think true. It is an object of animal faith, not of pure contemplation.

5. *Fact.*—Those who appeal to fact with unction are philosophers justly dissatisfied with theory and discourse : they are looking in the direction of substance. Yet in the conception of fact there is an element of an opposite kind, for fact is supposed to be obvious as well as fundamental. Not substance, says the empirical philosopher, which indeed would be the fact if it existed, but immediate fact, however unsubstantial, if I can only be sure of it. Unfortunately, the immediate datum is not a fact at all, but an essence : and even the intuition of that essence, which he may say is the fact he means, is only a bit of discourse or theory : the very thing of which he was so distrustful, and from which his common sense was appealing to the facts. The love of fact indeed has its revenges, and the word comes sometimes to be used for inarticulate feeling or intuition of the unutterable—a perfectly possible and rather common intuition. But at this point a triple confusion perhaps arises between the given essence of the unutterable, the incidental intuition of that essence, and the substance of the natural world which the philosopher is trying to discover. The unutterableness of the given essence is absurdly transferred to this substance, which would need to be no less articulate than appearance, if appearance was to arise from it or express it at all. Such a formless substance is as far as possible from being the object of animal faith posited in action and described in perception spontaneously and more

deliberately in theory and discourse. It is as far as possible from being a fact. And the intuition (which *is* a fact) will yield cold comfort to the philosopher who wanted "facts" rather than intuitions. The facts he wanted were things, and he has been looking for them in the wrong direction.

More often, however, fact is a name for any pronounced and conspicuous feature of the natural world, or event assumed to occur in that physical medium ; so that such a fact may well be a mode of substance. It obviously could neither arise nor be discovered except in a context no less substantial than itself ; for if each fact was a detached existence it would form a universe by itself, and the eulogistic title of fact could not belong to it with any better right than to any intuition. Intuitions, discourse, theories too, taken bodily, are facts ; but if they had no locus in nature, they could convey no knowledge of fact, being insignificant sensations or isolated worlds, occurring at no assignable time.

Fact, therefore, when honestly pointed to without metaphysical interpretation, means a thing or an event against which the speaker has indubitably run up : as it is a fact that the Atlantic Ocean separates Europe from America, or that men die. If understood not to mean such natural facts, but rather the impressions or notions of the mind that notes them, facts become an impossible sublimation of things : either actual intuitions, revealing not facts but essences : or alleged intuitions postulated by literary psychology (which assumes the natural world, without confessing it, as the field in which these intuitions are deployed) ; or finally an undiscoverable atom of sentience cut off from all relations in a metaphysical void. Such an atom, although it would be a substance in an absolute sense, if it existed, yet could neither act nor be acted upon, and therefore would not be the sort of substance that a practical mind, in love with facts, would be tempted to believe in.

6. *Events*.—Although things rather than events are the object of animal faith, ordinarily it is some event that calls attention to a thing : and it is intelligible that philosophers, reverting to the study of nature after their long quarantine in psychological scepticism, should dare to speak of events as constituting the woof of nature, before they dare to speak of them as things in flux or as modes of substance. Yet events can be nothing less. Events are changes, and change implies continuity and derivation of event from event : otherwise there might be variety in existence, but there could be no variation, since the phases of the alleged changes would not follow one another. This continuity and derivation essential to events suffice to render them events in substance, or changes in things. Both the medium of events (requisite to render any two events successive or contiguous) and the quantitative heritage of each (which it derives from the quantity of its antecedents) are substantial. Not so any event taken separately, and conceived merely as a passage of attention from one essence to another : for though the intuition spanning this transition would be a fact, neither it nor the terms it played with would be events. I can imagine an exception to this principle, if a total event exists including the whole process of creation. Such a total event (also any minute irreducible event if such existed) would be actually identical with a changing thing or a substance in flux. But every intermediate event would have arbitrary limits, being composed of minor events and embedded in greater ones. Perhaps there is no total and no rudimentary event : the men of science must decide that point if they can, although I am not confident, that after they had decided it on the best of evidence, their decision would prevent the flux of nature from

stopping, if they said it must go on, or from going on, if they said it must stop. However, the mere possibility that there should be no comprehensive and no least event shows on what slippery ground we stand if we attempt to make events the ultimate objects of belief. They are really only half of what changing existence implies : the other half is substance.

In the effort to halt at events without positing things there is some vestige of the psychological confusion which identifies intuition with the essences present to it. An intuition may present a specious event : it does not follow that it is an event itself, or occurs in time. Intuitions would indeed not be events if they had no locus in physical time, and were not members of a series of events occurring in quite another realm of being from the visionary events which those intuitions might picture. In order to be events in physical time (even so to speak by marriage) intuitions must have organs which are parts of the moving substance of nature. Otherwise they would be pure spirits, out of time, and out of relation to one another. They are events only because a natural event, not an intuition, envelops them and lends them a natural status. Were they only specious events present to another intuition they would not be events at all, but eternal essences contemplated by an eternal mind.

Nevertheless, the notion of events comes very near to that of things, as posited and required in action, and as analysed in physics. The substance of these things is, by definition, the ground of changing appearance and the agent in perpetual action : it is therefore essentially in flux. I cannot say whether this flux is pervasive, so that nothing whatever in substance remains for any time unchanged, the constant element in it being only a constant form or quantity of change : but on the level and scale of human experience, substance is everywhere the substance of events, not of things immutable. If Heraclitus and modern physics are right in telling us that the most stable of the Pyramids is but a mass of events, this truth about substance does not dissolve substance into events that happen nowhere and to nothing : that supposition, on the contrary, would paralyse the events. If an event is to have individual identity and a place amongst other events, it must be a change which substance undergoes in one of its parts. Otherwise, like facts and truths taken hypostatically, events would be metaphysical abstractions, utterly incompatible with that natural status which must belong to the things posited by animal faith in the heat of action —the only things in which there is any reason for believing.

CHAPTER XXII

BELIEF IN NATURE

BELIEF in substance, I have seen, is inevitable. The hungry dog *must* believe that the bone before him is a substance, not an essence ; and when he is snapping at it or gnawing it, that belief rises into conviction, and he would be a very dishonest dog if, at that moment, he denied it. For me, too, while I am alive, it would be dishonest to deny the belief in substance ; and not merely dishonest, but foolish : because if I am observant, observation will bring me strong corroborative evidence for that belief. Observation itself, of course, assumes a belief in discourse and in experience ; it assumes that I can recognise essences, remembering their former apparitions and contexts and comparing the earlier with the present instance of them, or with the different essences which now appear instead. When I survey my experience in this way, the order of appearances, as memory or presumption sets it before me, will confirm the suasion which these appearances exercised singly, and will show me how very well grounded was the instinct which told me, when I saw some casual essence, that it was a sign of something happening in an independent, persisting, self-evolving, indefinitely vast world. If experience, undergone, imposes belief in substance, experience studied imposes belief in nature.

The word nature is sometimes written with a

capital, as if nature were some sort of deity or person : and in ancient philosophy and common speech, powers and habits are attributed to nature which imply a certain moral idiosyncrasy in that personage. Poets also praise nature, and theologians rehearse her marvellous ways, in order to show that she could not have fallen into them of her own accord. All this mythology about nature is natural, and perhaps shows a better total appreciation of what nature is than would a precise physics. The precision of physics is mathematical ; it defines an essence ; and the attribution of this mathematical essence to nature, however legitimate, is sure to overlook many properties which belong to her just as truly, and appear in the realms of truth or of spirit. One such property, at least, is fundamental, and is better expressed by personifying nature than by describing her movements mathematically, I mean, her constancy, the assumption that we may trust her to be true to herself. In science, some observed or some hypothetical process is studied and the method or law of it is ascertained : but there is nothing particularly scientific in the presumption that this process is all that is going on in the given case, or that it will recur in other cases. What is called the uniformity of nature is an assumption made, in respect to the future, without any evidence, and with proportionately scanty evidence about the past : where experience confirms it in some particular, the confirmation itself is good for those instances, up to that time : it tells me nothing of anything beyond, or of the future. The source of my confidence is animal faith, the same that inspires confidence in a child towards his parents, or towards pet animals ; and the whole monstrous growth of human religion is an extension of this sense that nature is a person, or a set of persons, with constant but malleable characters. As experience remodels my impulses, I assume that

the world will remain amenable to my new ways ;
the convert feels he is saved ; the philosopher thinks
he has found the key to happiness ; the astronomer
tells you he has measured the infinite, and perhaps
rolled it up upon itself, and put it in his pocket.
They all express the infantile conviction that nature
cannot be false to what they have already learned or
instinctively affirmed of it : making nature a single
and quasi - personal entity, bound tragically to its
past, and pledged more or less wilfully to a particular
future. It is this sense that the world, like a person,
has a certain vital unity, and remains constant or at
least consequential in its moral aspects, that is expressed by calling it nature. Like a being born of a
seed, it has a determinate form, and a normal career,
a *nature*, which it cannot change.

What evidence is there for the existence of nature,
in this sense of the word ? If I speak of the universe
at large, there can be no evidence. Of course the
universe must be what it is, it must have a character,
it must exemplify an essence ; but taken as a whole, it
may be a chaos, in which nothing is predeterminate,
nor progressive, nor persistent, and in which the
parts are self-centred and the events spontaneous.
A philosopher who took his own life as a model for
conceiving all other things, ought perhaps to incline
to this view ; because he is himself, transcendentally
speaking, an absolute centre, and being ignorant of
the sources of his thoughts and actions, may presume
that they have no sources. If under these circumstances he still has the weakness (for it would be a
weakness) to believe in anything else, say in other
monads, he would doubtless allow them an equal
liberty ; so that in his universe of monads there would
be no common space, no common time, no common
type of character or development, no mutual influence
or kindred destiny. I think the inner life of animals,

if we treated each as a moral romance, apart from its physical setting and influence, would actually present such a chaos : especially if we imagine what may be the lives of creatures in other parts of the stellar universe, or out of any relation with ourselves at all. Such a loose universe could not properly be called nature. It would not have given us birth, it would not have nurtured us, it would not surround us with any constant influences or familiar aspects, it would not bring any seeds to maturity for our encouragement or warning.

Evidences for the existence of nature must be sought elsewhere, in a region which a monadologist would regard as internal to each monad, in that the substances posited by me in obedience to my vital instincts seem to me to behave as if they were parts of nature. Nature is the great counterpart of art. What I tuck under my pillow at night, I find there in the morning. Economy increases my possessions. People all grow old. Accidents have discoverable causes. There is a possible distinction between wisdom and folly. But how should all this be, and how could experience, or the shocks that punctuate it, teach me anything to the purpose, or lend me any assurance in life not merely a reinforced blindness and madness on my part, unless substances standing and moving in ordered ways surrounded me, and I was living in the midst of nature ? Certainly a partial sceptic like Berkeley, closing one eye in the interests of a sentimental religion, may conceive that nature is not a system of evolving substances round him affecting his own growth, but a perpetual illusion, like a dream : a story told him in the dark, a consecutive miracle of grace or of punishment by which a divine spirit dazzles and conducts his spirit, without any medium or any occasion. But if this fairy-tale is to hold good, and to justify the arts of life and maintain the distinction between vice and virtue, I must be able to discern the ways of Providence in their routine; everything will happen exactly as if nature existed, and unrolled itself in a mechanical, inexorable, and often shocking way; my idealism will merely allow me to admit miracles, and to hope that to-morrow everything will be well. If I regard the world of appearance as a mask which the deity wears inevitably, the very essence of the creator being to create such a world, the difference between belief in God and belief in nature will be merely verbal, and I may say with Spinoza, *Deus sive natura*. If on the contrary God is approachable in himself and would prove a better companion than nature and sweeter to commune with, why should he terrify me or delude me with this unworthy disguise? Why should he have preferred to manifest himself by creating appearances rather than by creating substances? What secret necessity could have compelled him to create anything at all, or whispered in his ear these irresponsible designs? If nature behaves as nature would, is it not simply nature? If God were there instead would he not behave like God? Or if I say that I have no right to presume how God should behave, but that wisdom counsels me to learn his ways by experience, what difference remains between God and nature, and are they more than two names for the same thing?

If by calling nature God or the work of God, or the language in which God speaks to us, nothing is meant except that nature is wonderful, unfathomed, alive, the source of our being, the sanction of morality, and the dispenser of happiness and misery, there can be no objection to such alternative terms in the mouth of poets; but I think a philosopher should avoid the ambiguities which a too poetical term often comports. The word nature is poetical enough: it suggests sufficiently the generative and controlling function, the endless vitality and changeful order of the world in which I live.

Faith in nature restores in a comprehensive way that sense of the permanent which is dear to animal life. The world then becomes a home, and I can be a philosopher in it. Perhaps nature is not really constant, nor single ; unless indeed I so stretch and eviscerate the notions of unity and constancy as to apply them to the total aspect of nature, under the form of eternity, however incoherent and loose the structure of that totality may be. But in this æon, in this portion or special plane of space, a sufficient constancy is discoverable : far greater than my scope can cover, or my interest require. It is inattention and prejudice in men, not inconstancy in nature, that keeps them so ignorant, and the art of government so chaotic. Whenever a little persistent study of nature is made (as recently in the interest of mechanical inventions) rapid progress at once follows in the arts : and art is the true discoverer, the unimpeachable witness to the reality of nature. The master of any art sees nature from the inside, and works with her, or she in him. Certainly he does not know *how* he operates, nor, at bottom, *why* he should : but no more does she. His mastery is a part of her innocence. It happens so, and within limits it prospers. To that extent he has assurance of power and of support. It is a faith congruous with his experience that if he could bend his faculties more accurately to their task, nature would prove indefinitely tractable : and if a given animal with special organs and a special form of imagination can progressively master the world, the fact proves that the world is con-natural with him. I do not mean that it favours his endeavours, much less that it is composed as his fancy pictures it ; I mean only that his endeavours express one of the for- mations which nature has fallen into, for the time in equilibrium with the surrounding formations ; and that his ideas too are in correspondence with the sphere of his motions, and express his real relations. The possibility of such correspondence and such equilibrium proves that nature exists, and that the creature that sustains them is a part of nature.

CHAPTER XXIII

EVIDENCES OF ANIMATION IN NATURE

THE sense that nature is animate, and in particular that men and brutes have feelings and thoughts, stands in greater need of criticism than of defence. I assume it before my notions of substance or of nature are clearly formed, and before I can distinguish animate from inanimate being. I assume it, not because it is at all evident or probable in itself, but because I fetch the materials for all my inchoate conceptions from my own sensibility : and in discourse (which I am busy with from the beginning) I unwittingly interweave the notion of animation in gathering my experience of essences and of things. I attribute an existence to these essences which is proper only to the light of intuition travelling over them : and I attribute to these substances moral attributes and sensuous perspectives also borrowed from my running discourse. This subjective matrix and envelope of all my knowledge, though I may overlook it, underlies knowledge to the end ; so that I shall never cease to conceive nature as animate and brutes and men as walking thoughts and passions until I have advanced very far in scepticism. Even then, except in deliberate theory, my apprehension of nature will be fabulous and dramatic ; so that now that I have officially reinstated my faith in nature, faith in the animation of nature will tend to slip in unannounced ; somewhat as when an exile is amnestied or a foreigner naturalised, his parasites (if any) are silently admitted too. Yet this is not, or need not be, the law ; and as it is legality in opinion that here occupies me, I will inquire whether evidence of animation (even supposing that nature is animate in fact) could by any possibility be found at all ; and having cleared up that point, I will inquire further under what control, and with what chances of truth, I may imaginatively attribute animation to nature in the absence of all evidence.

Why do I attribute animation to myself, that is, to my body ? That my spirit discovers a world with my body in it, is not the question ; the why of that would be a metaphysical enigma obviously insoluble, arising out of a trick of thought and inapt application of categories. The point is why, when I feel a pain, I suppose that it is my back or my stomach that aches, and not simply my spirit. I think we may distinguish two reasons. One is that the pain is an element in the perception of my back or stomach ; it is instinct with the loudest and most urgent animal faith ; and it imperatively summons my attention to those obscure regions, and makes me wonder what is happening there. The other reason is that the pain may be associated with another observed event in which my body appears as an integral element, as when my back aches because I am being thrashed. My nobler thoughts are also known to animate my body for this external reason. It is my tongue or gesture that announces them, even to myself. Bad observers, who suppose themselves to see or to discourse without intervention of their eyes or larynx, imagine that they are essentially disembodied spirits, to whom all things are directly perspicuous, and that only a hateful invention of philosophers, called introjection or bifurcation, has put their minds inside their bodies.

Whether incarnation is or is not a hateful fatality to spirit, I will not discuss here ; but that spirit *is* incarnate, that it lodges in the body and looks forth from it on the world, is a fact easily ascertained by closing the eyes, taking a glass of wine, or blushing at having made a fool of oneself.

Faith in memory (which is involved in dialectic and in perception) also reveals to me what animation means, and obliges me to assert its existence. In dialectic and in perception I assume that recurrent views are being taken by me of an object identical with itself if an essence, or continuous with itself if a substance. Such recurrent intuitions or mentions of the terms of discourse are posited in primary memory, as well as in reversion to the past after an interval of forgetfulness. This remembrance is remembrance of animation. It posits thought, cognitive, synthetic, immaterial ; but it posits it as having occurred in particular conjunctions at particular times, in the vicissitudes of a particular body, my own, in a material world. These alleged past intuitions could not be kept apart in memory, nor assumed to have been spaced at longer or shorter intervals of time, nor to have been enacted in a particular order, unless they were attributed to the past career of myself, an animal in the natural world, and grafted upon recognisable material situations and actions to which those intuitions were relevant. Nature is the canvas on which, in memory, I paint the perspective of my personal experience. Even a fictitious memory, or a false experience like that of a dream, is recognisable as having had a natural occasion and date, and as painting a particular incredible perspective of the same world. Otherwise, I should not think I was remembering my past thoughts, but I should be merely contemplating certain fresh essences.

By animation, then, I understand material life

quickened into intuitions, such as, if rehearsed and developed pertinently, make up a private experience. The question whether nature is animate does not regard its substance, but its moral individuation. In how many places is experience being gathered ? What evidence have I that nature thinks and feels, or that the men and animals think and feel who people nature ?

I must discard at once, as incompatible with the least criticism, the notion that nature or certain parts of nature are known to be animate because they *behave* in certain ways. The only behaviour that can give proof of thinking is thinking itself. If I have ever conceived intuition or discourse at all, and obtained assurance of its existence, it has been in my own person, by knowing what I mean and am meaning, what I feel and have felt ; and this posited discourse of mine has assumed, in my estimation, the character of animation of my body, by virtue of two additional dogmas which I have accepted : first, the dogma that I am a substantial being far deeper than my discourse, a psyche or self ; and second, the dogma that this substantial being is in dynamic interplay with a whole environing system of substances on the same plane with itself. In this way I have come by my initial instance of animation in nature, on the model of which I am able to conceive animation in its other parts.

Now it is obvious that in many parts of nature, and especially in the language and gestures of men of my own race, I find a setting for mental discourse exactly similar to the setting into which I have put my own intuitive experience ; so that their words and actions vividly suggest to me my own thoughts. Just as formerly I incorporated or introjected my thoughts into my own body, so now I incorporate or introject them into the bodies moving before me. Imitation contributes to this dramatic understanding, because I am not confined, when I watch other people, to remembering what I may have felt when I was in some such situation, or spoke some such words. Their attitude and language may be novel to me, and, as we say, a revelation : that is, they may by contagion arouse unprecedented intuitions in me now, which I unhesitatingly attribute to them, perhaps with indignation, swearing that such thoughts never could enter my head, and that I am utterly incapable of such feelings. Yet this is psychologically false ; because if I understand a thought, I have it ; though it may be present as an essence only, without carrying assent. The irony of the case is that very likely I alone have it, and not at all the man to whom I attribute it. Even the closest similarity in language or action is a very abstract similarity, and the concrete and full current of our two lives, on which the quality of intuitions depends, may be quite different. All dramatic understanding of which I am capable is, by hypothesis, *my* discourse. The most contagious feelings, the clearest thoughts, of others are clear or contagious only because I can readily make them my own. I cannot conceive deeper thoughts than my lead can plumb, nor feelings for which I lack the organ.

Of course by an abuse of language the word animation might be used to designate certain kinds of behaviour ; as the ancients said the world was rational because orderly, or the stars intelligent because they kept going round in circles. So men or women might be said to think because they speak or because they write books ; but it does not follow. The inner patter of words which I sometimes hear in myself, and which mystics have called inspiration or (when explosive) speaking with tongues, is not thinking ; it is an object of perception that may suggest to me a subsequent thought, although often I see, when I try to frame this thought, that those words make nonsense. It is very true, as I shall find later, that the fountain of my thoughts, that is, the self who thinks them, is my psyche, and that movements there guide my thoughts and render them, as the case may be, intelligent, confused, rapid, or halting; also supply my language, dictate my feelings, and determine when my thinking shall begin and where it shall end. But the light of thought is wanting there, which is the very thinking; and no fine inspection of behaviour nor interweaving of objects will ever transmute behaviour into intuition nor objects into the attention which, falling upon them, turns them from substances or essences into objects of actual thought. By animation I understand the incarnation in nature, when it behaves in these ways, of a pure and absolute spirit, an imperceptible cognitive energy, whose essence is intuition.

Animation being essentially imperceptible and not identical with any habit or act observable in nature, I see the justification of those philosophers who say that animals, in so far as science can study them, are machines; the discoverable part of them is material only, just as is the rest of nature. But this conclusion being implied only in my transcendental approach to nature and my knowledge of her, can in no way prejudge her real constitution, which may be as rich and superabundant as it likes, without asking my leave or reporting to me her domestic budget; nor is anything thereby prejudged in respect to the nature or laws of matter, or the simplicity of its mechanism. Nature seems, at first blush, to have many levels of habit, irreducible to one another. As it was only the other day that a hint reached us that gravity and the first law of motion might be forms of a single principle, so it may be long before we hear from the biologists that chemical reaction and animal instinct are forms of the same habit in matter. Even if they are irreducible to a common principle, they will be two habits of matter, and nothing more. There is a sense in which every different manifestation of a principle makes a different principle of it, as the language of the United States might be said not to be English ; but the alienation of form from form is not a departure from the habit of flux, complication, dissolution, and temporary arrest which runs through all language. So nature might be said to have as many irreducible habits as she has forms ; but she has an underlying ground of transformation as well, on which, I suspect, all those forms are grafted, no more wilfully diverse nor artificially identical than leaves upon a tree ; and when wiseacres, every day of every year, bring their ponderous proofs that life is not mechanical, that the human will, by exception, is free, and that a single disembodied purpose, by magic, makes all things dance contrarily to their own nature, nature and I wink at each other.

The circumstance that animation, by its very essence, must be imperceptible, and not a link in any traceable process, renders disproof of animation anywhere as impossible as proof of it. Those sentimentalists are short-sighted who in their desire to show that mind is everywhere, introduce mental forces or interpolate mental links into their account of physical economy. If thought was discoverable only in the gaps between motions, no thoughts would be discoverable in nature at all. I do not presume to say that nature can make no leaps ; I leave her to her own paces ; but I do not conceive that, if she shows gaps (and what is a gap but a transition ?) I must hasten to fill them up for her with alleged intuitions. She may be made up of gaps ; they may be her steps ; and if her limbs have strength in them for leaping, let her leap. Her strides are their own measure ; it is only my ignorance or egotism that can regard any of her ways as abnormal. Thought in myself has not appeared when my system has broken down, but rather when it has established quick connections with things about it. Thought is not a substitute for physical force or physical life, but an expression of them when they are working at their best. If I may read animation into nature at all, it must be where her mechanisms are sustained, not where they are suspended.

There are two stages in the criticism of myth, or dramatic fancy, or the sort of idealism that sees purposes and intentions and providential meanings in everything. The first stage treats them angrily as superstitions ; the second treats them smilingly as poetry. I think that most of the specific thoughts which men attribute to one another are proper only to the man who attributes them ; and the fabulous psychology of poets and theologians is easy to deride ; it has no specific justification, and the moral truth of it can be felt only by a poetic mind. Nevertheless, when I consider the inevitable egotism that presides over the understanding of mind in others, I fear that I am no less likely to sin through insensibility to the actual life of nature, because my tight little organs cannot vibrate to alien harmonies, than I am to sin through a childish anthropomorphism which makes not only the beasts but even the clouds and the gods discourse like myself. After all, in attributing human thoughts (with a difference) to non-human beings, I recognise their parity with myself ; my instinct is courteous or even humble ; and my incapacity to speak any moral language but my own is not only inevitable but healthy and manly. Sages and poets who have known no language but their own have a richer savour and a deeper wisdom than witlings full of miscellaneous accomplishments ; and when once

I have renounced the pedantic demand that poetry should be prose, I can allow that myth may do the life of nature less injustice than would the only alternative open to me, which is silence.

This may be said also about myth regarding myself, I mean the attempts of memory, self-justifying eloquence, or psycho-analysis to unfold the riches of my own mind. How much do I know about my own animation ? How much is too fluid to be caught in the sieve of memory, and to be officially assimilated in verbal soliloquy ? When any one asks me what I think of the weather or of the Prime Minister, does my answer report anything that I have previously thought ? Probably not ; my past impressions are lost, or obliterated by the very question put to me ; and I make bold to invent, on the spur of the moment, a myth about my sentiments on the subject. The present play of language and fancy may fairly bring to a head old impressions or ruling impulses ; or I may have occasion to amend my first expression, and obeying a fresh suggestion of my fancy I may say : No, no ; I meant rather this. Whereupon I may proceed laboriously to create and modulate my opinion, groping perhaps to a final epigram, which I say expresses just what I think, although I never thought it before. Such is my discourse when I am really thinking ; at other times it is but the echo of language which I remember to have formerly used, and therefore call my ideas. It is clear therefore that even in expressing my own mind when I conceive what I have felt, I have never really felt just that before. My report is an honest myth.

The case is even worse as regards the emotions. What do I mean when I talk of my desires, my intentions, or the motives of others ? Unless these things have been actually expressed in words which I can recover, neither I nor my neighbours have ever had in mind anything like what I now impute. My desire, in fact, was only a certain alacrity in doing things which afterwards I see leading to a certain issue ; my intention (if actual at all) was a certain foresight of what the issue might be ; and the motives I assigned to others were but ulterior events imagined by me which, if they had actually occurred, I suppose would have pleased those people. The sensations or ideas which may really have accompanied their actions, or the words they may really have pronounced mentally, are not within my view ; if they were they would probably go a very little way towards preparing or covering the actions in question. These actions would turn out to have had subjectively a totally different complexion from that which I assign to them on seeing them performed. The very abundance and incessant dream-like prolixity of mental discourse render it elusive ; and the discourse I officially impute to myself or to others is a subsequent literary fiction, apt if it suggests the events which the discourse concerned, or excites the emotions which those events if witnessed would have produced on an observer of my disposition, but by no means a fiction patterned on any actual former experience in anybody. My sense of animation in nature, and all my notions of human experience, are dramatic poetry, and nothing else.

There is therefore no direct evidence of animation in nature anywhere, but only a strong propensity in me to imagine nature discoursing as I discourse, because my apprehension of nature is embedded in my miscellaneous, serried, and private thoughts, and I can hardly clear it of the mental elements—emotional, pictorial, or dramatic—which encrust it there. On reflection, however, and by an indirect approach, I can see good reason for believing that some sort of animation (not at all such animation as my fancy attributes to it at first) pervades the organic world ; because my psyche is animate ; she is the source and seat, as I have learned to believe, of all my dis- course ; yet she is not different, in any observable respect, from the psyches of other animals, nor is she composed of a different sort of substance from the common earth, light, and air out of which she has arisen, and by which she is fed ; she is but one in the countless generations of living creatures. Accordingly the analogy of nature would suggest that the other living creatures in the world are animate too, and discourse privately no less assiduously and absurdly than I do. It would even suggest that all the substance of nature is ready to think, if circum- stances allow by presenting something to think about, and creating the appropriate organ.

The character of this universal animation, or readiness to think, is inconceivable by me, in so far as its organs or objects differ from my own. The forms of it are doubtless as various as the forms of material being ; a stone will think like me, in so far as it lives like me. There are actually some men, a few, who do live like me ; these also think like me ; and we can truly understand one another and impute to one another the very thoughts we severally have. In such rare cases, human discourse in one man may bring perfect knowledge (though no evidence) of human discourse in another. In doing the same things and uttering the same words we have instant assurance of unanimity, in this case not deceptive ; especially when it is not the outer stimulus that is common to us, but the spontaneous reaction. For this reason gesture or poetry is a better index to feeling than are events or information coming to men from outside. What happens to people will never tell you how they feel ; the alien observer misunder- stands everything ; only he understands a mind who can share its free and comic expression. For this reason too psychology is not a science unless it becomes the science of behaviour, when it ceases to be an account of mental discourse and traces only the material life of the psyche. In order to communicate thought it is necessary to impose it.

Moral communication becomes surer in proportion as the discourse to be reproduced involves more articulation, more distinct turns by which fidelity in the rendering may be controlled. The form of thought is more easily transferable than its sensuous elements. Under the same sky, with the same animal instincts, with the same experience of love, labour, and war, one race or one age may be totally cut off from another in spirit. The same language, on the contrary, the same myths, legends, or histories, may be carried almost unchanged across seas and ages, and may unite the happier moments of distant peoples. The range of such moral unity is also easy to discover ; I may learn how far languages or religions are diffused ; they create recognisable moral communities. Indeed, they tyrannise over society, so social are they ; and they often render people who share the same spirit cruel to heretics of their own flesh and blood. The humanities may prove inhuman ; and the less articulate, more robust instincts of mankind may take their revenge by stamping the humanities out. Yet the barbarians, who are not divided by rival traditions, fight all the more incessantly for food and space. Peoples cannot love one another unless they love the same ideas.

CHAPTER XXIV

LITERARY PSYCHOLOGY

SCIENTIFIC psychology is a part of physics, or the study of nature ; it is the record of how animals act. Literary psychology is the art of imagining how they feel and think. Yet this art and that science are practised together, because one characteristic habit of man, namely speech, yields the chief terms in which he can express his thoughts and feelings. Still it is not the words, any more than the action and attitude which accompany them, that are his *understanding* of the words, or his *sense* of his attitude and action. These can evidently be apprehended only dramatically, by imitative sympathy ; so that literary psychology, however far scientific psychology may push it back, always remains in possession of the moral field.

When nature was still regarded as a single animal, this confusion extended to science as a whole, and tinctured the observation of nature with some suggestion of how a being that so acts must be minded, and what thoughts and sentiments must animate it. Such myths cannot be true ; not because nature or its parts may not be animate in fact, but because there is no vital analogy between the cosmos and the human organism ; so that if nature is animate as a whole, or in her minute or gigantic cycles, animation there is sure not to resemble human discourse, which is all we can attribute to her. Myth and natural theology are accordingly fabulous essentially and irremediably. If literary psychology is to interpret the universe at large, it can be only very cautiously, after I have explored nature scientifically as far as I can, and am able to specify the degree of analogy and the process of concretion that connect my particular life with the universal flux.

Myth is now extinct (which is a pity) and theology discredited ; but the same confusion subsists in the quarters where it is not fashionable to doubt. History, for instance, is partly a science, since it contains archæological and antiquarian lore and a study of documents ; but it is also, in most historians, an essay in dramatic art, since it pretends to rehearse the ideas and feelings of dead men. These would not be recoverable even if the historian limited himself to quoting their recorded words, as he would if he was conscientious ; because even these words are hard to interpret afterwards, so as to recover the living sentiment they expressed. At least authentic phrases, like authentic relics, have an odour of antiquity about them which helps us to feel transported out of ourselves, even if we are transported in fact only into a more romantic and visionary stratum of our own being. Classic historians, however, are not content with quoting recorded words : they compose speeches for their characters, under the avowed inspiration of Clio ; or less honestly, in modern times, they explain how their heroes felt, or what influences were at work in the spirit of the age, or what dialectic drove public opinion from one sentiment to another. All this is shameless fiction ; and the value of it, when it has a value, lies exclusively in the eloquence, wisdom, or incidental information found in the historian. Such history can with advantage be written in verse, or put upon the stage ; its virtue is not at all to be true, but to be well invented.

Philosophy fell into the same snare when in modern times it ceased to be the art of thinking and tried to become that impossible thing, the science of thought. Thought can be found only by being enacted. I may therefore guide my thoughts according to some prudent rule, and appeal as often as I like to experience for a new starting-point or a controlling perception in my thinking ; but I cannot by any possibility make experience or mental discourse at large the object of investigation : it is invisible, it is past, it is nowhere. I can only surmise what it might have been, and rehearse it imaginatively in my own fancy. It is an object of literary psychology. The whole of British and German philosophy is only literature. In its deepest reaches it simply appeals to what a man says to himself when he surveys his adventures, re-pictures his perspectives, analyses his curious ideas, guesses at their origin, and imagines the varied experience which he would like to possess, cumulative and dramatically unified. The universe is a novel of which the ego is the hero ; and the sweep of the fiction (when the ego is learned and omnivorous) does not contradict its poetic essence. The composition is perhaps pedantic, or jejune, or overloaded ; but on the other hand it is sometimes most honest and appealing, like the autobiography of a saint ; and taken as the confessions of a romantic scepticism trying to shake itself loose from the harness of convention and of words, it may have a great dramatic interest and profundity. But not one term, not one conclusion in it has the least scientific value, and it is only when this philosophy is good literature that it is good for anything.

The literary character of such accounts of experience would perhaps have been more frankly avowed if the interest guiding them had been truly psychological, like that of pure dramatic poetry or fiction.

What kept philosophers at this task — often quite unsuited to their powers — was anxiety about the validity of knowledge in physics or in theology. They thought that by imagining how their ideas might have grown up they could confirm themselves in their faith or in their scepticism. Practising literary psychology with this motive, they did not practise it freely or sympathetically ; they missed, in particular, the decided dominance of the passions over the fancy, and the nebulous and volatile nature of fancy itself. For this reason the poets and novelists are often better psychologists than the philosophers. But the most pertinent effect of this appeal of science to a romantic psychology was the *hypostasis of an imagined experience*, as if experience could go on in a void without any material organs or occasions, and as if its entire course could be known by miracle, as the experiences of the characters in a novel are known to the author.

Criticism of knowledge is thus based on the amazing assumption that a man can have an experience which is past, or which was never his own. Although criticism can have no first principle, I have endeavoured in this book to show how, if genuinely and impartially sceptical, it may retreat to the actual datum and find there some obvious essence, necessarily without any given place, date, or inherence in any mind. But from such a datum it would not be easy to pass to belief in anything ; and if the leap was finally taken, it would be confessedly at the instance of animal faith, and in the direction of vulgar and materialistic convictions. Modern critics of knowledge have had more romantic prepossessions. Often they were not really critics, saying *It seems*, but rebels saying *I find*, *I know*, or empiricists saying *Everybody finds*, *Everybody knows*. Their alleged criticism of science is pure literary psychology, gossip, and story-telling. They are miraculously informed that there are many minds, and that these all have a conventional experience. What this experience contains, they think is easily stated. You have but to ask a friend, or make an experiment, or imagine how you would feel in another man's place. So confident is this social convention, that the natural world in which these experiences are reported to occur, and the assumed existence of which renders them imaginable, may be theoretically resolved into a picture contained in them. Thus the ground is removed which sustained all this literary psychology and suggested the existence of minds and their known experience at all ; yet the groundless belief in these minds, and in copious knowledge of their fortunes, is retained as obvious ; and this novelesque universe is called the region of facts, or of immediate experience, or of radical empiricism. Literary psychology thus becomes a metaphysics for novelists. It supplies one of the many thinkable systems of the universe, though a fantastic one ; and I shall return to it, under the name of psychologism, when considering the realm of matter. Here I am concerned only with the evidence that such masses of experience exist or are open to my inspection.

No inspection is competent to discover anything but an essence ; what social intuition touches is therefore always a dramatic illusion of life in others or in myself, never the actual experience that may have unfolded itself elsewhere as a matter of fact. Yet this dramatic illusion, like any given essence, may be a true symbol for the material events upon which the psyche is then directed ; in this case, the life of other people, or my own past life, as scientific psychology might describe it. A good literary psychologist, who can read people's minds intuitively, is likely to anticipate their conduct correctly. His psychological imagination is not a link in this practical sagacity but a symptom of it, a poetic by-product of fineness in instinct and in perception. Slight indications in the attitude or temper of the persons observed, much more than their words, will suggest to the sympathetic instinct of the observer what those persons are in the habit of doing, or are inclined to do ; and the stock idea assigned to them, or the stock passion attributed to them, will be but a sign in the observer's discourse for that true observation. I watch a pair of lovers ; and it requires no preternatural insight for me to see whether the love is genuine, whether it is mutual, whether it is waxing or waning, irritable or confident, sensual or friendly. I may make it the nucleus of a little novel in my own mind ; and it will be a question of my private fancy and literary gift whether I can evolve language and turns of sentiment capable of expressing all the latent dispositions which the behaviour of those lovers, unconscious of my observation, suggested to me. Have I read their minds ? Have I divined their fate ? It is not probable ; and yet it is infinitely probable that minds and fates were really evolving there, not generically far removed from those which I have imagined.

The only facts observable by the psychologist are physical facts, and the only events that can test the accuracy of his theories are material events ; he is therefore in those respects simply a scientific psychologist, even if his studies are casual and desultory. Whence, then, his literary atmosphere ? For there is not only the medium of words which intervenes in any science, but the ulterior sympathetic echo of feelings truly felt and thoughts truly rehearsed and intended. I reply that whereas scientific psychology is addressed to the bodies and the material events composing the animate world, literary psychology restores the essences intervening in the perception of those material events, and re-echoes the intuitions aroused in those bodies. This visionary stratum is the true immediate as well as the imagined ultimate. Even in the simplest perceptions on which scientific psychology, or any natural science, can be based, there is an essence present which only poetry can describe or sympathy conceive. Schoolroom experiments in optics, for instance, are initially a play of intuitions, and exciting in that capacity ; I see, and am confident and pleased that others see with me, this colour of an after-image, this straight stick bent at the surface of the water, the spokes of this wheel vanishing as it turns. For science, these given essences are only stepping-stones to the conditions under which they arise, and their proper æsthetic nature, which is trivial in itself, is forgotten in the curious knowledge I may acquire concerning light and perspective and refraction and the structure of the eye. Yet in that vast, vibrating, merciless realm of matter I am, as it were, a stranger on his travels. The adventure is exhilarating, and may be profitable, but it is endless and, in a sense, disappointing ; it takes me far from home. I may seem to myself to have gained the whole world and lost my own soul. Of course I am still at liberty to revert in a lyrical moment to the immediate, to the intuitions of my childish senses ; yet for an intelligent being such a reversion is a sort of *gran rifiuto* in the life of mind, a collapse into lotus-eating and dreaming. It is here that the Muses come to the rescue, with their dramatic and epic poetry, their constructive music, and their literary psychology. Knowledge of nature and experience of life are presupposed ; but as at first, in the beginnings of science, intuition was but a sign for material facts to be discovered, so now all material facts are but a pedestal for images of other intuitions. The poet feels the rush of emotion on the other side of the deployed events ; he wraps them in an atmosphere of immediacy, luminous or thunderous ; and his spirit, that piped so thin a treble in its solitude, begins to sing in chorus. Literary psychology pierces to the light, to the shimmer of passion and fancy, behind the body of nature, like Dante issuing from the bowels of the earth at the antipodes, and again seeing the stars.

Such a poetic interpretation of natural things has a double dignity not found in sensuous intuitions antecedent to any knowledge of the world. It has the dignity of virtual truth, because there are really intuitions in men and animals, varying with their fortunes, often much grander and sweeter than any that could come to me. The literary psychologist is like some antiquary rummaging in an old curiosity shop, who should find the score of some ancient composition, in its rude notation, and should sit down at a wheezy clavichord and spell out the melody, wondering at the depth of soul in that archaic art, so long buried, and now so feebly revealed. This curious music, he will say to himself, was mighty and glorious in its day ; this moonlight was once noon. There is no illusion in this belief in life long past or far distant ; on the contrary, the sentimentalist errs by defect of imagination, not by excess of it, and his pale water-colours do no justice to the rugged facts. The other merit that dignifies intuitions mediated by knowledge of things, is that they release capabilities in one's own soul which one's personal fortunes may have left undeveloped. This makes the mainspring of fiction, and its popular charm. The illusion of projecting one's own thoughts into remote or imaginary characters is only half an illusion : these thoughts were never there, but they were always here, or knocking at the gate ; and there is an indirect victory in reaching and positing elsewhere, in an explicit form, the life which accident denied me, and thereby enjoying it *sub rosa* in spite of fate. And there are many experiences which are only tolerable in this dream-like form, when their consequences are negligible and their vehemence is relieved by the distance at which they appear, and by the show they make. Thus both the truth and the illusion of literary psychology are blessings : the truth by revealing the minds of others, and the illusion by expanding one's own mind.

These imaginative blessings, however, are sometimes despised, and philosophers, when they suspect that they have no evidence for their psychological facts, or become aware of their literary flavour, sometimes turn away from this conventional miscellany of experience, and ask what is the substantial texture of experience beneath. Suppose I strain my introspection in the hope of discovering it ; the picture (for such a method can never yield anything but pictures) may be transformed in two ways, to which two schools of recent literary psychology are respectively wedded. One transformation turns experience, intensely gaped at, into a mere strain, a mere sense of duration or tension ; the other transformation unravels experience into an endless labyrinth of dreams. In the one case, experience loses its articulation to the extent of becoming a dumb feeling ; and it is hard to see how, if one dumb undifferentiated feeling is the only reality, the illusion of many events and the intuition of many pictures could be grafted upon it. In the other case experience increases its articulation to the extent of becoming a chaos ; and the sensitive psychology that dips into these subterranean dreams needs, and easily invents, guiding principles by which to classify them. Especially it reverts to sexual and other animal instincts, thus grafting literary psychology (which in this field is called psycho-analysis) again on natural substance and the life of animals, as scientific psychology may report it.

This natural setting restores literary psychology to its normal status ; it is no longer a chimerical metaphysics, but an imaginative version, like a historical novel, of the animation that nature, in some particular regions, may actually have possessed. The fineness and complexity of mental discourse within us may well be greater than we can easily remember or describe; and there is piety as well as ingenuity in rescuing some part of it from oblivion. But here, as elsewhere, myth is at work. We make a romance of our incoherence, and compose new unities in the effort to disentangle those we are accustomed to, and find their elements. Discourse is not a chemical compound ; its past formations are not embedded in its present one. It is a life with much iteration in it, much recapitulation, as well as much hopeless loss and forgetfulness. As the loom shifts, or gets out of order, the woof is recomposed or destroyed. It is a living, a perpetual creation ; and the very fatality that forces me, in conceiving my own past or future, or the animation of nature at large, to imagine that object afresh, with my present vital resources and on the scale and in the style of my present discourse— this very fatality, I say, reveals to me the nature of discourse everywhere, that it is poetry. But it is poetry about facts, or means to be ; and I need not fear to be too eloquent in expressing my forgotten sentiments, or the unknown sentiments of others. Very likely those sentiments, when living, were more eloquent than I am now.

CHAPTER XXV

THE IMPLIED BEING OF TRUTH

FROM the beginning of discourse there is a subtle reality posited which is not a thing : I mean the truth. If intuition of essence exists anywhere without discourse, the being of truth need not be posited there, because intuition of itself is intransitive, and having no object other than the datum, can be neither true nor false. Every essence picked up by intuition is equally real in its own sphere ; and every degree of articulation reached in intuition defines one of a series of essences, each contained in or containing its neighbour, and each equally central in that infinite progression. The central one, for apprehension, is the one that happens to appear at that moment. Therefore in pure intuition there is no fear of picking up the wrong thing, as if the object were a designated existence in the natural world ; and therefore the being of truth is not broached in pure intuition.

Truth is not broached even in pure dialectic, which is only the apprehension of a system of essences so complex and finely articulated, perhaps, as to tax human attention, or outrun it if unaided by some artifice of notation, but essentially only an essence like any other. Truth, therefore, is as irrelevant to dialectic as to merely æsthetic intuition. Logic and mathematics are not true inherently, however cogent or extensive. They are ideal constructions based on ideal axioms; and the question of truth or falsity does not arise in respect to them unless the dialectic is asserted to apply to the natural world, or perhaps when a dispute comes up as to the precise essence signified by some word, such as, for instance, infinity.

When men first invented language and other symbols, or fixed in reflection the master-images of their dreams and thoughts, it seemed to them that they were discovering parts of nature, and that even in those developments they must be either right or wrong. There was a *true* name for every object, a part of its nature. There was a *true* logic, and a *true* ethics, and a *true* religion. Certainly in so far as these mixed disciplines were assertions about alleged facts, they were either right or wrong; but in so far as they were systems of essences, woven together in fancy to express the instincts of the mind, they were only more or less expressive and fortunate and harmonious, but not at all true or false. Dialectic, though so fine-spun and sustained, is really a more primitive, a more dream-like, exercise of intuition than are animal faith and natural science. It is more spontaneous and less responsible, less controlled by secondary considerations, as poetry is in contrast with prose. If only the animals had a language, or some other fixed symbols to develop in thought, I should be inclined to believe them the greatest of dialecticians and the greatest of poets. But as they seem not to speak, and there is no ground for supposing that they rehearse their feelings reflectively in discourse, I will suppose them to be very empty-headed when they are not very busy; but I may be doing them an injustice. In any case their dreams would not suggest to them the being of truth; and even their external experience may hardly do so.

It might seem, perhaps, that truth must be envisaged even by the animals in action, when things are posited ; especially as uncertainty and change of tactics and purpose are often visible in their attitudes. Certainly truth is there, if the thing pursued is such as the animal presumes it to be ; and in searching for it in the right quarter and finding it, he enacts a true belief and a true perception, even if he does not realise them spiritually. What he realises spiritually, I suppose, is the pressure of the situation in which he finds himself, and the changes in his object ; but that his belief from moment to moment was right or wrong he probably never notices. Truth would then not come within his purview, nor be distinguished amongst his interests. He would want to be successful, not to be right.

So in a man, intent experience, when not reflective, need not disclose the being of truth. Sometimes, in a vivid dream, objects suffer a transformation to which I eagerly adapt myself, changing my feelings and actions with complete confidence in the new facts ; and I never ask myself which view was true, and which action appropriate. I live on in perfect faith, never questioning the present circumstances as they appear, nor do I follow my present policy with less assurance than I did the opposite policy a moment before. This happens to me in dreams ; but politicians do the same thing in real life, when the lives of nations are at stake. In general I think that the impulse of action is translated into a belief in changed things long before it reproaches itself with having made any error about them. The recognition of a truth to be discerned may thus be avoided ; because although a belief in things must actually be either true or false, it is directed upon the present existence and character of these things, not upon its own truth. The active object posited alone interests the man of action ; if he were interested in the rightness of the action, he would not be a man of action but a philosopher. So long as things continue to be perceived in one form or another, and can be posited accordingly, the active impulse is released, and the machine runs on prosperously until some hitch comes, or some catastrophe. It is then always the things that are supposed to have changed, not the forms of folly. Even the most pungent disappointment, as when a man loses a bet, is not regarded otherwise than as a misfortune. It is all the fault of the dice; they might and ought to have turned up differently. This, I say to myself, is an empirical world; all is novelty in it, and it is luck and free will that are to blame. My bet was really right when I made it; there was no error about the future then, for I acted according to the future my fancy painted, which was the only future there was. My act was a creative act of vitality and courage; but afterwards things accountably went wrong, and betrayed their own promise.

I am confirmed in this surmise about the psychology of action by the reasoning of empirical and romantic philosophers, who cling to this instinctive attitude and deny the being of truth. No substance exists, according to their view, but only things as they seem from moment to moment; so that it is idle to contrast opinion with truth, seeing that there is nothing, not even things, except in opinion. They can easily extend this view to the future of opinion or of experience, and maintain that the future does not exist except in expectation; and at a pinch, although the flesh may rebel against such heroic subjectivism, they may say that the past, too, exists only in memory, and that no other past can be thought of or talked about; so that there is no truth, other than current opinion, even about the past. If an opinion about the past, they say, seems problematical when it stands alone, we need but corroborate it by another opinion about the past in order to make it true. In other words, though the word truth is familiar to these philosophers, the idea of it is unintelligible to them, and absent altogether from their apprehension of the world.

The experience which perhaps makes even the empiricist awake to the being of truth, and brings it home to any energetic man, is the experience of other people lying. When I am falsely accused, or when I am represented as thinking what I do not think, I rebel against that contradiction to my evident self-knowledge ; and as the other man asserts that the liar is myself, and a third person might very well entertain that hypothesis and decide against me, I learn that a report may fly in the face of the facts. There is, I then see clearly, a comprehensive standard description for every fact, which those who report it as it happened repeat in part, whereas on the contrary liars contradict it in some particular. And a little further reflection may convince me that even the liar must recognise the fact to some extent, else it would not be *that* fact that he was misrepresenting ; and also that honest memory and belief, even when most unimpeachable, are not exhaustive and not themselves the standard for belief or for memory, since they are now clearer and now vaguer, and subject to error and correction. That standard comprehensive description of any fact which neither I nor any man can ever wholly repeat, is the truth about it.

The being of truth thus seems to be first clearly posited in disputation ; and a consequence of this accident (for it is an accident from the point of view of the truth itself under what circumstances men most easily acknowledge its authority)—a consequence is that truth is often felt to be somehow inseparable from rival opinions ; so that people say that if there was no mind and consequently no error there could be no truth. They mean, I suppose, that nothing can be correct or incorrect except some proposition or judgement regarding some specific fact ; and that the same constitution of the fact which renders one description correct, renders any contradictory description erroneous. " Truth " is often used in this abstract sense for correctness, or the quality which all correct judgements have in common ; and another word, perhaps " fact " or " reality," would then have to be used for that standard comprehensive description of the object to which correct judgements conform. But a fact is not a description of itself ; and as to the word " reality," if it is understood to mean existence, it too cannot designate a description, which is an essence only. Facts are transitory, and any part of existence to which a definite judgement is addressed is transitory too ; and when they have lapsed, it is only their essence that subsists and that, being partially recovered and assigned to them in a retrospective judgement, can render this judgement true. Opinions are true or false by repeating or contradicting some part of the truth about the facts which they envisage ; and this truth about the facts is the standard comprehensive description of them—something in the realm of essence, but more than the essence of any fact present within the limits of time and space which that fact occupies ; for a comprehensive description includes also all the radiations of that fact—I mean, all that perspective of the world of facts and of the realm of essence which is obtained by taking this fact as a centre and viewing everything else only in relation with it. The truth about any fact is therefore infinitely extended, although it grows thinner, so to speak, as you travel from it to further and further facts, or to less and less relevant ideas. It is the splash any fact makes, or the penumbra it spreads, by dropping through the realm of essence. Evidently no opinion can embrace it all, or identify itself with it ;

nor can it be identified with the facts to which it relates, since they are in flux, and it is eternal.

The word truth ought, I think, to be reserved for what everybody spontaneously means by it : the standard comprehensive description of any fact in all its relations.   Truth is not an opinion, even an ideally true one ;   because besides the limitation in scope which human opinions, at least, can never escape, even the most complete and accurate opinion would give precedence to some terms, and have a direction of survey ;   and this direction might be changed or reversed without lapsing into error ;   so that the truth is the field which various true opinions traverse in various directions, and no opinion itself.   An even more impressive difference between truth and any true discourse is that discourse is an event ;   it has a date not that of its subject-matter, even if the subject-matter be existential and roughly contemporary ;   and in human beings it is conversant almost entirely with the past only, whereas truth is dateless and absolutely identical whether the opinions which seek to reproduce it arise before or after the event which the truth describes.

The eternity of truth is inherent in it :   all truths— not a few grand ones—are equally eternal.   I am sorry that the word eternal should necessarily have an unction which prejudices dry minds against it, and leads fools to use it without understanding.   This unction is not rhetorical, because the nature of truth is really sublime, and its name ought to mark its sublimity.   Truth is one of the realities covered in the eclectic religion of our fathers by the idea of God. Awe very properly hangs about it, since it is the im- movable standard and silent witness of all our memories and assertions ;   and the past and the future, which in our anxious life are so differently interesting and so differently dark, are one seamless garment for the truth, shining like the sun. It is not necessary to offer any evidence for this eternity of truth, because truth is not an existence that asks to be believed in, and that may be denied. It is an essence involved in positing any fact, in remembering, expecting, or asserting anything; and while no truth need be acknowledged if no existence is believed in, and none would obtain if there was no existence in fact, yet on the hypothesis that anything exists, truth has appeared, since this existence must have one character rather than another, so that only one description of it in terms of essence will be complete; and this complete description, covering all its relations, will be the truth about it. No one who understands what is meant by this eternal being of truth can possibly deny it; so that no argument is required to support it, but only enough intensity of attention to express what we already believe.

Inspired people, who are too hot to think, often identify the truth with their own tenets, to signify by a bold hyperbole how certain they feel in their faith; but the effect is rather that they lead foolish people, who may see that this faith may be false, to suppose that therefore the truth may be false also. Eternal truths, in the mouth of both parties, are then tenets which the remotest ancestors of man are reputed to have held, and which his remotest descendants are forbidden to abandon. Of course there are no eternal tenets: neither the opinions of men, nor mankind, nor anything existent can be eternal; eternity is a property of essences only. Even if all the spirits in heaven and earth had been so far unanimous on any point of doctrine, there is no reason, except the monotony and inertia of nature, why their logic or religion or morals should not change to-morrow from top to bottom, if they all suddenly grew wiser or differently foolish.

At the risk of being scholastic I will suggest the uses to which the word eternal and the terms akin to it might be confined if they were made exact.

A thing that occupied but one point of physical time would be *instantaneous*. No essence is instantaneous, because none occupies any part of physical time or space; and I doubt whether any existence is instantaneous either; for if the mathematicians decide that the continuous or extended must be composed of an infinite number of inextended and non-contiguous units, in bowing to their authority I should retain a suspicion that nothing actual is confined to any of these units, but that the smallest event has duration and contains an infinite number of such units; so that one event (though not one instant) can be contiguous to another.

A given essence containing no specious temporal progression or perspective between its parts would be *timeless*. Colour, for instance, or number, is timeless. The timeless often requires to be abstracted from the total datum, because round any essence as actually given there is an atmosphere of duration and persistence, suggesting the existential flux of nature behind the essence. Colour seems to shine, that is, to vibrate. Number seems to mount, and to be built up. The timeless is therefore better illustrated in objects like laws or equations or definitions, which though intent on things in time, select relations amongst them which are not temporal.

A being that should have no external temporal relations and no locus in physical time would be *dateless*. Thus every given essence and every specious present is dateless, internally considered, and taken transcendentally, that is, as a station for viewing other things or a unit framing them in. Though dateless, the specious present is not timeless, and an instant, though timeless, is not dateless.

Whatsoever, having once arisen, never perishes, would be *immortal*. I believe there is nothing immortal.

Whatsoever exists through a time infinite in both directions is *everlasting*. Matter, time, the life of God, souls as Plato conceived them, and the laws of nature are commonly believed to be everlasting. In the nature of the case this can be only a presumption.

That which without existing is contemporary with all times is *eternal*. Truth is dateless and eternal, but not timeless, because, being descriptive of existence, it is a picture of change. It is frozen history. As Plato said that time was a moving image of eternity, we might say that eternity was a synthetic image of time. But it is much more than that, because, besides the description of all temporal things in their temporal relations, it contains everything that is not temporal at all ; in other words, the whole realm of essence, as well as the whole realm of truth.

CHAPTER XXVI

DISCERNMENT OF SPIRIT

Is the existence of spirit evident to spirit, and involved in the presence of anything ? Is its nature simple and obvious ? I think there is something of which this may be said, but not of spirit ; for by spirit I understand not only the passive intuition implied in any essences being given, but also the understanding and belief that may greet their presence. Even passive intuition is no datum ; there is nothing evident except the given essence itself. Yet, as I have seen above, the mere prolongation of this presence, the recognition of this essence as identical with itself, and the survey of its elements in various orders, very soon impose upon me a distinction between this essence and my intuition of it. This intuition is a fact and an event, as the essence cannot be ; so that even if spirit meant nothing but pure consciousness or the activity of a transcendental ego, it would need to be posited, in view of the felt continuity of discourse, and could not be an element in the given essences. If spirit were defined as the common quality of all appearances, distinguishing them from the rest of the realm of essence which does not appear, spirit would be reduced to an appearance itself. It would be like light, something seen, a luminousness in all objects, not what I understand by it, which is the seeing ; not the coloured lights I may observe, but the exercise of sight as distinguished from blindness.

The common quality of all appearances is not spirit but mere Being ; that simple and always obvious element to which I referred just now as given in all essences without distinction, and which some philosophers and saints have found so unutterably precious. This is all that is common to all possible appearances, considered in themselves ; but animal tension is not altogether absent even in this abstruse contemplation, and the sense that appearances are assaulting *me* thickens my intuition of their essence into an apprehension of existence, which existence, having no idea of myself, I of course attribute to them, or to the abstract common element in their essences, pure Being, which thus becomes in my eyes absolute existence.

The present stimulus that awakens me out of my material lethargy and keeps my attention more or less taut is not spirit, although, of course, the birth of spirit is involved in my awakening. That stimulus is the strain and rumble of the universal flux, audible in my little sea-shell. It preserves the same ground-tone (that of a disturbance or a strain) no matter what image it may bring forth, or even if it brings forth no images but only a pervasive sense of swimming in safety and bliss. This budding sentiment of existence is a recognition not of spirit but of substance, of fact, of force, of an unfathomable mystery.

By spirit I understand the light of discrimination that marks in that pure Being differences of essence, of time, of place, of value ; a living light ready to fall upon things, as they are spread out in their weight and motion and variety, ready to be lighted up. Spirit is a fountain of clearness, decidedly wind-blown and spasmodic, and possessing at each moment the natural and historical actuality of an event, not the imputed or specious actuality of a datum. Spirit, in a word, is no phenomenon, not sharing the æsthetic sort of reality proper to essences when given, nor that other sort proper to dynamic and material things; its peculiar sort of reality is to be intelligence in act. Spirit, or the intuitions in which it is realised, accordingly forms a new realm of being, silently implicated in the apparition of essences and in the felt pressure of nature, but requiring the existence of nature to create it, and to call up those essences before it. By spirit essences are transposed into appearances and things into objects of belief; and (as if to compensate them for that derogation from their native status) they are raised to a strange actuality in thought —a moral actuality which in their logical being or their material flux they had never aspired to have: like those rustics and servants at an inn whom a travelling poet may take note of and afterwards, to their astonishment, may put upon the stage with applause.

It is implied in these words, when taken as they are meant, that spirit is not a reality that can be observed; it does not figure among the *dramatis personæ* of the play it witnesses. As the author, nature, and the actors, things, do not emerge from the prompter's box, or remove their make-up so as to exhibit themselves to me in their unvarnished persons, but are satisfied that I should know them only as artists (and I for my part am perfectly willing to stop there in my acquaintance with them); so the spirit in me which their art serves is content not to be put on the stage; that would be far from being a greater honour, or expressing a truer reality, than that which belongs to it as spectator, virtually addressed and consulted and required in everything that the theatre contrives. Spirit can never be observed as an essence is observed, nor encountered as a thing is encountered. It must be enacted; and the essence of it (for of course it has an essence) can be described only circumstantially, and suggested pregnantly. It is actualised in actualising something else, an image or a feeling or an intent or a belief; and it can be discovered only by implication in all discourse, when discourse itself has been posited. The witnesses to the existence of spirit are therefore the same as those to the existence of discourse; but when once discourse is admitted, the existence of spirit in it becomes self-evident; because discourse is a perusal of essence, or its recurring presence to spirit.

Now in discourse there is more than passive intuition; there is intent. This element also implies spirit, and in spirit as man possesses it intent or intelligence is almost always the dominant element. For this reason I shall find it impossible, when I come to consider the realm of spirit, to identify spirit with simple awareness, or with consciousness in the abstract sense of this abused word. Pure awareness or consciousness suffices to exemplify spirit; and there may be cold spirits somewhere that have merely that function; but it is not the only function that only spirits could perform; and the human spirit, having intent, expectation, belief, and eagerness, runs much thicker than that. Spirit is a category, not an individual being: and just as the realm of essence contains an infinite number of essences, each different from the rest, and each nothing but an essence, so the realm of spirit may contain any number of forms of spirit, each nothing but a spiritual fact. Spirit is a fruition, and there are naturally as many qualities of fruition as there are fruits to ripen. Spirit is accordingly qualified by the types of life it actualises, and is individuated by the occasions on which it actualises them. Each occasion generates an intuition numerically distinct, and brings to light an essence qualitatively different.

Let me suppose, by way of illustration, that there was a disembodied spirit addressed to the realm of truth in general, and seeing all things under the form of eternity. This would be a very special kind of spirit, and many an essence would be excluded from its intuition ; for instance, the essence of surprise. No doubt it would congratulate itself on this incapacity, and say with Aristotle that there are things it is better not to know than to know, at least by experience. The essence of surprise involves ignorance of the future, and it could never be realised, or known by intuition, in a spirit to whom the future had always been known : and to know surprise by experience is the only way of knowing its essence. It might indeed be known by description, and defined as a feeling which animals have when they expect one thing and find another. Such a description may suggest the essence of surprise to me, who know by intuition what it is to expect and to find ; but it would never suggest that essence to a spirit that had only descriptions to go by, and who could reach a conception of " expecting " and of " finding " only in symbols that translated their transitive natures into synthetic pictures. Thus the essence of surprise would remain for ever excluded from intuition in a spirit that saw all things under the form of eternity.

The occasions on which spirit arises in man are the vicissitudes of his animal life : that is why spirit in him runs so thick. In intent, in belief, in emotion a given essence takes on a value which to pure spirit it could not have. The essence then symbolises an object to which the animal is tentatively addressed, or an event through which he has just laboured, or which he is preparing to meet. This attitude of the animal may be confined to inner readjustments in the psyche, not open to gross external observation ; yet it may all the more directly be raised to consciousness in the form of attention, expectation, deliberation, memory, or desire. These sentiments form a moving but habitual background for any particular essence considered ; they frame it in, not only pictorially in a sensuous perspective, but morally, by its ulterior suggestions, and by the way in which, in surveying the whole field of intuition, that particular feature in it is approached or attacked or rejected. In such settings given essences acquire their felt meanings ; and if they should be uprooted from that soil and exhibited in isolation, they would no longer mean the same thing to the spirit. Like a note in a melody, or a word in a sentence, they appeared in a field of essence greater than they ; they were never more than a term or a feature within it. For this reason I imagine that I see things and not essences ; the essences I see incidentally are embedded in the voluminous ever-present essences of the past, the world, myself, the future ; master-presences which express attitudes of mine appropriate not to an essence —which is given—but to a thing—which though not given enlists all my conviction and concern.

Thus intelligence in man, being the spiritual transcript of an animal life, is transitional and impassioned. It approaches its objects by a massive attack, groping for them and tentatively spying them before it discovers them unmistakably. It is energetic and creative, in the sense of slowly focussing its object within the field of intuition in the midst of felt currents with a felt direction, themselves the running expression of animal endeavours. All this intuition of turbulence and vitality, which a cold immortal spirit could never know, fills the spirit of man, and renders any contemplation of essences in their own realm only an interlude for him or a sublimation or an incapacity. It also renders him more conscious than a purer spirit would be of his own spirit. For just as I was able to find evidence of intuition in discourse, which in the motionless vision of essence would have eluded me, so in intent, expectation, belief, and emotion, the being of my thoughts rises up and almost hides the vision of my object. Although I myself am a substance in flux, on the same level as the material thing that confronts me, the essences that reveal my own being are dramatic and moral, whereas those that express the thing are sensuous ; and these dramatic and moral essences, although their presence involves spirit exactly in the same way, and no more deeply, than the presence of the sensuous essences does, yet seem to suggest its presence more directly and more voluminously.

Hence the popular identification of spirit with the heart, the breath, the blood, or the brain ; and the notion that my substantial self and the spirit within me are identical. In fact, they are the opposite poles of my being, and I am neither the one nor the other exclusively. If I am spiritually proud and choose to identify myself with the spirit, I shall be compelled to regard my earthly person and my human thoughts as the most alien and the sorriest of accidents ; and my surprise and mortification will never cease at the way in which my body and its world monopolise my attention. If on the contrary I modestly plead guilty to being the biped that I seem, I shall be obliged to take the spirit within me for a divine stranger, in whose heaven it is not given me to live, but who miraculously walks in my garden in the cool of the evening. Yet in reality, incarnation is no anomaly, and the spirit is no intruder. It is as much at home in any animal as in any heaven. In me, it takes my point of view ; it is the voice of my humanity ; and what other mansions it may have need not trouble me. Each will provide a suitable shrine for its resident deity and its native oracle. It is a prejudice to suppose that spirit is contaminated by the flesh ; it is generated there ; and the more varied its instruments and sources are, the more copiously it will be manifested, and the more unmistakably.

Spiritual minds are the first to recognise the empire of the flesh over the spirit in the senses, the passions, and even in a too vivid imagination ; and they call these influences the snares of the adversary. I think they are right in condemning as vain or carnal any impulses which would disrupt the health of the soul, either directly in the individual body, or indirectly by loosening such bonds with society as are requisite for human happiness. I also think, however, that moralists of this type overlook two considerations of the greatest moment, by which all the metaphysical background of their maxims is removed, and what is reasonable in them is put on a naturalistic basis. One consideration is that, on a small scale and in its own key, every impulse in man or beast bears its little flame of spirit. How much longing, how much laughter, how much perception, how much policy and art in those vices and crimes which the moralist thinks fatal to spirit ! They may render a finer thing impossible (which the moralist should bethink himself to depict more attractively), but in themselves they are full of life and light. For this reason crimes and vices, together with horrible adventures and the pomps and vanities of this wicked world, are the chosen theme of novelists and playwrights ; and the poor public, having hardly any other intellectual pleasure, gloats on these fictions, as an imaginative escape from the moral penury not only of their work, but of their religion. The poets are far more genuine lovers of spirit in this than their mentors, whose official morality is probably quite worldly, and insensible to any actually spiritual achievement, because such achievements are necessarily fugitive, invisible, and unproductive. The devil was an angel essentially; it was only in the complicated politics of this world that he missed his way, and became an enemy of the highest good.

The other consideration that is overlooked is that the spirit which may discern this highest good is itself a natural passion, and not less an expression of the flesh—though more justly and broadly—than the random impulses it condemns. Consider, for instance, the earnestness with which evil is condemned. If this evil is pain, the objection to it could not be more instinctive. Why should pure spirit detest pain? A material accident in the body here absorbs my attention, and strangely persuades me to be utterly rebellious and impatient at being so absorbed. The psyche, or the principle of bodily life, is somehow striving against the event or stimulus which produced the pain (a perfectly harmless essence to contemplate in itself), because the psyche is congenitally a system or cycle of habits which that obnoxious event interrupts. It is this material pressure and effort not to be stifled or rent in any of her operations that the psyche imposes on the spirit, commanding it to pronounce it a terrible evil that she should be rent or stifled. These strange and irrational pronouncements of spirit, calling events good or evil, are accordingly grounded on nothing but on a creeping or shrinking of the flesh. If the evil is moral—the eventual defeat of some ideal I cherish for myself, my children, or my country—what has fixed this ideal, or declared it to be a good? Suppose this ideal is a life glorious and unending; is it not obvious that nothing but the momentum of life, already accidentally working in myself, my children, or my country, could possibly demand life or determine what forms of life would be glorious for us? I will not pursue this topic: if the reader does not understand, he probably never will.

Let me turn to the most intellectual powers of spirit—attention, synthesis, perception. These too are voices .loudly issuing from the heart of material existence, and proclaiming their origin there not only by their occasions and external connections, but by their inmost moral nature. Why does the spirit stop to collect or to recollect anything ? Why not range undisturbed and untrammelled over image after image, without referring one to another or attempting (always in vain) to preserve the design of vanished images, or the order of their appearance, even through the lapse of the sensible elements that filled them in ? Because the animal is forming habits. The psyche is plastic ; no impression can endure unchanged, as if it had been a substantial little thing in itself, and not a mode, a ripple, in an inherited, transmissible, ever rejuvenated substance. Scarcely is the impression received, but it merges in the general sensitiveness or responsiveness of the organ affected, modifying its previous way of reacting on some natural object, an object reported not by that impression alone, but by many others : so that the synthetic unity of apperception (that most radical of transcendental principles) obeys a compulsion peculiar to animal economy, which no pure spirit would need to share, the compulsion to use things as materials, to drop them and forge ahead, or to eat and to digest them : for the drinking in of light through the eyes, or of currents from other organs, thereby rearranging the habits of the nervous system, is very like the consumption of food, restoring the vegetative functions. Synthesis in thought, correlation, scope, or (as the phrase is) taking things in, is laborious piety on the spirit's part in subservience to the flesh. It is the mental fruit of training, of care : an inner possession rewarding an outer fidelity.

Pure spirit would never need to *apperceive* at all ; this is an animal exigency that distracts it from intuition. There is unity in intuition too, of a nebulous sort, as there must be unity in the universe, since it is all there is, however loose its structure or unmarked its limits. Yet in intuition, as in cloud-land, the field is in the act of changing pervasively ; every part shifts more or less. Any feature you may distinguish fades and refashions itself irresponsibly ; and pure spirit would be perfectly content that it should do so. Perhaps, if it was a young spirit, it would positively whip up the hoop, or blow and distend the bubble, for the fun of seeing it run or burst more gloriously ; and it would be happy to think there was no harm done, and nothing left over. The scene would then be cleared for something utterly fresh. The synthetic unity of apperception is something imposed by things on animals, when these things exercise a seductive charm or threaten mischief. Attention cries halt, it reconnoitres, it takes note, it throws a lassoo over the horses of Poseidon, lord of the flux. And why ? Because the organs of spirit are structures ; they are mechanisms instituted in nature to keep doing certain things, roughly appropriate to the environment, itself roughly constant. It is to this approximate fixity of function and habit that spirit owes its distinct ideas, the names it gives to things, and its faith in things, which is a true revelation of their existence—knowledge of them stored for use.

Perception, too, would be a miracle and an impossibility to a spirit conceived as alien to matter. Perception is a stretching forth of intent beyond intuition ; it is an exercise of intelligence. Intelligence, the most ideal function of spirit, is precisely its point of closest intimacy with matter, of most evident subservience to material modes of being. The life of matter (at least on the human scale, if not at every depth) is a flux, a passage from this to that, almost forbidding anything to be simply itself, by immediately turning it, in some respect, into something different. If the psyche were a closed round of motions, the spirit it generated (if it generated spirit at all) would certainly not be perceptive or cognitive, but in some way emotional or musical—the music of those spheres. But the round of motions which the psyche is actually wound up to make must be executed in a changeful and precarious environment, not to speak of changes in her own substance. She must hunt, fight, find a mate, protect the offspring, defend the den and the treasure. Perception, intelligence, knowledge accurately transcribe this mode of being, profoundly alien to repose in intuition or to drifting reverie. Perception points to what it does not, save by pointing, know to exist; knowledge is only of the past or the future, both of which are absent; and intelligence talks and talks to an interlocutor—the mind of another man or god or an eventual self of one's own—whom it can never see and whose replies, conveyed (if at all) through material channels, it is never sure exist morally, or could be understood if they did exist. There is no dilemma in the choice between animal faith and reason, because reason is only a form of animal faith, and utterly unintelligible dialectically, although full of a pleasant alacrity and confidence, like the chirping of birds. The suasion of sanity is physical : if you cut your animal traces, you run mad.

It is impossible to say everything at once, and I have been contrasting intelligence with intuition, as if intuition were less subject than intelligence to physical inspiration, or had an independent source. This is not the case; intuition is itself pathetically animal. Why should I have awaked at all? Can anything, inwardly considered, be more gratuitous than consciousness? I am afraid I must be constituted differently from other people, at least in the reflective faculty, because it astonishes me to hear so many philosophers talking of spirit as if its existence explained itself, and denying the possibility of matter; whereas to me it seems credible, though certainly unnecessary *a priori*, that matter should exist without being consulted, for it cannot help itself, suffers nothing, and has no reason to protest; and its existence is antecedently just as plausible as its non-existence. But the existence of spirit really demands an explanation; it is a tremendous paradox to itself, not to say a crying scandal—I mean from a scientific or logical point of view, because treated as a family secret the scandal is often delicious, and privately it is in this festive and poetic medium that I love to dwell. Spirit, since it *can* ask how it came to exist, has a right to put the question and to look for an answer. And it may perhaps find an answer of a sort, although not one which spirit, in all its moods, will think satisfactory.

Fact can never be explained, since only another fact could explain it: therefore the existence of a universe rather than no universe, or of one sort of universe rather than another, must be accepted without demur. In this very irrationality or contingency of existence, which is inevitable in any case, I find a clue to the strange presence of spirit in this world. Spirit, the wakefulness of attention, could not have arisen of its own accord; it contains no bias, no principle of choice, but is an impartial readiness to know. It never could have preferred one thing to another, nor preferred existence for itself to non-existence, nor *vice versa*. Attention is not a principle that can select the themes that shall attract attention: to select them it must already have thought of them. As far as its own nature is concerned, attention is equally ready to fall on the just and on the unjust; spirit is equally ready to speak any language, to quicken any body, and to adopt any interest. An instance of spirit cannot be determined by spirit itself either in its occasion, its intensity, or the æsthetic character of the essence presented to it. Chance, matter, fate —some non-spiritual principle or other—must have determined what the spirit in me shall behold, and what it shall endure. Some internal fatality, their own brute existence and wilfulness, must be responsible for the fact that things are as they are, and not other-wise. If any instance of spirit was to arise anywhere, the ground of it (if I speak of grounds at all) must have been irrational. Spirit has the innocence of a child ; it pleads not guilty ; at most it has become, without knowing how, an accomplice after the fact. It is astonished at everything. It is essentially, wherever it may be found, unsubstantial and ex-pressive ; it is essentially secondary. Even if in fact some instance of spirit, some isolated intuition, sprang miraculously into being in an absolute void, and nothing else had ever existed or would exist, yet logically and in its own eyes that intuition would be secondary, since no principle internal to spirit, but only brute chance, would be expressed in the existence of that intuition, and in the arbitrary choice of the essence that happened to appear there. Spirit is therefore of its very nature and by its own confession the voice of something else : it speaks not of itself, but of the Father that sent it. I am accordingly prepared to find some arbitrary world or other in existence; and since this arbitrary world obviously has spirit in it, my problem is reduced to inquiring what features, in this arbitrary existing world, can have called spirit forth, and made it their living witness.

I postpone the detail of this inquiry, but I have already indicated how the life of nature is expressed in the chief phases of spirit. Wakefulness, common to all these phases, is itself a witness to animal unrest, appetition, alarm, concern, preparation. It would be inane, as well as impossible, for me to open my eyes, if in looking I did not identify my spirit with my material person in its material predicaments, raising to an actual hypostasis in consciousness its material sensitiveness to outlying things. Electric influences issuing from these allow my organs to adjust themselves before grosser contact occurs ; and then intuition is a premonition of material fusion. Organic systems about to collide send forth this conscious cry or salutation. The current established may prevent a ruder shock, or may precipitate it, according to the prepared instinct of the receivers. The intuition expresses the initial fusion involved in the distant response, as if a ghostly messenger of oncoming things had rushed like a forerunner into the audience chamber, announcing their arrival. It is only messengers that reach the spirit, even in the thick of the fray ; but by lending credence to their hot reports, it can live through the battle, lost in its mists and passions, and thinking itself to give and to receive the blows.

For a man, and especially for a philosopher, to suggest that spirit does not exist may accordingly pass for a delicious absurdity, and the best of unconscious comedy. If it had been some angel that denied it, because in his serenity and selflessness he could not discover that he was alive, we might regard the denial of spirit as the highest proof of spirituality : but in a material creature struggling to see and to think, and tossed from one illusion and passion to another, such a denial seems not only stupid, but ungracious ; for a man ought to be very proud of this dubious spark in his embers, and nurse it more tenderly than the life of a frail child. Nevertheless I think that those who deny the existence of spirit, although their language is rash and barbarous, are honestly facing the facts, and are on the trail of a truth. Spirit is too near them for them to stop at it in their eagerness to count their visible possessions; and when they hear the word used, it irritates them, because they suppose it means some sort of magical power or metaphysical caloric, alleged to keep bodies alive, and to impose purposes on nature; purposes which such a prior spirit, being supernatural and immortal, could have had no reason for choosing. Such a dynamic spirit would indeed be nothing but an immaterial matter, a second physical substance distinguished from its grosser partner only in that we know nothing of it, but assign to its operation all those results which seem to us inexplicable. Belief in such a spirit is simply belief in magic; innocent enough at first when it is merely verbal and childish, but becoming perverse when defended after it has ceased to be spontaneous. I am not concerned with spirit of that sort, nor with any kind of nether influences. The investigation of substance and of the laws of events is the province of physics, and I call everything that science may discover in that direction physical and not spiritual. Even if the substance of things should be sentiency, or a bevy of souls, or a single intense Absolute, it would be nothing but matter to what I call spirit. It would exercise only material functions in kindling the flame of actual intuition, and bearing my light thoughts like bubbles upon its infinite flood. I do not know what matter is in itself: but what metaphysical idealists call spirit, if it is understood to be responsible for what goes on in the world and in myself, and to be the " reality " of these appearances, is, in respect to my spiritual existence, precisely what I call matter; and I find the description of this matter which the natural sciences supply much more interesting than that given by the idealists, much more beautiful, and much more likely to be true. That there is no spirit in the interstices of matter, where the magicians look for it, nor at the heart of matter, where many metaphysicians would place it, needs no proof to one who understands what spirit is ; because spirit is in another realm of being altogether, and needs the being and movement of matter, by its large sweeping harmonies, to generate it, and give it wings. It would be a pity to abandon this consecrated word to those who are grubbing for the atoms of substance, or speculating about a logic in history, or tabulating the capers of ghosts ; especially as there is the light of intuition, the principle of actuality in vision and feeling, to call by that name. The popular uses of the word spiritual support this definition of it ; because intuition, when it thoroughly dominates animal experience, transmutes it into pure flame, and renders it religious or poetical, which is what is commonly meant by spiritual.

CHAPTER XXVII

COMPARISON WITH OTHER CRITICISMS OF KNOWLEDGE

DESCARTES was the first to begin a system of philosophy with universal doubt, intended to be only provisional and methodical ; but his mind was not plastic nor mystical enough to be profoundly sceptical, even histrionically. He could doubt any particular fact easily, with the shrewdness of a man of science who was also a man of the world ; but this doubt was only a more penetrating use of intelligence, a sense that the alleged fact might be explained away. Descartes could not lend himself to the disintegration of reason, and never doubted his principles of explanation. For instance, in order to raise a doubt about the applicability of mathematics to existence (for their place in the realm of essence would remain the same in any case) he suggested that a malign demon might have been the adequate cause of our inability to doubt that science. He thus assumed the principle of sufficient reason, a principle for which there is no reason at all. If any idea or axiom were really *a priori* or spontaneous in the human mind, it would be infinitely improbable that it should apply to the facts of nature. Every genius, in this respect, is his own malign demon. Nor was this the worst ; for Descartes was not content to assume that reason governs the world—a notion scandalously contrary to fact, and at bottom contrary to reason itself, which is but the grammar of human discourse and aspiration linking mere essences. He set accidental limits to his scepticism even about facts. " I think, therefore I am," if taken as an inference is sound because analytical, only repeating in the conclusion, for the sake of emphasis, something assumed in the premise. If taken as an attestation of fact, as I suppose it was meant, it is honest and richly indicative, all its terms being heavy with empirical connotations. What is " thinking," what is " I," what is " therefore," and what is " existence " ? If there were no existence there would certainly be no persons and no thinking, and it may be doubted (as I have indicated above) that anything exists at all. That any being exists that may be called " I," so that I am not a mere essence, is a thousand times more doubtful, and is often denied by the keenest wits. The persuasion that in saying " I am " I have reached an indubitable fact, can only excite a smile in the genuine sceptic. No *fact* is self-evident ; and what sort of fact is this " I," and in what sense do I " exist " ? Existence does not belong to a mere datum, nor am I a datum to myself ; I am a somewhat remote and extremely obscure object of belief. Doubtless what I *mean* by myself is an existence and even a substance ; but the rudimentary phantoms that suggest that object, or that suggest the existence of anything, need to be trusted and followed out by a laborious empirical exploration, before I can make out at all what they signify. Variation alleged, strain endured, persistence assumed—notions which when taken on faith lead to the assertion of existence and of substance, if they remained merely notions would prove nothing, disclose nothing, and assert nothing. Yet such, I suppose, are the notions actually before me when I say " I am." As to myself, when I proceed to distinguish that object in the midst of the moving world, I am roughly my body, or more accurately, its living centre, master of its organs and seat of its passions ; and this inner life of the body, I suspect, was the rock of vulgar belief which Descartes found at hand, easy to mount on, after his not very serious shipwreck. And the rock was well chosen ; not because the existence of my inner man is a simpler or a surer fact than any other ; to a true sceptic this alleged being so busily thinking and willing and fuming within my body is but a strange feature in the fantastic world that appears for the moment. Yet the choice of the inner man as the one certain existence was a happy one, because this sense of life within me is more constant than other perceptions, and not wholly to be shaken off except in profound contemplation or in some strange forms of madness. It was a suitable first postulate for the romantic psychologist. On this stepping-stone to idealism the father of modern philosophy, like another Columbus, set his foot with elegance. His new world, however, would be but an unexplored islet in the world of the ancients if all he discovered was himself thinking.

Thinking is another name for discourse ; and perhaps Descartes, in noting his own existence, was really less interested in the substance of himself, or in the fact that he was alive, than in the play of terms in discourse, which seemed to him obvious. Discourse truly involves spirit, with its intuition and intent, surveying those terms. And the definition of the soul, that its essence is to think, being a definition of spirit and not of a man's self, supports this interpretation. But discourse, no less than the existence of a self, needs to be posited, and the readiness with which a philosopher may do so yields only a candid confession of personal credulity, not the proof of anything. The assumption that spirit discoursing exists, and is more evident than any other existence, leads by a slightly different path to the same conclusion as the assumption of the self as the fundamental fact. In the one case discourse will soon swallow up all existence, and in the other this chosen existence, myself, will evaporate into discourse: but it will remain an insoluble problem whether I am a transcendental spirit, not a substance, holding the whole imaginary universe in the frame of my thought, or whether I am an instance of thinking, a phase of that flux of sentience which will then be the substance of the world. It is only if we interpret and develop the Cartesian axiom in the former transcendental sense that it supplies an instrument for criticism. Understood in an empirical way, as the confident indication of a particular fact, it is merely a chance dogma, betraying the psychological bias of reflection in modern man, and suggesting a fantastic theory of the universe, conveniently called psychologism; a theory which fuses the two disparate substances posited by Descartes, and maintains that while the inner essence of substance everywhere is to think, or at least to feel, its distribution, movement, and aspect, seen from without, are those of matter.

In adopting the method of Descartes, I have sought to carry it further, suspending all conventional categories as well as all conventional beliefs; so that not only the material world but all facts and all existences have lost their status, and become simply the themes or topics which intrinsically they are. Neither myself nor pure spirit is at all more real in that realm of essence than any other mentionable thing. When it comes to assertion (which is belief) I follow Descartes in choosing discourse and (as an implication of discourse) my substantial existence as the objects of faith least open to reasonable doubt; not because they are the first objects asserted, nor because intrinsically they lend themselves to existence better than anything else, but simply because in taking note of anything whatever I find that I am assuming the validity of primary memory ; in other words, that the method and the fact of observation are adventitious to the theme. But the fact that observation is involved in observing anything does not imply that observation is the only observed fact : yet in this gross sophism and insincerity the rest of psychologism is entangled.

Hume and Kant seemed sceptics in their day and were certainly great enemies of common sense, not through any perversity of temper (for both were men of wise judgement) but through sophistical scruples and criticism halting at unfortunate places. They disintegrated belief on particular points of scholastic philosophy, which was but common sense applied to revelation ; and they made no attempt to build on the foundations so laid bare, but rather to comfort themselves with the assurance that what survived was practically sufficient, and far simpler, sounder, and purer than what they had demolished. After the manner of the eighteenth century, they felt that convention was a burden and an imposture, not because here and there it misinterpreted nature, but because it interpreted or defined nature at all ; and in their criticism they ran for a fall. They had nothing to offer in the place of what they criticised, except the same cheque dishonoured. All their philosophy, where it was not simply a collapse into living without philosophy, was retrenchment ; and they retrenched in that hand-to-mouth fashion which Protestantism had introduced and which liberalism was to follow. They never touched bottom, and nothing could be more gratuitous or more helpless than their residual dogmas. These consisted in making metaphysics out of literary psychology ; not seeing that the discourse or experience to which they appealed was a social convention, roughly dramatising those very facts of the material world, and of animal life in it, which their criticism had denied.

Hume seems to have assumed that every perception perceived itself. He assumed further that these perceptions lay in time and formed certain sequences. Why a given perception belonged to one sequence rather than to another, and why all simultaneous perceptions were not in the same mind, he never considered ; the questions were unanswerable, so long as he ignored or denied the existence of bodies. He asserted also that these perceptions were repeated, and that the repetitions were always fainter than the originals—two groundless assertions, unless the transitive force of memory is admitted, and impressions are distinguished from ideas externally, by calling an intuition an impression when caused by a present object, visible to a third person, and calling it an idea when not so caused. Furthermore, he invoked an alleged habit of perceptions always to follow one another in the same order—something flatly contrary to fact ; but the notion was made plausible by confusion with the habits of the physical world, where similar events recur when the conditions are similar. Intuitions no doubt follow the same routine ; but the conditions for an intuition are not the previous intuitions, but the whole present state of the psyche and of the environment, something of which the previous intuitions were at best prophetic symptoms, symptoms often falsified by the event.

All these haltings and incoherences arose in the attempt to conceive experience divorced from its physical ground and from its natural objects, as a dream going on *in vacuo*. So artificial an abstraction, however, is hard to maintain consistently, and Hume, by a happy exercise of worldly wit, often described the workings of the mind as our social imagination leads us all vaguely to conceive them. In these

inspired moments he made those acute analyses of
our notions of material things, of the soul, and of cause,
which have given him his name as a sceptic. These
analyses are bits of plausible literary psychology,
essays on the origin of common sense. They are
not accounts of what the notions analysed mean, much
less scientific judgements of their truth. They are
supposed, however, by Hume and by the whole
modern school of idealists, to destroy both the meaning
of these notions and the existence of their intended
objects. Having explained how, perhaps, early man,
or a hypothetical infant, might have reached his first
glimmerings of knowledge that material things exist,
or souls, or causes, we are supposed to have proved
that no causes, no souls, and no material things can
exist at all. We are not allowed to ask how, in that
case, we have any evidence for the existence of early
man, or of the hypothetical infant, or of any general
characteristics of the human mind, and its tendencies
to feign. The world of literature is sacred to these
bookish minds ; only the world of nature and science
arouses their suspicion and their dislike. They think
that " experience," with the habits of thought and
language prevalent in all nations, from Adam down,
needs only to be imagined in order to be known truly.
All but this imagined experience seems to them the
work of imagination. While their method of criticism
ought evidently to establish not merely solipsism, but
a sort of solipsism of the present datum, yet they
never stop to doubt the whole comedy of human
intercourse, just as the most uncritical instinct and
the most fanciful history represent it to be. How can
such a mass of ill-attested and boldly dogmatic assumptions fail to make the critics of science uncomfortable
in their own house ? Is it because the criticism of
dogma in physics, without this dogma in psychology,
could never so much as begin ? Is not their criticism

at bottom a work of edification or of malice, not of philosophic sincerity, so that they reject the claim to knowledge only in respect to certain physical, metaphysical, or religious objects which the modern mind has become suspicious of, and hopes to feel freer without ? Meantime, they keep their conventional social assumptions without a qualm, because they need them to justify their moral precepts and to lend a false air of adequacy to their view of the world. Thus we are invited to believe that our notions of material things do not mean what they assert, but being illusions in their deliverance, really signify only the series of perceptions that have preceded them, or that, for some unfathomable reason, may be expected to ensue.

All this is sheer sophistry, and limping scepticism. Certainly the vulgar notions of nature, and even the scientific ones, are most questionable ; and they may have grown up in the way these critics suggest ; in any case they have grown up humanly. But they are not mere images ; they are beliefs ; and the truth of beliefs hangs on what they assert, not on their origin. The question is whether such an object as they describe lies in fact in the quarter where they assert it to lie ; the genealogy of these assertions in the mind of the believer, though interesting, is irrelevant. *It is for science and further investigation of the object to pronounce on the truth of any belief.* It will remain a mere belief to the end, no matter how much corroborated and corrected ; but the fact that it is a belief, far from proving that it must be false, renders it possibly true, as it could not be if it asserted nothing and had no object beyond itself which it pointed to and professed to describe. This whole school criticises knowledge, not by extending knowledge and testing it further, but by reviewing it maliciously, on the tacit assumption that knowledge is impossible.

But in that case this review of knowledge and all this shrewd psychology are themselves worthless ; and we are reduced, as Hume was in his deeper moments of insight, to a speechless wonder. So that whilst all the animals trust their senses and live, philosophy would persuade man alone not to trust them and, if he was consistent, to stop living.

This tragic conclusion might not have daunted a true philosopher, if like the Indians he had reached it by a massive moral experience rather than by incidental sophistries with no hold on the spirit. In that case the impossibility of knowledge would have seemed but one illustration of the vanity of life in general. That all is vanity was a theme sometimes developed by Christian preachers, and even in some late books of the Bible, with special reservations ; but it is an insight contrary to Hebraic religion, which invokes supernatural or moral agencies only in the hope of securing earthly life and prosperity for ever. The wisdom demanded could, therefore, not be negative or merely liberating ; and scepticism in Christian climes has always seemed demoralising. When it forced itself on the reluctant mind, people either dismissed it as a game not worth playing and sank back, like Hume, into common sense, though now with a bad conscience ; or else they sought some subterfuge or equivocation by which knowledge, acknowledged to be worthless, was nevertheless officially countersigned and passed as legal tender, so that the earnest practice of orthodoxy, religious or worldly, or both at once, might go on without a qualm. Evidently, to secure this result, it was necessary to set up some oracle, independent of natural knowledge, that should represent some deeper reality than natural knowledge could profess to reach ; and it was necessary that this oracle itself, by a pious or a wilful oversight, should escape criticism ; for otherwise all was lost.

It escaped criticism by virtue of the dramatic illusion which always fills the sails of argument, and renders the passing conviction the indignant voice of omniscience and justice. The principle invoked in criticism, whatever it might be, could not be criticised. It did not need to be defended : its credentials were the havoc it wrought among more explicit conventions. And yet, by a mocking fatality, those discredited conventions had to be maintained in practice, since they are inevitable for mankind, and the basis, even by their weaknesses, of the appeal to that higher principle which, in theory, was to revise and reject them. This higher principle was no alternative view of the world, no revelation of further facts or destinies ; it was the thinking or dreaming spirit that posited those necessary conventions, and would itself die if it ceased to posit them. In discrediting the fictions of spirit we must, therefore, beware of suspending them. We are not asked to abolish our conception of the natural world, nor even, in our daily life, to cease to believe in it ; we are to be idealists only north-north-west, or transcendentally ; when the wind is southerly, we are to remain realists. The pronouncements of animal faith have no doubt been reversed in a higher court, but with this singular proviso, that the police and the executioner, while reverently acknowledging the authority of the higher tribunal, must unflinchingly carry out the original sentence passed by the lower. This escape from scepticism by ambiguity, and by introducing only cancelled dogmas, was chosen by German philosophy at the beginning of the nineteenth century, and by modernism and pragmatism at the end of it.

Kant was thought a sceptic in his day, and called his philosophy criticism ; but his scepticism was very impure and his criticism, though laborious, was very uncritical. That he was regarded as a great philosopher in the nineteenth century is due to the same causes that made Locke seem a great philosopher in the eighteenth, not to any intrinsic greatness. He announced some revolutionary principles, which alarmed and excited the public, but he did not carry them out, so that the public was reassured. In his criticism of knowledge he assumed without question the Humian sequences of perceptions, although contrary to his doctrine of time ; and, more wisely than Hume, he never abandoned the general sense that these perceptions had organs and objects beneath and beyond them ; but having cut off, by his malicious criticism of knowledge, the organs and objects which perceptions notoriously have, he was forced to forge others, artificial and metaphysical. Instead of the body, he posited a transcendental ego, the categories of thought, and a disembodied law of duty ; instead of natural substances he posited the unknowable. I shall revert to these subjects in discussing the realm of matter, which is where they belong. Here I am concerned only with the analysis of knowledge, which in Kant was most conscientious, and valuable in spite of its rationalistic bias and its mythical solutions.

Any intelligent mind comes upon data and takes them for signs of things. Empirical criticism consists in reverting from these objects of intent, the things of common sense and science, to the immediate data by which they are revealed. But since data are not vacantly stared at by an intelligent being, but are interpreted and combined, there is evidently a subtler element in knowledge of things than the data which empirical criticism reverts to : namely, the principles of interpretation, since the data are read and taken to be significant of existing objects, far richer and more persistent and more powerful than themselves. These principles I have summarily called animal faith, not being concerned to propose any analysis of them that should apply to all minds or to all objects ; for I conceive, for instance, that the future, in other animals, may be a more frequent and vivid object of animal faith than the past or the material environment posited by human beings. But Kant, assuming that mind everywhere must have a single grammar, investigated very ingeniously what he conceived to be its recondite categories, and schemata, and forms of intuition : all pompous titles for what Hume had satirically called tendencies to feign. But Kant, in dishonouring the intellect, at least studied it devotedly, like an alienist discovering the logic of madness ; and he gave it so elaborate an articulation, and imposed it so rigorously on all men for ever, that people supposed he was establishing the sciences on a solid foundation rather than prescribing for all men a gratuitous uniformity in error. Yet this was his true meaning : and in spite of its psychological prefaces and metaphysical epilogues, and in spite of this pedantry about the necessary forms of all the sciences, the heart of the Kantian system was the most terrible negation. Among transcendental principles he placed space, time, and causality ; so that, if he had been consistent, he would have had to regard all multiple and successive existence as imagined only. Everything conceivable would have collapsed into the act of conceiving it, and this act itself would have lost its terms and its purpose, and evaporated into nothing. But not at all ; as if aware that all his conclusions were but curiosities in speculation and academic humours, he continued to think of experience as progressing in time, trifled most earnestly with astronomy and geography, and even comforted the pious with a postulate of immortality, as if time existed otherwise than in imagination. In fact, these backslidings were his amiable side : he always retained a certain humanity and wisdom, being much more thoroughly saturated with his conventional presuppositions than with his extravagant conclusions.

A philosopher, however, must be taken at his best, or at his worst ; in any case, his pure doctrine must be freed as far as possible from its personal alloy : and the pure doctrine of Kant was that knowledge is impossible. Anything I could perceive or think was *ipso facto* a creature of my sense or thought. Nature, history, God and the other world, even a man's outspread experience, could be things imagined only. Thought—for it was still assumed that there was thought—was a bubble, self-inflated at every moment, in an infinite void. All else was imaginary ; no world could be anything but the iridescence of that empty sphere. And this transcendental thought, so rich in false perspectives, could it be said to exist anywhere, or at any time, or for any reason ?

Here we touch one of those ambiguities and mystifications in which German philosophy takes refuge when pressed ; strong in the attack, it dissolves if driven to the defensive. Transcendentalism, in so far as it is critical, is a method only ; the principles by which data are interpreted come into play whenever intelligence is at work. The occasions for this exercise, as a matter of fact, are found in animal life ; and while every mind, at every moment, is the seat and measure of its own understanding, and creates its own knowledge (though, of course, not the objects on which animal life is directed and which it professes to know) yet the quality and degree of this intelligence may vary indefinitely from age to age and from animal to animal. Transcendental principles are accordingly only principles of local perspective, the grammar of fancy in this or that natural being quickened to imagination, and striving to understand what it endures and to utter what it deeply wills. The study of transcendental logic ought, therefore, to be one of the most humane, tender, tentative of studies : nothing but sympathetic poetry and insight into the hang and rhythm of various thoughts. It should be the finer part of literary psychology. But such is not the transcendentalism of the absolute transcendentalists. For them the grammar of thought is single and compulsory. It is the method of the creative fiat by which not this or that idea of the universe, but the universe itself, comes into being. The universe has only a specious existence ; and the method by which specious existence is evoked in thought is divine and identical in all thinking.

But why divine, and why always identical ? And why any thinking at all, or any process or variation in discourse, other than the given perspectives of the present vision ? At this point vertigo seizes the transcendentalist, and he no longer knows what he means. On the one hand, phenomena cannot be produced by an agency prior to them, for his first principle is that all existence is phenomenal and exists only in being posited or discovered. Will, Life, Duty, or whatever he calls this transcendental agency, by which the illusions of nature and history are summoned from the vasty deep, cannot be a fact, since all facts are created by its incantations. On the other hand phenomena cannot be substantial on their own account, for then they would not be phenomena but things, and no transcendental magician, himself non-existent and non-phenomenal, would be needed to produce them.

Absolute transcendentalism—the only radical form of a psychological criticism of knowledge—is accordingly not a thinkable nor a stable doctrine. It is merely a habit of speaking ambiguously, with a just sense for the living movement of thought and a romantic contempt for its deliverance. Self-consciousness cannot be, as this school strove to make it, a first principle of criticism : it is far too complex and derivative for that. But transcendentalism is a legitimate attitude for a poet in his dramatic reflections and romantic soliloquies ; it is the principle of perspective in thought, the scenic art of the mental theatre. The fully awakened soul, looking about it in this strange world, may well believe that it is dreaming. It may review its shifting memories, with a doubt whether they were ever anything in themselves. It may marshal all things in ideal perspectives about the present moment, and esteem them important and even real only in so far as they diversify the mental landscape. And to compensate it for the visionary character which the world takes on, it may cultivate the sense (by no means illusory) of some deep fountain of feeling and fancy within the self. Such wistful transcendentalism is akin to principles which in India long ago inspired very deep judgements upon life. It may be practised at will by any reflective person who is minded to treat the universe, for the time being, as so much furniture for his dreams.

Yet this attitude, seeing that man is not a solitary god but an animal in a material and social world, must be continually abandoned. It must be abandoned precisely when a man does or thinks anything important. Its own profundity is dreamful, and, so to speak, digestive : action, virtue, and wisdom sound another note. It is therefore no worthy philosophy ; and in fact the Germans, whose philosophy it is, while so dutiful in their external discipline, are sentimental and immoral in their spiritual economy. If a learned and placid professor tells me he is creating the universe by positing it in his own mind according to eternal principles of logic and duty, I may smile and admire such an inimitable mixture of enthusiasm and pedantry, profundity and innocence. Yet there is something sinister in this transcendentalism, apparently so pure and blameless ; it really expresses and sanctions the absoluteness of a barbarous soul, stubborn in its illusions, vulgar in its passions, and cruel in its zeal—cruel especially to itself, as barbarism always is, because it feeds and dilates its will as if its will were an absolute power, whereas it is nothing but a mass of foolish impulses and boasts ending in ignominy. Moreover, transcendentalism cannot even supply a thorough criticism of knowledge, which would demand that the ideas of self, of activity, and of consciousness should be disintegrated and reduced to the immediate. In the immediate, however, there is no transcendental force nor transcendental machinery, not even a set of perceptions nor an experience, but only some random essence, staring and groundless.

I hope I have taken to heart what the schools of Hume and Kant have to offer by way of disintegrating criticism of knowledge, and that in positing afresh the notions of substance, soul, nature, and discourse, I have done so with my eyes open. These notions are all subject to doubt; but so, also, are the notions proposed instead by psychological philosophers. None of these have reached the limit of possible doubt ; yet the dogmas they have retained, being romantic prejudices, are incoherent and incapable of serving as the basis for any reasonable system : and in a moral sense they are the very opposite of philosophy. When pressed, their negations end in solipsism and their affirmations in rhapsody. Far from purging the mind and strengthening it, that it might gain a clearer and more stable vision of the world, these critics have bewildered it with a multitude of methods and vistas, the expression of the confusion reigning in their day between natural science and religious faith, and between psychology and scepticism.

My endeavour has been to restore these things to their natural places, without forgetting the assumptions on which they rest. But the chief difference between my criticism of knowledge and theirs lies in the conception of knowledge itself. The Germans call knowledge *Wissenschaft*, as if it were something to be found in books, a catalogue of information, and an encyclopædia of the sciences. But the question is whether all this *Wissenschaft* is knowledge or only learning. My criticism is criticism of myself : I am talking of what I believe in my active moments, as a living animal, when I am really believing something : for when I am reading books belief in me is at its lowest ebb ; and I lend myself to the suasion of eloquence with the same pleasure (when the book is well written) whether it be the *Arabian Nights* or the latest philosophy. My criticism is not essentially a learned pursuit, though habit may sometimes make my language scholastic ; it is not a choice between artificial theories ; it is the discipline of my daily thoughts and the account I actually give to myself from moment to moment of my own being and of the world around me. I should be ashamed to countenance opinions which, when not arguing, I did not believe. It would seem to me dishonest and cowardly to militate under other colours than those under which I live. Merely learned views are not philosophy ; and therefore no modern writer is altogether a philosopher in my eyes, except Spinoza ; and the critics of knowledge in particular seem to me as feeble morally as they are technically.

I should like, therefore, to turn to the ancients and breathe again a clear atmosphere of frankness and honour ; but in the present business they are not very helpful. The Indians were poets and mystics ; and while they could easily throw off the conventions of vulgar reason, it was often only to surrender themselves to other conventions, far more misleading to a free spirit, such as the doctrine of transmigration of souls ; and when, as in Buddhism, they almost vanquished that illusion, together with every other, their emasculated intellect had nothing to put in its place. The Greeks on the contrary were rhetoricians ; they seldom or never reverted to the immediate for a foothold in thought, because the immediate lies below the level of language and of political convention. But they were disputatious, and in that sense no opinion escaped their criticism. In this criticism they simply pitted one plausible opinion against another, supporting each in turn by all conceivable arguments, based on no matter what prejudices or presumptions. The result of this forensic method was naturally a suspense of rational judgement, favourable now to frivolity and now to superstition. The frivolity appeared in the Sophists who, seeing that nothing was certain, impudently assumed as true whatever it was socially convenient to advocate. Protagoras seems to have reduced this bad habit to an honest system, when he taught that each occasion is, for itself, the ultimate judge of truth. This, taken psychologically, is evidently the case : a mind cannot judge on other subjects nor on other evidences than are open to it when judging. But the judging moment need not judge truly ; and to maintain (as Protagoras does in Plato's *Dialogue* and as some pragmatists have done in our day) that all momentary opinions are equal in truth, though not equal in value, is to fail in radical scepticism : for it is to assume many moments, and knowledge (utterly inexplicable on these principles) of their several sequences and import ; and to assume something even more wanton, a single standard of value by which to judge them all. Such incoherence is not surprising in sophists whose avowed purpose in philosophising is to survive and succeed in this world, or perhaps in the next. Worldly people will readily admit that some ideas are better than others, even if both sets are equally false. The interest in truth for its own sake is not a worldly interest, but the human soul is capable of it ; and there might be spirits directed on the knowledge of truth as upon their only ultimate good, as there might be spirits addressed exclusively to music. Which arts and sciences are worth pursuing, and how far, is a question for the moralist, to be answered in each case in view of the faculties and genius of the persons concerned, and their opportunities. Socrates may humorously eschew all science that is useless to cobblers ; he thereby expresses his plebeian hard sense, and his Hellenic joy in discourse and in moral apologues ; but if he allows this pleasant prejudice to blind him to the possibility of physical discoveries, or of cogent mathematics, he becomes a simple sophist. The moralist needs true knowledge of nature—even a little astronomy—in order to practise the art of life in a becoming spirit ; and an agnosticism which was not merely personal, provisional, and humble would be the worst of dogmas.

A sinking society, with its chaos of miscellaneous opinions, touches the bottom of scepticism in this sense, that it leaves no opinion unchallenged. But as a complete suspense of judgement is physically impossible in a living animal, every sceptic of the decadence has to accept some opinion or other. Which opinions he accepts, will depend on his personal character or his casual associations. His philosophy therefore deserts him at the threshold of life, just when it might cease to be a verbal accomplishment ; in other words, he is at intervals a sophist, but at no time a philosopher. Nevertheless, among the Greek sceptics there were noble minds. They turned their scepticism into an expression of personal dignity and an argument for detachment. In such scepticism every one who practises philosophy must imitate them ; for why should I pledge myself absolutely to what in fact is not certain ? Physics and theology, to which most philosophies are confined, are dubious in their first principles : which is not to say that nothing in them is credible. If we assert that one thing is more probable than another, as did the sceptics of the Academy, we have adopted a definite belief, we profess to have some hold on the nature of things at large, a law seems to us to rule events, and the lust of scepticism in us is chastened. This belief in nature, with a little experience and good sense to fill in the picture, is almost enough by way of belief. Nor can a man honestly believe less. An active mind never really loses the conviction that it is scenting the way of the world.

Living when human faith is again in a state of dissolution, I have imitated the Greek sceptics in calling doubtful everything that, in spite of common sense, any one can possibly doubt. But since life and even discussion forces me to break away from a complete scepticism, I have determined not to do so surreptitiously nor at random, ignominiously taking cover now behind one prejudice and now behind another. Instead, I have frankly taken nature by the hand, accepting as a rule in my farthest speculations the animal faith I live by from day to day. There are many opinions which, though questionable, are inevitable to a thought attentive to appearance, and honestly expressive of action. These natural opinions are not miscellaneous, such as those which the Sophists embraced in disputation. They are superposed in a biological order, the stratification of the life of reason. In rising out of passive intuition, I pass, by a vital constitutional necessity, to belief in discourse, in experience, in substance, in truth, and in spirit. All these objects may conceivably be illusory. Belief in them, however, is not grounded on a prior probability, but all judgements of probability are grounded on them. They express a rational instinct or instinctive reason, the waxing faith of an animal living in a world which he can observe and sometimes remodel.

This natural faith opens to me various Realms of Being, having very different kinds of reality in themselves and a different status in respect to my knowledge of them. I hope soon to invite the friendly reader to accompany me in a further excursion through those tempting fields.

INDEX

THE END

A CATALOGUE OF SELECTED DOVER BOOKS
IN ALL FIELDS OF INTEREST

A CATALOGUE OF SELECTED DOVER BOOKS
IN ALL FIELDS OF INTEREST

AMERICA'S OLD MASTERS, James T. Flexner. Four men emerged unexpectedly from provincial 18th century America to leadership in European art: Benjamin West, J. S. Copley, C. R. Peale, Gilbert Stuart. Brilliant coverage of lives and contributions. Revised, 1967 edition. 69 plates. 365pp. of text.
21806-6 Paperbound $3.00

FIRST FLOWERS OF OUR WILDERNESS: AMERICAN PAINTING, THE COLONIAL PERIOD, James T. Flexner. Painters, and regional painting traditions from earliest Colonial times up to the emergence of Copley, West and Peale Sr., Foster, Gustavus Hesselius, Feke, John Smibert and many anonymous painters in the primitive manner. Engaging presentation, with 162 illustrations. xxii + 368pp.
22180-6 Paperbound $3.50

THE LIGHT OF DISTANT SKIES: AMERICAN PAINTING, 1760-1835, James T. Flexner. The great generation of early American painters goes to Europe to learn and to teach: West, Copley, Gilbert Stuart and others. Allston, Trumbull, Morse; also contemporary American painters—primitives, derivatives, academics—who remained in America. 102 illustrations. xiii + 306pp. 22179-2 Paperbound $3.00

A HISTORY OF THE RISE AND PROGRESS OF THE ARTS OF DESIGN IN THE UNITED STATES, William Dunlap. Much the richest mine of information on early American painters, sculptors, architects, engravers, miniaturists, etc. The only source of information for scores of artists, the major primary source for many others. Unabridged reprint of rare original 1834 edition, with new introduction by James T. Flexner, and 394 new illustrations. Edited by Rita Weiss. 6⅝ x 9⅝.
21695-0, 21696-9, 21697-7 Three volumes, Paperbound $13.50

EPOCHS OF CHINESE AND JAPANESE ART, Ernest F. Fenollosa. From primitive Chinese art to the 20th century, thorough history, explanation of every important art period and form, including Japanese woodcuts; main stress on China and Japan, but Tibet, Korea also included. Still unexcelled for its detailed, rich coverage of cultural background, aesthetic elements, diffusion studies, particularly of the historical period. 2nd, 1913 edition. 242 illustrations. lii + 439pp. of text.
20364-6, 20365-4 Two volumes, Paperbound $6.00

THE GENTLE ART OF MAKING ENEMIES, James A. M. Whistler. Greatest wit of his day deflates Oscar Wilde, Ruskin, Swinburne; strikes back at inane critics, exhibitions, art journalism; aesthetics of impressionist revolution in most striking form. Highly readable classic by great painter. Reproduction of edition designed by Whistler. Introduction by Alfred Werner. xxxvi + 334pp.
21875-9 Paperbound $2.50

THE ARCHITECTURE OF COUNTRY HOUSES, Andrew J. Downing. Together with Vaux's *Villas and Cottages* this is the basic book for Hudson River Gothic architecture of the middle Victorian period. Full, sound discussions of general aspects of housing, architecture, style, decoration, furnishing, together with scores of detailed house plans, illustrations of specific buildings, accompanied by full text. Perhaps the most influential single American architectural book. 1850 edition. Introduction by J. Stewart Johnson. 321 figures, 34 architectural designs. xvi + 560pp.

22003-6 Paperbound $4.00

LOST EXAMPLES OF COLONIAL ARCHITECTURE, John Mead Howells. Full-page photographs of buildings that have disappeared or been so altered as to be denatured, including many designed by major early American architects. 245 plates. xvii + 248pp. 7⅞ x 10¾.

21143-6 Paperbound $3.00

DOMESTIC ARCHITECTURE OF THE AMERICAN COLONIES AND OF THE EARLY REPUBLIC, Fiske Kimball. Foremost architect and restorer of Williamsburg and Monticello covers nearly 200 homes between 1620-1825. Architectural details, construction, style features, special fixtures, floor plans, etc. Generally considered finest work in its area. 219 illustrations of houses, doorways, windows, capital mantels. xx + 314pp. 7⅞ x 10¾.

21743-4 Paperbound $3.50

EARLY AMERICAN ROOMS: 1650-1858, edited by Russell Hawes Kettell. Tour of 12 rooms, each representative of a different era in American history and each furnished, decorated, designed and occupied in the style of the era. 72 plans and elevations, 8-page color section, etc., show fabrics, wall papers, arrangements, etc. Full descriptive text. xvii + 200pp. of text. 8⅜ x 11¼.

21633-0 Paperbound $5.00

THE FITZWILLIAM VIRGINAL BOOK, edited by J. Fuller Maitland and W. B. Squire. Full modern printing of famous early 17th-century ms. volume of 300 works by Morley, Byrd, Bull, Gibbons, etc. For piano or other modern keyboard instrument; easy to read format. xxxvi + 938pp. 8⅜ x 11.

21068-5, 21069-3 Two volumes, Paperbound $8.00

HARPSICHORD MUSIC, Johann Sebastian Bach. Bach Gesellschaft edition. A rich selection of Bach's masterpieces for the harpsichord: the six English Suites, six French Suites, the six Partitas (Clavierübung part I), the Goldberg Variations (Clavierübung part IV), the fifteen Two-Part Inventions and the fifteen Three-Part Sinfonias. Clearly reproduced on large sheets with ample margins; eminently playable. vi + 312pp. 8⅛ x 11.

22360-4 Paperbound $5.00

THE MUSIC OF BACH: AN INTRODUCTION, Charles Sanford Terry. A fine, nontechnical introduction to Bach's music, both instrumental and vocal. Covers organ music, chamber music, passion music, other types. Analyzes themes, developments, innovations. x + 114pp.

21075-8 Paperbound $1.25

BEETHOVEN AND HIS NINE SYMPHONIES, Sir George Grove. Noted British musicologist provides best history, analysis, commentary on symphonies. Very thorough, rigorously accurate; necessary to both advanced student and amateur music lover. 436 musical passages. vii + 407 pp.

20334-4 Paperbound $2.25

THE PHILOSOPHY OF THE UPANISHADS, Paul Deussen. Clear, detailed statement of upanishadic system of thought, generally considered among best available. History of these works, full exposition of system emergent from them, parallel concepts in the West. Translated by A. S. Geden. xiv + 429pp.
21616-0 Paperbound $3.00

LANGUAGE, TRUTH AND LOGIC, Alfred J. Ayer. Famous, remarkably clear introduction to the Vienna and Cambridge schools of Logical Positivism; function of philosophy, elimination of metaphysical thought, nature of analysis, similar topics. "Wish I had written it myself," Bertrand Russell. 2nd, 1946 edition. 160pp.
20010-8 Paperbound $1.35

THE GUIDE FOR THE PERPLEXED, Moses Maimonides. Great classic of medieval Judaism, major attempt to reconcile revealed religion (Pentateuch, commentaries) and Aristotelian philosophy. Enormously important in all Western thought. Unabridged Friedländer translation. 50-page introduction. lix + 414pp.
(USO) 20351-4 Paperbound $2.50

OCCULT AND SUPERNATURAL PHENOMENA, D. H. Rawcliffe. Full, serious study of the most persistent delusions of mankind: crystal gazing, mediumistic trance, stigmata, lycanthropy, fire walking, dowsing, telepathy, ghosts, ESP, etc., and their relation to common forms of abnormal psychology. Formerly *Illusions and Delusions of the Supernatural and the Occult.* iii + 551pp. 20503-7 Paperbound $3.50

THE EGYPTIAN BOOK OF THE DEAD: THE PAPYRUS OF ANI, E. A. Wallis Budge. Full hieroglyphic text, interlinear transliteration of sounds, word for word translation, then smooth, connected translation; Theban recension. Basic work in Ancient Egyptian civilization; now even more significant than ever for historical importance, dilation of consciousness, etc. clvi + 377pp. 6½ x 9¼.
21866-X Paperbound $3.75

PSYCHOLOGY OF MUSIC, Carl E. Seashore. Basic, thorough survey of everything known about psychology of music up to 1940's; essential reading for psychologists, musicologists. Physical acoustics; auditory apparatus; relationship of physical sound to perceived sound; role of the mind in sorting, altering, suppressing, creating sound sensations; musical learning, testing for ability, absolute pitch, other topics. Records of Caruso, Menuhin analyzed. 88 figures. xix + 408pp.
21851-1 Paperbound $2.75

THE I CHING (THE BOOK OF CHANGES), translated by James Legge. Complete translated text plus appendices by Confucius, of perhaps the most penetrating divination book ever compiled. Indispensable to all study of early Oriental civilizations. 3 plates. xxiii + 448pp. 21062-6 Paperbound $2.75

THE UPANISHADS, translated by Max Müller. Twelve classical upanishads: Chandogya, Kena, Aitareya, Kaushitaki, Isa, Katha, Mundaka, Taittiriyaka, Brhadaranyaka, Svetasvatara, Prasna, Maitriyana. 160-page introduction, analysis by Prof. Müller. Total of 826pp. 20398-0, 20399-9 Two volumes, Paperbound $5.00

PLANETS, STARS AND GALAXIES: DESCRIPTIVE ASTRONOMY FOR BEGINNERS, A. E. Fanning. Comprehensive introductory survey of astronomy: the sun, solar system, stars, galaxies, universe, cosmology; up-to-date, including quasars, radio stars, etc. Preface by Prof. Donald Menzel. 24pp. of photographs. 189pp. 5¼ x 8¼.
21680-2 Paperbound $1.50

TEACH YOURSELF CALCULUS, P. Abbott. With a good background in algebra and trig, you can teach yourself calculus with this book. Simple, straightforward introduction to functions of all kinds, integration, differentiation, series, etc. "Students who are beginning to study calculus method will derive great help from this book." Faraday House Journal. 308pp. 20683-1 Clothbound $2.00

TEACH YOURSELF TRIGONOMETRY, P. Abbott. Geometrical foundations, indices and logarithms, ratios, angles, circular measure, etc. are presented in this sound, easy-to-use text. Excellent for the beginner or as a brush up, this text carries the student through the solution of triangles. 204pp. 20682-3 Clothbound $2.00

TEACH YOURSELF ANATOMY, David LeVay. Accurate, inclusive, profusely illustrated account of structure, skeleton, abdomen, muscles, nervous system, glands, brain, reproductive organs, evolution. "Quite the best and most readable account,' Medical Officer. 12 color plates. 164 figures. 311pp. 4¾ x 7.
21651-9 Clothbound $2.50

TEACH YOURSELF PHYSIOLOGY, David LeVay. Anatomical, biochemical bases; digestive, nervous, endocrine systems; metabolism; respiration; muscle; excretion; temperature control; reproduction. "Good elementary exposition," The Lancet. 6 color plates. 44 illustrations. 208pp. 4¼ x 7. 21658-6 Clothbound $2.50

THE FRIENDLY STARS, Martha Evans Martin. Classic has taught naked-eye observation of stars, planets to hundreds of thousands, still not surpassed for charm, lucidity, adequacy. Completely updated by Professor Donald H. Menzel, Harvard Observatory. 25 illustrations. 16 x 30 chart. x + 147pp. 21099-5 Paperbound $1.25

MUSIC OF THE SPHERES: THE MATERIAL UNIVERSE FROM ATOM TO QUASAR, SIMPLY EXPLAINED, Guy Murchie. Extremely broad, brilliantly written popular account begins with the solar system and reaches to dividing line between matter and nonmatter; latest understandings presented with exceptional clarity. Volume One: Planets, stars, galaxies, cosmology, geology, celestial mechanics, latest astronomical discoveries; Volume Two: Matter, atoms, waves, radiation, relativity, chemical action, heat, nuclear energy, quantum theory, music, light, color, probability, antimatter, antigravity, and similar topics. 319 figures. 1967 (second) edition. Total of xx + 644pp. 21809-0, 21810-4 Two volumes, Paperbound $4.00

OLD-TIME SCHOOLS AND SCHOOL BOOKS, Clifton Johnson. Illustrations and rhymes from early primers, abundant quotations from early textbooks, many anecdotes of school life enliven this study of elementary schools from Puritans to middle 19th century. Introduction by Carl Withers. 234 illustrations. xxxiii + 381pp.
21031-6 Paperbound $2.50

A HISTORY OF COSTUME, Carl Köhler. Definitive history, based on surviving pieces of clothing primarily, and paintings, statues, etc. secondarily. Highly readable text, supplemented by 594 illustrations of costumes of the ancient Mediterranean peoples, Greece and Rome, the Teutonic prehistoric period; costumes of the Middle Ages, Renaissance, Baroque, 18th and 19th centuries. Clear, measured patterns are provided for many clothing articles. Approach is practical throughout. Enlarged by Emma von Sichart. 464pp. 21030-8 Paperbound $3.00

ORIENTAL RUGS, ANTIQUE AND MODERN, Walter A. Hawley. A complete and authoritative treatise on the Oriental rug—where they are made, by whom and how, designs and symbols, characteristics in detail of the six major groups, how to distinguish them and how to buy them. Detailed technical data is provided on periods, weaves, warps, wefts, textures, sides, ends and knots, although no technical background is required for an understanding. 11 color plates, 80 halftones, 4 maps. vi + 320pp. 6⅛ x 9⅛. 22366-3 Paperbound $5.00

TEN BOOKS ON ARCHITECTURE, Vitruvius. By any standards the most important book on architecture ever written. Early Roman discussion of aesthetics of building, construction methods, orders, sites, and every other aspect of architecture has inspired, instructed architecture for about 2,000 years. Stands behind Palladio, Michelangelo, Bramante, Wren, countless others. Definitive Morris H. Morgan translation. 68 illustrations. xii + 331pp. 20645-9 Paperbound $2.50

THE FOUR BOOKS OF ARCHITECTURE, Andrea Palladio. Translated into every major Western European language in the two centuries following its publication in 1570, this has been one of the most influential books in the history of architecture. Complete reprint of the 1738 Isaac Ware edition. New introduction by Adolf Placzek, Columbia Univ. 216 plates. xxii + 110pp. of text. 9½ x 12¾. 21308-0 Clothbound $10.00

STICKS AND STONES: A STUDY OF AMERICAN ARCHITECTURE AND CIVILIZATION, Lewis Mumford.One of the great classics of American cultural history. American architecture from the medieval-inspired earliest forms to the early 20th century; evolution of structure and style, and reciprocal influences on environment. 21 photographic illustrations. 238pp. 20202-X Paperbound $2.00

THE AMERICAN BUILDER'S COMPANION, Asher Benjamin. The most widely used early 19th century architectural style and source book, for colonial up into Greek Revival periods. Extensive development of geometry of carpentering, construction of sashes, frames, doors, stairs; plans and elevations of domestic and other buildings. Hundreds of thousands of houses were built according to this book, now invaluable to historians, architects, restorers, etc. 1827 edition. 59 plates. 114pp. 7⅞ x 10¾. 22236-5 Paperbound $3.00

DUTCH HOUSES IN THE HUDSON VALLEY BEFORE 1776, Helen Wilkinson Reynolds. The standard survey of the Dutch colonial house and outbuildings, with constructional features, decoration, and local history associated with individual homesteads. Introduction by Franklin D. Roosevelt. Map. 150 illustrations. 469pp. 6⅝ x 9¼. 21469-9 Paperbound $3.50

AMERICAN FOOD AND GAME FISHES, David S. Jordan and Barton W. Evermann. Definitive source of information, detailed and accurate enough to enable the sportsman and nature lover to identify conclusively some 1,000 species and sub-species of North American fish, sought for food or sport. Coverage of range, physiology, habits, life history, food value. Best methods of capture, interest to the angler, advice on bait, fly-fishing, etc. 338 drawings and photographs. 1 + 574pp. 6⅝ x 9⅜.

22383-1 Paperbound $4.50

THE FROG BOOK, Mary C. Dickerson. Complete with extensive finding keys, over 300 photographs, and an introduction to the general biology of frogs and toads, this is the classic non-technical study of Northeastern and Central species. 58 species; 290 photographs and 16 color plates. xvii + 253pp.

21973-9 Paperbound $4.00

THE MOTH BOOK: A GUIDE TO THE MOTHS OF NORTH AMERICA, William J. Holland. Classical study, eagerly sought after and used for the past 60 years. Clear identification manual to more than 2,000 different moths, largest manual in existence. General information about moths, capturing, mounting, classifying, etc., followed by species by species descriptions. 263 illustrations plus 48 color plates show almost every species, full size. 1968 edition, preface, nomenclature changes by A. E. Brower. xxiv + 479pp. of text. 6½ x 9¼.

21948-8 Paperbound $5.00

THE SEA-BEACH AT EBB-TIDE, Augusta Foote Arnold. Interested amateur can identify hundreds of marine plants and animals on coasts of North America; marine algae; seaweeds; squids; hermit crabs; horse shoe crabs; shrimps; corals; sea anemones; etc. Species descriptions cover: structure; food; reproductive cycle; size; shape; color; habitat; etc. Over 600 drawings. 85 plates. xii + 490pp.

21949-6 Paperbound $3.50

COMMON BIRD SONGS, Donald J. Borror. 33⅓ 12-inch record presents songs of 60 important birds of the eastern United States. A thorough, serious record which provides several examples for each bird, showing different types of song, individual variations, etc. Inestimable identification aid for birdwatcher. 32-page booklet gives text about birds and songs, with illustration for each bird.

21829-5 Record, book, album. Monaural. $2.75

FADS AND FALLACIES IN THE NAME OF SCIENCE, Martin Gardner. Fair, witty appraisal of cranks and quacks of science: Atlantis, Lemuria, hollow earth, flat earth, Velikovsky, orgone energy, Dianetics, flying saucers, Bridey Murphy, food fads, medical fads, perpetual motion, etc. Formerly "In the Name of Science." x + 363pp.

20394-8 Paperbound $2.00

HOAXES, Curtis D. MacDougall. Exhaustive, unbelievably rich account of great hoaxes: Locke's moon hoax, Shakespearean forgeries, sea serpents, Loch Ness monster, Cardiff giant, John Wilkes Booth's mummy, Disumbrationist school of art, dozens more; also journalism, psychology of hoaxing. 54 illustrations. xi + 338pp.

20465-0 Paperbound $2.75

JOHANN SEBASTIAN BACH, Philipp Spitta. One of the great classics of musicology, this definitive analysis of Bach's music (and life) has never been surpassed. Lucid, nontechnical analyses of hundreds of pieces (30 pages devoted to St. Matthew Passion, 26 to B Minor Mass). Also includes major analysis of 18th-century music. 450 musical examples. 40-page musical supplement. Total of xx + 1799pp.
(EUK) 22278-0, 22279-9 Two volumes, Clothbound $15.00

MOZART AND HIS PIANO CONCERTOS, Cuthbert Girdlestone. The only full-length study of an important area of Mozart's creativity. Provides detailed analyses of all 23 concertos, traces inspirational sources. 417 musical examples. Second edition. 509pp.
(USO) 21271-8 Paperbound $3.50

THE PERFECT WAGNERITE: A COMMENTARY ON THE NIBLUNG'S RING, George Bernard Shaw. Brilliant and still relevant criticism in remarkable essays on Wagner's Ring cycle, Shaw's ideas on political and social ideology behind the plots, role of Leitmotifs, vocal requisites, etc. Prefaces. xxi + 136pp.
21707-8 Paperbound $1.50

DON GIOVANNI, W. A. Mozart. Complete libretto, modern English translation; biographies of composer and librettist; accounts of early performances and critical reaction. Lavishly illustrated. All the material you need to understand and appreciate this great work. Dover Opera Guide and Libretto Series; translated and introduced by Ellen Bleiler. 92 illustrations. 209pp.
21134-7 Paperbound $1.50

HIGH FIDELITY SYSTEMS: A LAYMAN'S GUIDE, Roy F. Allison. All the basic information you need for setting up your own audio system: high fidelity and stereo record players, tape records, F.M. Connections, adjusting tone arm, cartridge, checking needle alignment, positioning speakers, phasing speakers, adjusting hums, trouble-shooting, maintenance, and similar topics. Enlarged 1965 edition. More than 50 charts, diagrams, photos. iv + 91pp. 21514-8 Paperbound $1.25

REPRODUCTION OF SOUND, Edgar Villchur. Thorough coverage for laymen of high fidelity systems, reproducing systems in general, needles, amplifiers, preamps, loudspeakers, feedback, explaining physical background. "A rare talent for making technicalities vividly comprehensible," R. Darrell, High Fidelity. 69 figures. iv + 92pp.
21515-6 Paperbound $1.00

HEAR ME TALKIN' TO YA: THE STORY OF JAZZ AS TOLD BY THE MEN WHO MADE IT, Nat Shapiro and Nat Hentoff. Louis Armstrong, Fats Waller, Jo Jones, Clarence Williams, Billy Holiday, Duke Ellington, Jelly Roll Morton and dozens of other jazz greats tell how it was in Chicago's South Side, New Orleans, depression Harlem and the modern West Coast as jazz was born and grew. xvi + 429pp.
21726-4 Paperbound $2.50

FABLES OF AESOP, translated by Sir Roger L'Estrange. A reproduction of the very rare 1931 Paris edition; a selection of the most interesting fables, together with 50 imaginative drawings by Alexander Calder. v + 128pp. 6½x9¼.
21780-9 Paperbound $1.25

CATALOGUE OF DOVER BOOKS

AGAINST THE GRAIN (A REBOURS), Joris K. Huysmans. Filled with weird images, evidences of a bizarre imagination, exotic experiments with hallucinatory drugs, rich tastes and smells and the diversions of its sybarite hero Duc Jean des Esseintes, this classic novel pushed 19th-century literary decadence to its limits. Full unabridged edition. Do not confuse this with abridged editions generally sold. Introduction by Havelock Ellis. xlix + 206pp. 22190-3 Paperbound $2.00

VARIORUM SHAKESPEARE: HAMLET. Edited by Horace H. Furness; a landmark of American scholarship. Exhaustive footnotes and appendices treat all doubtful words and phrases, as well as suggested critical emendations throughout the play's history. First volume contains editor's own text, collated with all Quartos and Folios. Second volume contains full first Quarto, translations of Shakespeare's sources (Belleforest, and Saxo Grammaticus), Der Bestrafte Brudermord, and many essays on critical and historical points of interest by major authorities of past and present. Includes details of staging and costuming over the years. By far the best edition available for serious students of Shakespeare. Total of xx + 905pp. 21004-9, 21005-7, 2 volumes, Paperbound $5.25

A LIFE OF WILLIAM SHAKESPEARE, Sir Sidney Lee. This is the standard life of Shakespeare, summarizing everything known about Shakespeare and his plays. Incredibly rich in material, broad in coverage, clear and judicious, it has served thousands as the best introduction to Shakespeare. 1931 edition. 9 plates. xxix + 792pp. (USO) 21967-4 Paperbound $3.75

MASTERS OF THE DRAMA, John Gassner. Most comprehensive history of the drama in print, covering every tradition from Greeks to modern Europe and America, including India, Far East, etc. Covers more than 800 dramatists, 2000 plays, with biographical material, plot summaries, theatre history, criticism, etc. "Best of its kind in English," New Republic. 77 illustrations. xxii + 890pp. 20100-7 Clothbound $7.50

THE EVOLUTION OF THE ENGLISH LANGUAGE, George McKnight. The growth of English, from the 14th century to the present. Unusual, non-technical account presents basic information in very interesting form: sound shifts, change in grammar and syntax, vocabulary growth, similar topics. Abundantly illustrated with quotations. Formerly Modern English in the Making. xii + 590pp. 21932-1 Paperbound $3.50

AN ETYMOLOGICAL DICTIONARY OF MODERN ENGLISH, Ernest Weekley. Fullest, richest work of its sort, by foremost British lexicographer. Detailed word histories, including many colloquial and archaic words; extensive quotations. Do not confuse this with the Concise Etymological Dictionary, which is much abridged. Total of xxvii + 830pp. 6½ x 9¼. 21873-2, 21874-0 Two volumes, Paperbound $5.50

FLATLAND: A ROMANCE OF MANY DIMENSIONS, E. A. Abbott. Classic of science-fiction explores ramifications of life in a two-dimensional world, and what happens when a three-dimensional being intrudes. Amusing reading, but also useful as introduction to thought about hyperspace. Introduction by Banesh Hoffmann. 16 illustrations. xx + 103pp. 20001-9 Paperbound $1.00

POEMS OF ANNE BRADSTREET, edited with an introduction by Robert Hutchinson. A new selection of poems by America's first poet and perhaps the first significant woman poet in the English language. 48 poems display her development in works of considerable variety—love poems, domestic poems, religious meditations, formal elegies, "quaternions," etc. Notes, bibliography. viii + 222pp.
22160-1 Paperbound $2.00

THREE GOTHIC NOVELS: THE CASTLE OF OTRANTO BY HORACE WALPOLE; VATHEK BY WILLIAM BECKFORD; THE VAMPYRE BY JOHN POLIDORI, WITH FRAGMENT OF A NOVEL BY LORD BYRON, edited by E. F. Bleiler. The first Gothic novel, by Walpole; the finest Oriental tale in English, by Beckford; powerful Romantic supernatural story in versions by Polidori and Byron. All extremely important in history of literature; all still exciting, packed with supernatural thrills, ghosts, haunted castles, magic, etc. xl + 291pp.
21232-7 Paperbound $2.00

THE BEST TALES OF HOFFMANN, E. T. A. Hoffmann. 10 of Hoffmann's most important stories, in modern re-editings of standard translations: Nutcracker and the King of Mice, Signor Formica, Automata, The Sandman, Rath Krespel, The Golden Flowerpot, Master Martin the Cooper, The Mines of Falun, The King's Betrothed, A New Year's Eve Adventure. 7 illustrations by Hoffmann. Edited by E. F. Bleiler. xxxix + 419pp.
21793-0 Paperbound $2.50

GHOST AND HORROR STORIES OF AMBROSE BIERCE, Ambrose Bierce. 23 strikingly modern stories of the horrors latent in the human mind: The Eyes of the Panther, The Damned Thing, An Occurrence at Owl Creek Bridge, An Inhabitant of Carcosa, etc., plus the dream-essay, Visions of the Night. Edited by E. F. Bleiler. xxii + 199pp.
20767-6 Paperbound $1.50

BEST GHOST STORIES OF J. S. LeFANU, J. Sheridan LeFanu. Finest stories by Victorian master often considered greatest supernatural writer of all. Carmilla, Green Tea, The Haunted Baronet, The Familiar, and 12 others. Most never before available in the U. S. A. Edited by E. F. Bleiler. 8 illustrations from Victorian publications. xvii + 467pp.
20415-4 Paperbound $2.50

THE TIME STREAM, THE GREATEST ADVENTURE, AND THE PURPLE SAPPHIRE—THREE SCIENCE FICTION NOVELS, John Taine (Eric Temple Bell). Great American mathematician was also foremost science fiction novelist of the 1920's. *The Time Stream,* one of all-time classics, uses concepts of circular time; *The Greatest Adventure,* incredibly ancient biological experiments from Antarctica threaten to escape; The *Purple Sapphire,* superscience, lost races in Central Tibet, survivors of the Great Race. 4 illustrations by Frank R. Paul. v + 532pp.
21180-0 Paperbound $3.00

SEVEN SCIENCE FICTION NOVELS, H. G. Wells. The standard collection of the great novels. Complete, unabridged. *First Men in the Moon, Island of Dr. Moreau, War of the Worlds, Food of the Gods, Invisible Man, Time Machine, In the Days of the Comet.* Not only science fiction fans, but every educated person owes it to himself to read these novels. 1015pp.
20264-X Clothbound $5.00

THE RED FAIRY BOOK, Andrew Lang. Lang's color fairy books have long been children's favorites. This volume includes Rapunzel, Jack and the Bean-stalk and 35 other stories, familiar and unfamiliar. 4 plates, 93 illustrations x + 367pp.
21673-X Paperbound $1.95

THE BLUE FAIRY BOOK, Andrew Lang. Lang's tales come from all countries and all times. Here are 37 tales from Grimm, the Arabian Nights, Greek Mythology, and other fascinating sources. 8 plates, 130 illustrations. xi + 390pp.
21437-0 Paperbound $1.95

HOUSEHOLD STORIES BY THE BROTHERS GRIMM. Classic English-language edition of the well-known tales — Rumpelstiltskin, Snow White, Hansel and Gretel, The Twelve Brothers, Faithful John, Rapunzel, Tom Thumb (52 stories in all). Translated into simple, straightforward English by Lucy Crane. Ornamented with headpieces, vignettes, elaborate decorative initials and a dozen full-page illustrations by Walter Crane. x + 269pp.
21080-4 Paperbound $1.75

THE MERRY ADVENTURES OF ROBIN HOOD, Howard Pyle. The finest modern versions of the traditional ballads and tales about the great English outlaw. Howard Pyle's complete prose version, with every word, every illustration of the first edition. Do not confuse this facsimile of the original (1883) with modern editions that change text or illustrations. 23 plates plus many page decorations. xxii + 296pp.
22043-5 Paperbound $2.00

THE STORY OF KING ARTHUR AND HIS KNIGHTS, Howard Pyle. The finest children's version of the life of King Arthur; brilliantly retold by Pyle, with 48 of his most imaginative illustrations. xviii + 313pp. 6⅛ x 9¼.
21445-1 Paperbound $2.00

THE WONDERFUL WIZARD OF OZ, L. Frank Baum. America's finest children's book in facsimile of first edition with all Denslow illustrations in full color. The edition a child should have. Introduction by Martin Gardner. 23 color plates, scores of drawings. iv + 267pp.
20691-2 Paperbound $1.95

THE MARVELOUS LAND OF OZ, L. Frank Baum. The second Oz book, every bit as imaginative as the Wizard. The hero is a boy named Tip, but the Scarecrow and the Tin Woodman are back, as is the Oz magic. 16 color plates, 120 drawings by John R. Neill. 287pp.
20692-0 Paperbound $1.75

THE MAGICAL MONARCH OF MO, L. Frank Baum. Remarkable adventures in a land even stranger than Oz. The best of Baum's books not in the Oz series. 15 color plates and dozens of drawings by Frank Verbeck. xviii + 237pp.
21892-9 Paperbound $2.00

THE BAD CHILD'S BOOK OF BEASTS, MORE BEASTS FOR WORSE CHILDREN, A MORAL ALPHABET, Hilaire Belloc. Three complete humor classics in one volume. Be kind to the frog, and do not call him names . . . and 28 other whimsical animals. Familiar favorites and some not so well known. Illustrated by Basil Blackwell. 156pp.
(USO) 20749-8 Paperbound $1.25

THE PRINCIPLES OF PSYCHOLOGY, William James. The famous long course, complete and unabridged. Stream of thought, time perception, memory, experimental methods—these are only some of the concerns of a work that was years ahead of its time and still valid, interesting, useful. 94 figures. Total of xviii + 1391pp.
20381-6, 20382-4 Two volumes, Paperbound $6.00

THE STRANGE STORY OF THE QUANTUM, Banesh Hoffmann. Non-mathematical but thorough explanation of work of Planck, Einstein, Bohr, Pauli, de Broglie, Schrödinger, Heisenberg, Dirac, Feynman, etc. No technical background needed. "Of books attempting such an account, this is the best," Henry Margenau, Yale. 40-page "Postscript 1959." xii + 285pp.
20518-5 Paperbound $2.00

THE RISE OF THE NEW PHYSICS, A. d'Abro. Most thorough explanation in print of central core of mathematical physics, both classical and modern; from Newton to Dirac and Heisenberg. Both history and exposition; philosophy of science, causality, explanations of higher mathematics, analytical mechanics, electromagnetism, thermodynamics, phase rule, special and general relativity, matrices. No higher mathematics needed to follow exposition, though treatment is elementary to intermediate in level. Recommended to serious student who wishes verbal understanding. 97 illustrations. xvii + 982pp.
20003-5, 20004-3 Two volumes, Paperbound $5.50

GREAT IDEAS OF OPERATIONS RESEARCH, Jagjit Singh. Easily followed non-technical explanation of mathematical tools, aims, results: statistics, linear programming, game theory, queueing theory, Monte Carlo simulation, etc. Uses only elementary mathematics. Many case studies, several analyzed in detail. Clarity, breadth make this excellent for specialist in another field who wishes background. 41 figures. x + 228pp.
21886-4 Paperbound $2.25

GREAT IDEAS OF MODERN MATHEMATICS: THEIR NATURE AND USE, Jagjit Singh. Internationally famous expositor, winner of Unesco's Kalinga Award for science popularization explains verbally such topics as differential equations, matrices, groups, sets, transformations, mathematical logic and other important modern mathematics, as well as use in physics, astrophysics, and similar fields. Superb exposition for layman, scientist in other areas. viii + 312pp.
20587-8 Paperbound $2.25

GREAT IDEAS IN INFORMATION THEORY, LANGUAGE AND CYBERNETICS, Jagjit Singh. The analog and digital computers, how they work, how they are like and unlike the human brain, the men who developed them, their future applications, computer terminology. An essential book for today, even for readers with little math. Some mathematical demonstrations included for more advanced readers. 118 figures. Tables. ix + 338pp.
21694-2 Paperbound $2.25

CHANCE, LUCK AND STATISTICS, Horace C. Levinson. Non-mathematical presentation of fundamentals of probability theory and science of statistics and their applications. Games of chance, betting odds, misuse of statistics, normal and skew distributions, birth rates, stock speculation, insurance. Enlarged edition. Formerly "The Science of Chance." xiii + 357pp.
21007-3 Paperbound $2.00

CATALOGUE OF DOVER BOOKS

TWO LITTLE SAVAGES; BEING THE ADVENTURES OF TWO BOYS WHO LIVED AS INDIANS AND WHAT THEY LEARNED, Ernest Thompson Seton. Great classic of nature and boyhood provides a vast range of woodlore in most palatable form, a genuinely entertaining story. Two farm boys build a teepee in woods and live in it for a month, working out Indian solutions to living problems, star lore, birds and animals, plants, etc. 293 illustrations. vii + 286pp.

20985-7 Paperbound $1.95

PETER PIPER'S PRACTICAL PRINCIPLES OF PLAIN & PERFECT PRONUNCIATION. Alliterative jingles and tongue-twisters of surprising charm, that made their first appearance in America about 1830. Republished in full with the spirited woodcut illustrations from this earliest American edition. 32pp. 4½ x 6⅜.

22560-7 Paperbound $1.00

SCIENCE EXPERIMENTS AND AMUSEMENTS FOR CHILDREN, Charles Vivian. 73 easy experiments, requiring only materials found at home or easily available, such as candles, coins, steel wool, etc.; illustrate basic phenomena like vacuum, simple chemical reaction, etc. All safe. Modern, well-planned. Formerly *Science Games for Children*. 102 photos, numerous drawings. 96pp. 6⅛ x 9¼.

21856-2 Paperbound $1.25

AN INTRODUCTION TO CHESS MOVES AND TACTICS SIMPLY EXPLAINED, Leonard Barden. Informal intermediate introduction, quite strong in explaining reasons for moves. Covers basic material, tactics, important openings, traps, positional play in middle game, end game. Attempts to isolate patterns and recurrent configurations. Formerly *Chess*. 58 figures. 102pp. (USO) 21210-6 Paperbound $1.25

LASKER'S MANUAL OF CHESS, Dr. Emanuel Lasker. Lasker was not only one of the five great World Champions, he was also one of the ablest expositors, theorists, and analysts. In many ways, his Manual, permeated with his philosophy of battle, filled with keen insights, is one of the greatest works ever written on chess. Filled with analyzed games by the great players. A single-volume library that will profit almost any chess player, beginner or master. 308 diagrams. xli x 349pp.

20640-8 Paperbound $2.50

THE MASTER BOOK OF MATHEMATICAL RECREATIONS, Fred Schuh. In opinion of many the finest work ever prepared on mathematical puzzles, stunts, recreations; exhaustively thorough explanations of mathematics involved, analysis of effects, citation of puzzles and games. Mathematics involved is elementary. Translated by F. Göbel. 194 figures. xxiv + 430pp. 22134-2 Paperbound $3.00

MATHEMATICS, MAGIC AND MYSTERY, Martin Gardner. Puzzle editor for Scientific American explains mathematics behind various mystifying tricks: card tricks, stage "mind reading," coin and match tricks, counting out games, geometric dissections, etc. Probability sets, theory of numbers clearly explained. Also provides more than 400 tricks, guaranteed to work, that you can do. 135 illustrations. xii + 176pp.

20338-2 Paperbound $1.50

LAST AND FIRST MEN AND STAR MAKER, TWO SCIENCE FICTION NOVELS, Olaf Stapledon. Greatest future histories in science fiction. In the first, human intelligence is the "hero," through strange paths of evolution, interplanetary invasions, incredible technologies, near extinctions and reemergences. Star Maker describes the quest of a band of star rovers for intelligence itself, through time and space: weird inhuman civilizations, crustacean minds, symbiotic worlds, etc. Complete, unabridged. v + 438pp. 21962-3 Paperbound $2.00

THREE PROPHETIC NOVELS, H. G. WELLS. Stages of a consistently planned future for mankind. *When the Sleeper Wakes,* and *A Story of the Days to Come,* anticipate *Brave New World* and *1984,* in the 21st Century; *The Time Machine,* only complete version in print, shows farther future and the end of mankind. All show Wells's greatest gifts as storyteller and novelist. Edited by E. F. Bleiler. x + 335pp. (USO) 20605-X Paperbound $2.00

THE DEVIL'S DICTIONARY, Ambrose Bierce. America's own Oscar Wilde—Ambrose Bierce—offers his barbed iconoclastic wisdom in over 1,000 definitions hailed by H. L. Mencken as "some of the most gorgeous witticisms in the English language." 145pp. 20487-1 Paperbound $1.25

MAX AND MORITZ, Wilhelm Busch. Great children's classic, father of comic strip, of two bad boys, Max and Moritz. Also Ker and Plunk (Plisch und Plumm), Cat and Mouse, Deceitful Henry, Ice-Peter, The Boy and the Pipe, and five other pieces. Original German, with English translation. Edited by H. Arthur Klein; translations by various hands and H. Arthur Klein. vi + 216pp. 20181-3 Paperbound $1.50

PIGS IS PIGS AND OTHER FAVORITES, Ellis Parker Butler. The title story is one of the best humor short stories, as Mike Flannery obfuscates biology and English. Also included, That Pup of Murchison's, The Great American Pie Company, and Perkins of Portland. 14 illustrations. v + 109pp. 21532-6 Paperbound $1.00

THE PETERKIN PAPERS, Lucretia P. Hale. It takes genius to be as stupidly mad as the Peterkins, as they decide to become wise, celebrate the "Fourth," keep a cow, and otherwise strain the resources of the Lady from Philadelphia. Basic book of American humor. 153 illustrations. 219pp. 20794-3 Paperbound $1.25

PERRAULT'S FAIRY TALES, translated by A. E. Johnson and S. R. Littlewood, with 34 full-page illustrations by Gustave Doré. All the original Perrault stories—Cinderella, Sleeping Beauty, Bluebeard, Little Red Riding Hood, Puss in Boots, Tom Thumb, etc.—with their witty verse morals and the magnificent illustrations of Doré. One of the five or six great books of European fairy tales. viii + 117pp. 8⅛ x 11. 22311-6 Paperbound $2.00

OLD HUNGARIAN FAIRY TALES, Baroness Orczy. Favorites translated and adapted by author of the *Scarlet Pimpernel.* Eight fairy tales include "The Suitors of Princess Fire-Fly," "The Twin Hunchbacks," "Mr. Cuttlefish's Love Story," and "The Enchanted Cat." This little volume of magic and adventure will captivate children as it has for generations. 90 drawings by Montagu Barstow. 96pp. (USO) 22293-4 Paperbound $1.95

EAST O' THE SUN AND WEST O' THE MOON, George W. Dasent. Considered the best of all translations of these Norwegian folk tales, this collection has been enjoyed by generations of children (and folklorists too). Includes True and Untrue, Why the Sea is Salt, East O' the Sun and West O' the Moon, Why the Bear is Stumpy-Tailed, Boots and the Troll, The Cock and the Hen, Rich Peter the Pedlar, and 52 more. The only edition with all 59 tales. 77 illustrations by Erik Werenskiold and Theodor Kittelsen. xv + 418pp.
22521-6 Paperbound $3.00

GOOPS AND HOW TO BE THEM, Gelett Burgess. Classic of tongue-in-cheek humor, masquerading as etiquette book. 87 verses, twice as many cartoons, show mischievous Goops as they demonstrate to children virtues of table manners, neatness, courtesy, etc. Favorite for generations. viii + 88pp. 6½ x 9¼.
22233-0 Paperbound $1.25

ALICE'S ADVENTURES UNDER GROUND, Lewis Carroll. The first version, quite different from the final Alice in Wonderland, printed out by Carroll himself with his own illustrations. Complete facsimile of the "million dollar" manuscript Carroll gave to Alice Liddell in 1864. Introduction by Martin Gardner. viii + 96pp. Title and dedication pages in color.
21482-6 Paperbound $1.00

THE BROWNIES, THEIR BOOK, Palmer Cox. Small as mice, cunning as foxes, exuberant and full of mischief, the Brownies go to the zoo, toy shop, seashore, circus, etc., in 24 verse adventures and 266 illustrations. Long a favorite, since their first appearance in St. Nicholas Magazine. xi + 144pp. 6⅝ x 9¼.
21265-3 Paperbound $1.50

SONGS OF CHILDHOOD, Walter De La Mare. Published (under the pseudonym Walter Ramal) when De La Mare was only 29, this charming collection has long been a favorite children's book. A facsimile of the first edition in paper, the 47 poems capture the simplicity of the nursery rhyme and the ballad, including such lyrics as I Met Eve, Tartary, The Silver Penny. vii + 106pp. 21972-0 Paperbound $1.25

THE COMPLETE NONSENSE OF EDWARD LEAR, Edward Lear. The finest 19th-century humorist-cartoonist in full: all nonsense limericks, zany alphabets, Owl and Pussycat, songs, nonsense botany, and more than 500 illustrations by Lear himself. Edited by Holbrook Jackson. xxix + 287pp. (USO) 20167-8 Paperbound $1.75

BILLY WHISKERS: THE AUTOBIOGRAPHY OF A GOAT, Frances Trego Montgomery. A favorite of children since the early 20th century, here are the escapades of that rambunctious, irresistible and mischievous goat—Billy Whiskers. Much in the spirit of Peck's Bad Boy, this is a book that children never tire of reading or hearing. All the original familiar illustrations by W. H. Fry are included: 6 color plates, 18 black and white drawings. 159pp.
22345-0 Paperbound $2.00

MOTHER GOOSE MELODIES. Faithful republication of the fabulously rare Munroe and Francis "copyright 1833" Boston edition—the most important Mother Goose collection, usually referred to as the "original." Familiar rhymes plus many rare ones, with wonderful old woodcut illustrations. Edited by E. F. Bleiler. 128pp. 4½ x 6⅜.
22577-1 Paperbound $1.25

HOW TO KNOW THE WILD FLOWERS, Mrs. William Starr Dana. This is the classical book of American wildflowers (of the Eastern and Central United States), used by hundreds of thousands. Covers over 500 species, arranged in extremely easy to use color and season groups. Full descriptions, much plant lore. This Dover edition is the fullest ever compiled, with tables of nomenclature changes. 174 full-page plates by M. Satterlee. xii + 418pp. 20332-8 Paperbound $2.50

OUR PLANT FRIENDS AND FOES, William Atherton DuPuy. History, economic importance, essential botanical information and peculiarities of 25 common forms of plant life are provided in this book in an entertaining and charming style. Covers food plants (potatoes, apples, beans, wheat, almonds, bananas, etc.), flowers (lily, tulip, etc.), trees (pine, oak, elm, etc.), weeds, poisonous mushrooms and vines, gourds, citrus fruits, cotton, the cactus family, and much more. 108 illustrations. xiv + 290pp. 22272-1 Paperbound $2.00

HOW TO KNOW THE FERNS, Frances T. Parsons. Classic survey of Eastern and Central ferns, arranged according to clear, simple identification key. Excellent introduction to greatly neglected nature area. 57 illustrations and 42 plates. xvi + 215pp. 20740-4 Paperbound $1.75

MANUAL OF THE TREES OF NORTH AMERICA, Charles S. Sargent. America's foremost dendrologist provides the definitive coverage of North American trees and tree-like shrubs. 717 species fully described and illustrated: exact distribution, down to township; full botanical description; economic importance; description of subspecies and races; habitat, growth data; similar material. Necessary to every serious student of tree-life. Nomenclature revised to present. Over 100 locating keys. 783 illustrations. lii + 934pp. 20277-1, 20278-X Two volumes, Paperbound $6.00

OUR NORTHERN SHRUBS, Harriet L. Keeler. Fine non-technical reference work identifying more than 225 important shrubs of Eastern and Central United States and Canada. Full text covering botanical description, habitat, plant lore, is paralleled with 205 full-page photographs of flowering or fruiting plants. Nomenclature revised by Edward G. Voss. One of few works concerned with shrubs. 205 plates, 35 drawings. xxviii + 521pp. 21989-5 Paperbound $3.75

THE MUSHROOM HANDBOOK, Louis C. C. Krieger. Still the best popular handbook: full descriptions of 259 species, cross references to another 200. Extremely thorough text enables you to identify, know all about any mushroom you are likely to meet in eastern and central U. S. A.: habitat, luminescence, poisonous qualities, use, folklore, etc. 32 color plates show over 50 mushrooms, also 126 other illustrations. Finding keys. vii + 560pp. 21861-9 Paperbound $3.95

HANDBOOK OF BIRDS OF EASTERN NORTH AMERICA, Frank M. Chapman. Still much the best single-volume guide to the birds of Eastern and Central United States. Very full coverage of 675 species, with descriptions, life habits, distribution, similar data. All descriptions keyed to two-page color chart. With this single volume the average birdwatcher needs no other books. 1931 revised edition. 195 illustrations. xxxvi + 581pp. 21489-3 Paperbound $3.25

CATALOGUE OF DOVER BOOKS

ALPHABETS AND ORNAMENTS, Ernst Lehner. Well-known pictorial source for decorative alphabets, script examples, cartouches, frames, decorative title pages, calligraphic initials, borders, similar material. 14th to 19th century, mostly European. Useful in almost any graphic arts designing, varied styles. 750 illustrations. 256pp. 7 x 10.
21905-4 Paperbound $4.00

PAINTING: A CREATIVE APPROACH, Norman Colquhoun. For the beginner simple guide provides an instructive approach to painting: major stumbling blocks for beginner; overcoming them, technical points; paints and pigments; oil painting; watercolor and other media and color. New section on "plastic" paints. Glossary. Formerly *Paint Your Own Pictures*. 221pp.
22000-1 Paperbound $1.75

THE ENJOYMENT AND USE OF COLOR, Walter Sargent. Explanation of the relations between colors themselves and between colors in nature and art, including hundreds of little-known facts about color values, intensities, effects of high and low illumination, complementary colors. Many practical hints for painters, references to great masters. 7 color plates, 29 illustrations. x + 274pp.
20944-X Paperbound $2.50

THE NOTEBOOKS OF LEONARDO DA VINCI, compiled and edited by Jean Paul Richter. 1566 extracts from original manuscripts reveal the full range of Leonardo's versatile genius: all his writings on painting, sculpture, architecture, anatomy, astronomy, geography, topography, physiology, mining, music, etc., in both Italian and English, with 186 plates of manuscript pages and more than 500 additional drawings. Includes studies for the Last Supper, the lost Sforza monument, and other works. Total of xlvii + 866pp. 7⅞ x 10¾.
22572-0, 22573-9 Two volumes, Paperbound $10.00

MONTGOMERY WARD CATALOGUE OF 1895. Tea gowns, yards of flannel and pillow-case lace, stereoscopes, books of gospel hymns, the New Improved Singer Sewing Machine, side saddles, milk skimmers, straight-edged razors, high-button shoes, spittoons, and on and on . . . listing some 25,000 items, practically all illustrated. Essential to the shoppers of the 1890's, it is our truest record of the spirit of the period. Unaltered reprint of Issue No. 57, Spring and Summer 1895. Introduction by Boris Emmet. Innumerable illustrations. xiii + 624pp. 8½ x 11⅝.
22377-9 Paperbound $6.95

THE CRYSTAL PALACE EXHIBITION ILLUSTRATED CATALOGUE (LONDON, 1851). One of the wonders of the modern world—the Crystal Palace Exhibition in which all the nations of the civilized world exhibited their achievements in the arts and sciences—presented in an equally important illustrated catalogue. More than 1700 items pictured with accompanying text—ceramics, textiles, cast-iron work, carpets, pianos, sleds, razors, wall-papers, billiard tables, beehives, silverware and hundreds of other artifacts—represent the focal point of Victorian culture in the Western World. Probably the largest collection of Victorian decorative art ever assembled—indispensable for antiquarians and designers. Unabridged republication of the Art-Journal Catalogue of the Great Exhibition of 1851, with all terminal essays. New introduction by John Gloag, F.S.A. xxxiv + 426pp. 9 x 12.
22503-8 Paperbound $4.50

"ESSENTIAL GRAMMAR" SERIES

All you really need to know about modern, colloquial grammar. Many educational shortcuts help you learn faster, understand better. Detailed cognate lists teach you to recognize similarities between English and foreign words and roots—make learning vocabulary easy and interesting. Excellent for independent study or as a supplement to record courses.

ESSENTIAL FRENCH GRAMMAR, Seymour Resnick. 2500-item cognate list. 159pp.
(EBE) 20419-7 Paperbound $1.25

ESSENTIAL GERMAN GRAMMAR, Guy Stern and Everett F. Bleiler. Unusual short-cuts on noun declension, word order, compound verbs. 124pp.
(EBE) 20422-7 Paperbound $1.25

ESSENTIAL ITALIAN GRAMMAR, Olga Ragusa. 111pp.
(EBE) 20779-X Paperbound $1.25

ESSENTIAL JAPANESE GRAMMAR, Everett F. Bleiler. In Romaji transcription; no characters needed. Japanese grammar is regular and simple. 156pp.
21027-8 Paperbound $1.25

ESSENTIAL PORTUGUESE GRAMMAR, Alexander da R. Prista. vi + 114pp.
21650-0 Paperbound $1.25

ESSENTIAL SPANISH GRAMMAR, Seymour Resnick. 2500 word cognate list. 115pp.
(EBE) 20780-3 Paperbound $1.25

ESSENTIAL ENGLISH GRAMMAR, Philip Gucker. Combines best features of modern, functional and traditional approaches. For refresher, class use, home study. x + 177pp.
21649-7 Paperbound $1.25

A PHRASE AND SENTENCE DICTIONARY OF SPOKEN SPANISH. Prepared for U. S. War Department by U. S. linguists. As above, unit is idiom, phrase or sentence rather than word. English-Spanish and Spanish-English sections contain modern equivalents of over 18,000 sentences. Introduction and appendix as above. iv + 513pp.
20495-2 Paperbound $2.00

A PHRASE AND SENTENCE DICTIONARY OF SPOKEN RUSSIAN. Dictionary prepared for U. S. War Department by U. S. linguists. Basic unit is not the word, but the idiom, phrase or sentence. English-Russian and Russian-English sections contain modern equivalents for over 30,000 phrases. Grammatical introduction covers phonetics, writing, syntax. Appendix of word lists for food, numbers, geographical names, etc. vi + 573 pp. 6⅛ x 9¼.
20496-0 Paperbound $3.00

CONVERSATIONAL CHINESE FOR BEGINNERS, Morris Swadesh. Phonetic system, beginner's course in Pai Hua Mandarin Chinese covering most important, most useful speech patterns. Emphasis on modern colloquial usage. Formerly *Chinese in Your Pocket.* xvi + 158pp.
21123-1 Paperbound $1.50

CATALOGUE OF DOVER BOOKS

MATHEMATICAL PUZZLES FOR BEGINNERS AND ENTHUSIASTS, Geoffrey Mott-Smith. 189 puzzles from easy to difficult—involving arithmetic, logic, algebra, properties of digits, probability, etc.—for enjoyment and mental stimulus. Explanation of mathematical principles behind the puzzles. 135 illustrations. viii + 248pp.
20198-8 Paperbound $1.25

PAPER FOLDING FOR BEGINNERS, William D. Murray and Francis J. Rigney. Easiest book on the market, clearest instructions on making interesting, beautiful origami. Sail boats, cups, roosters, frogs that move legs, bonbon boxes, standing birds, etc. 40 projects; more than 275 diagrams and photographs. 94pp.
20713-7 Paperbound $1.00

TRICKS AND GAMES ON THE POOL TABLE, Fred Herrmann. 79 tricks and games—some solitaires, some for two or more players, some competitive games—to entertain you between formal games. Mystifying shots and throws, unusual caroms, tricks involving such props as cork, coins, a hat, etc. Formerly *Fun on the Pool Table*. 77 figures. 95pp.
21814-7 Paperbound $1.00

HAND SHADOWS TO BE THROWN UPON THE WALL: A SERIES OF NOVEL AND AMUSING FIGURES FORMED BY THE HAND, Henry Bursill. Delightful picturebook from great-grandfather's day shows how to make 18 different hand shadows: a bird that flies, duck that quacks, dog that wags his tail, camel, goose, deer, boy, turtle, etc. Only book of its sort. vi + 33pp. 6½ x 9¼. 21779-5 Paperbound $1.00

WHITTLING AND WOODCARVING, E. J. Tangerman. 18th printing of best book on market. "If you can cut a potato you can carve" toys and puzzles, chains, chessmen, caricatures, masks, frames, woodcut blocks, surface patterns, much more. Information on tools, woods, techniques. Also goes into serious wood sculpture from Middle Ages to present, East and West. 464 photos, figures. x + 293pp.
20965-2 Paperbound $2.00

HISTORY OF PHILOSOPHY, Julián Marías. Possibly the clearest, most easily followed, best planned, most useful one-volume history of philosophy on the market; neither skimpy nor overfull. Full details on system of every major philosopher and dozens of less important thinkers from pre-Socratics up to Existentialism and later. Strong on many European figures usually omitted. Has gone through dozens of editions in Europe. 1966 edition, translated by Stanley Appelbaum and Clarence Strowbridge. xviii + 505pp.
21739-6 Paperbound $3.00

YOGA: A SCIENTIFIC EVALUATION, Kovoor T. Behanan. Scientific but non-technical study of physiological results of yoga exercises; done under auspices of Yale U. Relations to Indian thought, to psychoanalysis, etc. 16 photos. xxiii + 270pp.
20505-3 Paperbound $2.50

Prices subject to change without notice.
Available at your book dealer or write for free catalogue to Dept. GI, Dover Publications, Inc., 180 Varick St., N. Y., N. Y. 10014. Dover publishes more than 150 books each year on science, elementary and advanced mathematics, biology, music, art, literary history, social sciences and other areas.